RANDALL L, BISHOP
RT #1 BOX 128B
PAW PAW WV,
25434

SONG OF THE WHALE

ACKNOWLEDGMENTS

The author wishes to thank the following people who played a role in bringing this book to print. Foremost, I would like to thank Paul Spong, Linda Spong, Yashi Spong, and Helena Symonds for telling me their stories. Catherine Ingram, Shivon Robinsong, Joanne Goodwin-Weyler, Peg Post, Robert Hunter, Flora Cook, Liz Jackson, Karol Sinats, Peter Ballem, John-Peter Bradford, and Jill Carlino read the first draft of the manuscript and offered valuable suggestions for improvements. James Raines at Doubleday first conceived the idea. I also wish to thank all the editors at Doubleday who played a role, and particularly copy editor Viera Morse, who offered vast improvements to the text. Michael Bigg provided the genealogy of the whale families, and Peter Thomas provided many of the excellent photographs. And I thank Ron Bernstein for his professional help.

NOTE: I Ching quotes on pp. 26, 50, 74, 210–11 are from *The I Ching,* The Richard Wilhelm Translation, Bollinger Series XIX, Princeton University Press, Princeton, New Jersey, 1967.

Rex Weyler

SONG
of the
WHALE

1986
ANCHOR PRESS/DOUBLEDAY
GARDEN CITY, NEW YORK

Library of Congress Cataloging-in-Publication Data
Weyler, Rex, 1947–
Song of the whale.
1. Spong, Paul. 2. Killer whale. 3. Whales.
4. Wildlife conservation. 5. Mammalogists—British
Columbia—Biography.   I. Title.
QL31.S64W49 1986   599.5′3   85-20033
ISBN 0-385-19938-4

Dedicated to my mother,
Joanne Goodwin-Weyler

CONTENTS

SONG OF THE WHALE

1

Skana

The midsummer skyline remained bright azure though the sun had gone down over English Bay and Vancouver Island. Paul Spong's weathered Volkswagen van hummed through the arch of fir and maple and dogwood boughs that led from Stanley Park into the evening traffic of West End Vancouver. Paul was thinking of Skana. His work at the university, where he was Dr. Paul Spong, assistant professor of psychiatry, had begun recently to drift from his mind. He performed his duties in the lab, but his mind was on the whale.

Paul drove along the familiar seawall in something of a trance, absorbed by thoughts of Skana and his own research into the workings of her mind. He drove up the shop-lined hill into the electric buzz of Vancouver. Near the center of town Paul automatically began the right turn that would take him over the bridge to his home, but at the last minute he went straight ahead. At Granville Street, where office workers waited for buses and street people panhandled for quarters, Paul pulled his van to the curb and parked. He dodged traffic across Granville Street and leaped onto the sidewalk. Over his shoulder swung a leather bag in which he carried his notebooks. He pushed slowly through the door of the Cecil Hotel

Public House. The street noise died out and the hum of pub chatter grew in the smoky yellow light.

It was July 17, 1968. Paul looked at the familiar faces as he walked through the pub. He often came to the Cecil since his arrival in Vancouver a year earlier. A far corner of the old hotel bar harbored an enclave of street intelligentsia, unpublished poets, and jobless philosophers whose company and conversation Paul sometimes preferred to the shop talk at the university or at the aquarium. Pool balls cracked, laughter and arguments echoed in the nooks and crannies, and beer glasses thudded heavily as they were set down on the aged terry-cloth covers on the small round tables.

Paul sat in his familiar corner, caught the eye of a waiter, smiled, and held up two fingers. After paying fifty cents for the two beers and tipping the waiter a quarter, he sat back to think. Skana had taken an unexpectedly long time to learn the first simple test that Paul had given her, to discriminate visually between two lines and one line on a card in her pool and to push the appropriate lever. They had performed some two thousand trials over the previous several months, and Skana was just beginning to get it.

The results induced a familiar sigmoid learning curve, but the lethargic pace had surprised Paul. "She's got more wits than that," Paul was hypothesizing to himself when his drifting thoughts were interrupted with a "Hi, man" directed at him from short range.

Paul looked up to see a recognizable face, one of the Cecil regulars, holding a beer glass and nodding. "Oh, hi mate," replied Paul, motioning the young man to sit down. "I forget your name."

"Walt. I was out at UBC for a while in the anthropology department, then I quit and went tree planting up north. How's it going with the whale? Aren't they s'posed to be really smart? Someone told—"

"I don't know how smart she is," Paul interrupted. "I'm still trying to find out how well she can see. I was just figuring today that she can see underwater about as well as a cat sees in the air, somewhere in the vicinity of one tenth the power of visual resolution that we have. But I suspect sight isn't that important to whales; they probably use echolocation—you know, like bats, sonar—more than they use sight for getting around in the ocean, navigating, finding food, and so on."

"But I heard they have huge brains, and might—"

"Like I said, I don't know how smart they are," Paul interrupted again. "Skana took a long time to learn some pretty simple behavioral responses to stimuli. But something puzzles me about it. She just *seems* smarter than that. I'm beginning to think maybe half a dead herring isn't all that exciting a reward for her. A flippin' rat would have learned to work the food dispenser faster than Skana."

"Do you know what Skana means?" asked Walt with a gleam in his eye.

"Oh, it's an Indian name for the killer whale," said Paul, shrugging his shoulders.

"It's a Haida name," explained Walt. "All the bands along the coast had different names for killer whales. But it doesn't mean just killer whale, it means 'Supernatural One.' They revered the killer whale. It was the worst of bad luck to ever injure or kill a whale. The killer whales lived in families, like humans, with chiefs, and they could turn into humans and—"

"Oh wow, that reminds me, mate. I better call my family. We just had a baby, eh?"

"Yeah? How old?"

"Two and a half months—a boy. His name is Yashi." Paul stood up, hitched his bag over his shoulder, and downed the last drop of his second beer. "See ya, mate."

"See ya later, Paul," Walt called as Paul disappeared into the sea of big-bodied Canadian beer drinkers. Paul's eyes were so piercing, and his talk so magnetic, that people often did not notice he was a short man until they could see him from a distance. His face had gaunt features that were softened by his long, flowing hair and full beard. Paul could exude gentleness at one moment and deep intensity the next. To an outsider he might at times have seemed absentminded, his thoughts flitting from one subject to another. Paul's mind, however, was in non-stop calculation, computation, and he had a natural penchant for picking out meaningful details from the mass of information that swirled through his brain.

Paul called his wife, Linda, from the pay phone by the door, then started back to his seat. However, on the way he changed his mind; he had an urge to go back to the aquarium to see Skana. He had never seen her at night when she didn't know he was there. He wondered what she did at night.

It was dark when he pulled into the empty aquarium parking lot in Stanley Park. In the still air he heard Skana's massive breath, a long "whooooooo" out-breath followed by a shorter windy "uhhhh" in-breath that trailed off into silence. He unlocked the door, walked past the offices, through the public fish display, and stood by a big glass window where he could see Skana rising from the water to breathe. He walked out onto the deck by the pool, reentered the building, and walked to his lab. From inside he could see the small pool that held Tung Jen, the young male killer whale captured just a few months earlier. Paul had been holding Tung Jen in isolation. Once he had finished the experiments with Skana, he wanted a naive whale on which to run a fresh battery of tests. Tung Jen lived in a small pool measuring fifty by thirty by eight feet deep. When he first arrived he had vocalized continually, but Paul noticed that lately he just floated in one corner, breathing slowly. For a closer look, Paul stepped out beside Tung Jen's pool.

In the cool night air Tung Jen breathed even more slowly than he usually did, dropping just below the surface between breaths. In the distance Skana was also breathing slowly. Paul noticed that Skana's breaths were following almost immediately after Tung Jen's. "Whoooooooo . . . uhhhhhh." "Whooooooo . . . uhhhhh." The two whales were breathing almost at the same time. Paul pulled out his notebook and wrote down the observation. "Maybe a coincidence," he thought; "but maybe not."

Paul had read John Lilly's papers on dolphin sleep; he knew that unlike land mammals, whales and dolphins were voluntary breathers. Living in the water but breathing air, they could not go to sleep for more than a few minutes at a time. Whales took the ultimate catnap. They would wake up, rise to the surface, breathe, and then go back to sleep. Lilly had even noticed that dolphins sometimes alternated eyes, keeping one eye open, breathing, then keeping the other eye open, resting half the brain at a time.

Paul watched for thirty or forty minutes in the total darkness. Skana and Tung Jen did not break their pattern. Paul folded his notebook into his bag, swung it over his shoulder, walked back through the aquarium and stood again behind the glass, watching Skana's pool. Skana dove, swam under the water, and surfaced at the near edge of the pool. She held her head sideways, eye above the water, looking in the direction of the window. Paul stopped still, looking back at her. He knew that she could not see him as she ducked below the water, swam around, and came up on the other side, slapping her pectoral fin on the surface of the water. Paul watched, motionless, as Skana swam around slowly. He took out his notebook and wrote down what he had witnessed. "Good night, Skana," he said out loud. "Get some sleep. If you're so smart, let's see if you can get a hundred percent tomorrow." He laughed at his little joke and walked back through the offices to the back door of the aquarium.

Stepping out into the parking lot, he found himself staring into a bright flashlight. "Hello?" he questioned.

"Oh, it's you, Dr. Spong. I was wondering what was going on. I saw the van there and no lights on inside."

Paul recognized the night patrolman.

"How's your whales doin'?" asked the officer.

"They're sleeping. Or at least they were; I think I disturbed them."

"You better get some sleep yourself—you look tired. You're going to fall into the pool some night and get eaten." Paul heard Skana slap the water again with her flipper.

"Yes," said Paul, "I am tired. Good night."

"Good night, Dr. Spong."

Paul drove back through the park the long way, through the trees. He drove through the city, over the Burrard Street Bridge, and into Kitsilano, a pleasant university neighborhood of 1930s wooden houses and streets lined with cherry trees. He drove along Fourth Avenue, where the shops catered to the "youth

movement," as the newspapers called it, that was just beginning to invade Vancouver from the south.

At Vine Street he doubled back along Third Avenue and
parked in front of his house. A new moon was shining, a little
sliver like a fingernail clipping. Paul walked quietly to his door,
opened it slowly, took off his shoes, and stepped in, walking
through to the bedroom. He tiptoed across the floor to Yashi's
bed in the corner. He gazed for a few moments at his new son,
who was sleeping soundly. Yashi emitted some baby sound as
if he were dreaming. "Paul?" whispered Linda from the bed.
"Yes," answered Paul in a whisper.

Paul snuggled in beside her, and slept like a baby himself.

Just over a year earlier, in the spring of 1967, Paul Spong had
flown to Vancouver from Los Angeles to be interviewed for a
highly specialized research job at the University of British Columbia. He had met with Dr. Patrick McGeer, head of the Kinsmen Laboratory of Neurological Sciences; Dr. Jim Tyhurst,
head of the department of psychiatry; and Dr. Murray Newman, director of the Vancouver Public Aquarium from its incep-
tion in 1956.

Paul had been recommended for the job by a senior professor at the Brain Research Institute at UCLA, who had plucked
Paul from the University of Auckland in New Zealand at the
beginning of 1963 and brought him to UCLA to work in his
laboratory. In four years Paul had completed his Ph.D. in physiological psychology; his thesis had been on the relationship
between brain mechanisms and behavior in humans. He had
earned a postdoctoral fellowship at UCLA, and, like most of
his young colleagues, sought a tenured position in academia.

Paul was single-mindedly on a career path in the neurological sciences. He had loved the high-tech atmosphere of the
UCLA lab, where he performed computer analyses of brain-
wave patterns in humans. He had also learned how to implant
electrodes into animals' brains with precision, locating the various cerebral functions and differentiating among them. Paul
was on the cutting edge of physiological psychology, mapping
the brain, identifying the areas responsible for arousal, decod-

ing the mysterious brain stem, and tracking sensory input from nerve endings to consciousness.

When the job interview was offered by McGeer at UBC, Paul was confident except for one disturbing matter. Half the job involved working in McGeer's neurological lab, but the other half was at the Vancouver Public Aquarium, performing behavioral research on the newly acquired *Orcinus orca,* or killer whale, known as Skana. This was to be groundbreaking work. No such research had yet been done on killer whales. Indeed, at that time only four such animals had been captured, and three had died. Skana was the first *Orcinus orca* to be held in an aquarium successfully so that scientists could investigate her.

But Paul knew almost nothing about whales. In the lab at UCLA he had witnessed the work of Austrian biologist Manfred Haider, who was analyzing microvibrations of the skin in dolphins, but Paul had not been interested in the dolphins per se; he had only been interested in the physiology of their nervous system. He had watched patterns on the oscilloscope, but had not interacted with the animal itself or learned much about its behavior.

Prior to his visit to Vancouver, therefore, Paul had read just about every existing scientific paper written about cetaceans—dolphins and whales. He consumed the work of Lilly, Gregory Bateson, Dr. Peter Morgane of the Communication Research Institute in Miami, and Drs. Eugene Nagle, Will McFarland, and Paul Yakovlev of Harvard University. Then he went to talk with Dr. Ken Norris, a cetacean researcher at UCLA. Norris advised Paul, "Most of what we know about cetaceans is about their hearing and vocalizing; we know a little about their diets and migrations because of the whaling industry. What is needed is knowledge of their vision. We don't have much yet on that."

As Paul sat on the airplane descending into Vancouver International Airport in the spring of 1967, he felt confident. He felt he knew almost as much about whales as any scientist at that time could know; he had nudged the frontier of neurological psychology, and he was at ease with the latest in computer technology.

He was unaware that his biggest stumbling block to landing his job would be his liberal demeanor, his outspoken frankness, and his UCLA graduate-student wardrobe. He thought he looked great. Under his corduroy suit he wore a lovely velvet vest made by Linda, who had also trimmed his hair and beard for the occasion. By UCLA standards he looked like quite the sharp candidate. He was not prepared, however, for the colonial conservatism and stately sobriety of the University of British Columbia; nor was he prepared for the political machinations and social economics of the Vancouver Public Aquarium. Nor for the effect that Skana subsequently would have on his understanding of science.

Paul watched from a window seat as the plane circled over Vancouver. Scattered clouds hung above English Bay, once "White Bay" to British Captain George Vancouver, who named it after the white dogwood blossoms that ringed the shoreline upon his first visit to the sheltered harbor in 1789. Before that it was Eealmu, home to the Salish bands of Chief Capilano on the north shore, and Chief Khitsilano on the south shore. The Salish met here with the Haida, Nootka, Kwakiutl, and Cowichan for ceremonies on a shore that later became known as Jericho Park in Kitsilano.

Jutting out from the bay, west of Kitsilano, were the crumbling sandstone bluffs of Point Grey, and the dignified graystone buildings of the University of British Columbia, ringed majestically by a thin band of fir and cedar trees. Snow still clung to the mountains, which rose straight out of the bay.

At the airport Paul was met by a former colleague from New Zealand, who drove him directly to the Kinsmen Laboratory of Neurological Sciences, where he was met by Dr. Jim Tyhurst.

Jim Tyhurst's office was a well-organized professor's study. The desk, table, and shelves bespoke a busy but disciplined worker. Dr. Tyhurst was friendly, sharp, and receptive, and he listened intently as Paul talked.

"I really want this job," said Paul, sitting forward in his chair. "I'm glad you are interested in the brain-wave work.

This is exciting for me. We're just looking at the tip of the iceberg with this alpha monitoring and computer analysis of brain activity. It's a big field."

Paul had hardly noticed that half an hour had passed when Pat McGeer walked into the office. Paul was cut off in mid-sentence. "Hi, Jim," said McGeer. "Dr. Spong? Hello, sir, it's good to meet you." Dr. Pat McGeer had an authoritative presence. He let his status of boss be known with a serious and hurried manner. He wore a distinguished gray suit; his hair was short and neatly combed back against his round face.

"I'm sorry I'm late, Jim," said McGeer. "Dr. Spong, we have a lot to talk about. We'll have a busy day tomorrow. Dr. Tyhurst can give you a tour of the lab in the morning. Let's meet in my office after lunch, say about one o'clock. I've scheduled a meeting with Dr. Newman at the aquarium for three."

McGeer did not sit down. Paul tried to speak, but he felt a bit uneasy. He began to feel a little ragtag under McGeer's stare. "I'm sorry I can't stay and talk right now Dr. Spong," said McGeer. "I can find out all about you tomorrow night at dinner. I've made reservations at the Faculty Club. You do have a tie, don't you?"

"Uh, yes," said Paul.

McGeer chuckled. "See you tomorrow, Jim. Can you join us for dinner?"

Dr. Tyhurst nodded.

"Great," said McGeer. "See you tomorrow, Dr. Spong."

Paul stood up to shake his hand. The Canadian and the New Zealander were about the same size; they met eye to eye somewhere at the level of Jim Tyhurst's shoulders. McGeer's handshake was firm and his gaze steady. "Nice to meet you," said Paul.

After McGeer left, Tyhurst cast a fatherly look across the desk toward Paul. "It looks pretty good, Paul. Murray Newman at the aquarium has the final say, but you come with high recommendations, and I think you'd fit in fine here."

On the following morning Paul toured the laboratory with Jim Tyhurst, had lunch by himself at a Chinese restaurant near the university, and then went to Dr. McGeer's office at one o'clock for his scheduled meeting. Paul expected McGeer to be late, but he was waiting when Paul arrived. The two men talked for about an hour; McGeer outlined the projects going on in the neurological lab and questioned Paul thoroughly. Paul was impressed with his knowledge, and he sensed another side to the brusque man he had met the day before.

Following their interview, McGeer took Paul over to the department of zoology, where they met Dr. Dean Fisher, professor of zoology, the local specialist on marine mammals. They talked about Skana. Both Fisher and McGeer were quite excited about the captive whale. "She's a healthy specimen," said Dr. Fisher. "We've looked over your proposal about visual-acuity studies, and we like the idea. This is the only *Orcinus orca* available for research anywhere in the world. We have quite an opportunity here."

As the three men drove across town, Fisher and McGeer talked university business in the front seat while Paul stared out the window from the back. Paul liked Vancouver; he liked the water, the clean air, and the tree-lined streets. When they entered Stanley Park from downtown, he was stunned by the immense cedar trees and charmed by the Canada geese that led their goslings along the roadside.

Inside the aquarium office Paul met Murray Newman, a quiet man who seemed to be somewhat preoccupied. He also met the president of the Vancouver Aquarium Association, and aquarium curator Vince Penfold. Newman asked Paul about his proposal to do visual acuity tests with Skana. "It's really the next thing that needs to be done with cetaceans," offered Paul, echoing the sentiments of Ken Norris. Newman was very practical; he asked Paul what he would need. Paul outlined his equipment needs, including computer specifications.

Paul tried to make a good impression, but Dr. Newman seemed distant. He looked at the floor while the others spoke, nodding introspectively. Vince Penfold seemed interested in what Paul had to say. Paul was somewhat intimidated by the affluent appearance of the men in the room. He had borrowed a tie for the occasion, but his velvet vest and corduroy suit were beginning to show signs of travel fatigue. He felt uncomfortably underdressed, and he found himself wishing that Jim Tyhurst had come.

When they finished talking, Newman led them out onto the concrete deck surrounding the whale pool. Paul caught his first glimpse of the killer whale. "That's Skana," said Vince Penfold. The six men chatted as Skana floated in the background. Paul kept his eyes on Newman, but he could not quite engage him. The aquarium director's thoughts seemed to be on some next order of business. McGeer cut the conversation off. "I'll give you a call in the morning, Murray," he said. He nodded at Vince Penfold and headed for the exit. Paul shook hands all around. He looked at Skana quickly as he left. He realized that she was the biggest animal he had ever seen, in or out of a zoo.

At dinner that night at the Faculty Club the conversation was jovial, but Paul felt uneasy. McGeer had hardly mentioned the job during dinner.

Paul flew back to Los Angeles, and within a week he heard from McGeer, who offered him the job. Paul and Linda spent the rest of the summer on Venice Beach near their rented Twenty-sixth Avenue house, contemplating their rosy future in Vancouver.

Before moving into the home at 2021 West Third Avenue in Kitsilano, near the university, Paul and Linda had rented an upstairs suite from Reg and Edith Parmenter in Deep Cove, twenty minutes out of Vancouver. Edith, fifty years old, was a sensitive, loving first-grade schoolteacher who more or less adopted Paul and Linda, showering Linda with motherly kindness. Paul was commuting between Deep Cove, UBC, and the aquarium in Stanley Park. One day while Paul was at the aquarium, Edith visited Linda in her kitchen. At one point in their conversation Edith told her thoughtfully, "You know, I have this feeling, and I don't know why, but I feel like someday Paul is going to be very famous for this work he is doing with the whales."

Yashi was born the following spring, and the little family moved to Kitsilano. Paul's work with Skana began to consume most of his days, and eventually his nights.

Paul slept late on the morning after his late-night observation of Skana and Tung Jen. Over coffee he told Linda about it as he held Yashi in his lap. "They seemed to be synchronizing their breathing. It's fascinating; according to Lilly, they only sleep for a few minutes at a time, then they wake up to breathe. Imagine, Linda, having to wake up for every breath."

"We'd never make it as whales," she laughed. While they talked, the phone rang. Paul answered.

"Hi, Paul," said Jim Tyhurst on the other end of the line. "I just wanted to catch you before you went over to the aquarium. They need you in the lab today."

"I'll be over this morning. I guess I've been spending a lot of time at the aquarium."

"That's all right, Paul. McGeer and Newman are pleased with the progress, but don't forget about us over here."

"Thanks, Jim. I'll stop by the lab shortly." Paul hung up the phone. "Well," he said ruefully, "I'm off to the lab to cut up some cats."

"Sick!" said Linda.

At the neurological laboratory Paul was implanting electrodes into cats' brains. A cat lay motionless on the table. Though he had performed the simple operation dozens of times, Paul felt queasy as his scalpel slid across the skull. The tightly stretched skin sprang open, exposing the bone; blood vessels popped, and the sedated cat twitched. Paul hurried through the routine. He wanted to get out of the lab as soon as possible. He finished his work by noon, leaving the experiments in the hands of the lab technicians.

He drove quickly through town to Stanley Park. The aquarium and zoo swarmed with tourists. Children fed popcorn to the ducks. An old man had two black squirrels running up and down his back and over his shoulders, to the delight of the crowd. Paul watched with interest as a squirrel took bread from the man's lips. At the end of his act, the old man bowed to the crowd and passed his hat. Happy children ran forward to give him coins.

Inside the aquarium Paul went directly to his lab. Tung Jen

was floating listlessly in his pool; Skana swam and splashed. On this particular day Paul had high hopes for Skana.

Several months earlier he had begun to teach Skana to distinguish between one line and two lines on cards that he lowered into the water. Performing seventy-two trials per day, Paul began to narrow the gap between the lines from four inches down to an inch, then to a half inch, a quarter, an eighth, and then to one sixteenth of an inch. It took Skana two hundred trials to reach 90 percent accuracy in recognizing the sixteenth-of-an-inch gap.

However, when Paul reduced the gap to one thirty-second of an inch, Skana's behavior became erratic. Paul figured that he was near the limits of Skana's powers of visual resolution. His plan then was to present the gap widths in random order, but before doing that he wanted to return to the sixteenth-of-an-inch test in order to bring her performance up to a high level again.

On July 18, 1968, Paul set up the experiment again at one sixteenth of an inch. He lowered his apparatus into the small gateway between Skana's pool and an adjacent holding pool. He loaded the food dispenser and placed two cards into the viewing slots. One card had a single line, and the second card had two lines separated by a sixteenth-of-an-inch space. Paul rang a bell to signal the start of a trial, and Skana obediently, though sluggishly, swam over to the apparatus. She was quite familiar with the procedure—some twenty-four hundred times Skana had read the cards, pushed the proper lever indicating which card had two lines, and received half a dead herring as a reward. The herring was dispensed from an automatic stainless-steel fish feeder with a carousel tray that advanced one slot at a time, dropping the fish into the pool, where Skana swallowed it.

On the previous seventy-two trials at the sixteenth-of-an-inch gap, Skana had performed at the 90 percent level throughout. Paul planned to do another seventy-two trials, and he expected Skana to execute the test effortlessly at 90 or even 100 percent. He initiated trial number one. Skana's answer was incorrect: She had pushed the lever on the right, but the two lines were on the left side. Paul triggered a second trial; Skana answered correctly and ate the herring. On the third trial Skana's answer was again incorrect. On the fourth trial she was incorrect. "Come on, Skana," said Paul. "Let's get on with it."

Skana signaled the one-line card again on the fifth trial, vocalizing both before and after pushing the lever. Again on the sixth, seventh, eighth, ninth, and tenth trials Skana pushed the wrong lever, vocalizing audibly above the water. "ReeeEEEE, ReeeeeeeEEEEEEE."

Paul walked to the side of the oval pool. Through the huge windows of the aquarium gift shop he could see tourists milling about. He stood between the tiers of empty benches and the concrete edge of the pool. Skana swam about in the turquoise water, making shrill calls and slapping the water with her pectoral fins. Park visitors, hearing the sound, gathered by the rail at the perimeter of the aquarium to behold the spectacle. "Come on, Skana!" muttered Spong. "I know that you know how to do this; now cut it out!" He rang the bell again.

Paul ran twenty more trials. Skana pushed the wrong lever on every test, issuing a chorus of screeches each time. Paul stood and breathed deeply, quieting his frustration. He unfolded his notebook and wrote down his observations of Skana's behavior. She was one-for-thirty for the day, her worst performance ever. Paul checked the apparatus. Everything worked. He sat on his heels at the edge of the water and looked at the whale. She swam about lazily and then surfaced in front of him, floating under his glare. "What's going on, Skana?" Paul asked softly. He looked up and saw Murray Newman standing on the deck by the aquarium windows.

It was five o'clock, and the aquarium staff was going home. Paul left Skana and stopped to talk with Newman. "How's it going?" the director asked.

Paul checked himself; he wanted to think about the events of the day before he talked about them. "Okay," he said. "We have a fairly accurate measure of Skana's visual acuity; it's about the same as the dolphins'."

"You look tired, Paul."

"Yeah," said Paul, laughing nervously. "Well, I'm through for the day."

"I hear you were working late last night. Don't overwork yourself, Paul."

"No," said Paul. "I won't."

Paul went back to the lab to collect his things. He folded up his notebook, turned off the equipment and lights, and then returned to Skana's pool, leaning against the glass, staring out at the whale. For fifteen minutes he watched her swim with grace and pliancy through the water. Leaving the aquarium, he walked to his van and drove straight home.

When he got home, Paul curled up with Yashi and took a short nap. Later, over supper, he was taciturn. Linda probed his quiet thoughts. "What's wrong Paul?" she asked.

"I don't know."

"Is it the lab? I don't blame you for being tired of cutting up cats."

"No," said Paul. "Well, yes, I guess that's part of it. . . . I don't know. The experiment at the aquarium isn't going so well either."

"I thought it was going great."

"It was. I thought I was almost done. It seemed as if Skana's visual acuity—you know, her ability to resolve the width between two lines—was about the same as the dolphin's. It worked out to be about six minutes of arc—that is, from a distance of eighteen inches she could distinguish a sixteenth-of-an-inch gap. At one thirty-second of an inch she had trouble. I thought I had it pretty well nailed down; now I'm not so sure. Suddenly, today, she falls apart. She gets all wrong answers at a sixteenth. So the data is totally skewed. I can't be certain about anything."

Yashi woke up, and Linda started for the bedroom to pick him up. "Hold on, Linda," Paul stopped her. "You only condition them to cry if you pick them up every time they cry. They learn that they get rewarded for crying."

"I don't know about that," she answered. "If they're crying they must be needing something. They'll stop crying when they get older. It seems that if you give them what they need now, they'll learn to feel safe and secure. It must be frustrating being a baby, always having to get someone else to help you get what you want. I'm getting to know his different cries," she said. "I think you should just trust your instinct. You know, if I really listen I can tell if he's honestly needing attention or if he's just crying to let off steam. They need to cry. It's about the only thing they can do."

Paul and Linda spent the evening playing and laughing with their baby. Yashi kept them up late.

Paul went straight to the aquarium the next morning. With his assistant, Don White, he set up the cards and signaled for Skana to start the first trial. "Oooookay, Skana," said Paul, "let's try this again."

He triggered the first trial of the day. Skana pushed the wrong lever. Paul stopped for a moment and stared at Skana. Then he flicked his switch and again Skana pushed the wrong lever. Paul shook his head. He watched her closely, flicking the switch for the third time. With the tip of her rostrum (the foremost part of her head) against her little viewing screen, Skana screeched and pushed the wrong lever for the third time.

Paul heard her shrill call. He hadn't noticed whether or not she had vocalized during the first two trials. He noted her vocalizations in his notebook. For over an hour Paul and Don ran the experiment, and stopped after twenty trials. On every single trial Skana had vocalized before and after pushing the lever, and on each trial she pushed the wrong lever. Paul was dumbfounded. His prior statistics were useless. Skana had dropped from 90 percent to zero. The experiment was collapsing.

Paul turned off his apparatus, folded up his notebook, and walked through the aquarium office at an uncharacteristically quick pace, shaking his head to himself. Avoiding everyone's eyes, he headed for the back door as if he had somewhere important to go.

Once out the door he slowed down. He walked toward his van, but turned into the park at the last moment and walked among the summer zoo visitors. He was going to have to confide in someone, but in whom, he wondered. Murray Newman?

Vince? No, he thought, no one at the aquarium yet. McGeer was his boss. No . . . Jim. He'd talk with Jim Tyhurst; Jim would have a good suggestion.

Paul drove out to the university. He revved his van through the park, past the bathers of English Bay. He drove over the Burrard Street Bridge, along the south shore on Point Grey Road, up the hill, and through the forested endowment lands to the campus. He parked in the Kinsmen Lab parking lot and walked inside. Jim's office was empty. He checked with the secretary, who told him that Dr. Tyhurst would be in a meeting all afternoon. Paul went home early and took a walk on the beach with Linda and Yashi, forgetting, for a few hours, his dilemma.

On the following morning Paul again went directly to the aquarium. During the night he had concluded that Skana must be confused. He was going to go back to a simpler test, increasing the width of the gap between the two lines. He set the width to a quarter inch. As he had done hundreds of times before, Paul rang the bell to start the day's trials.

When Skana got that test wrong five times, he methodically increased the width to two and a half inches, the width at which Skana had originally learned the procedure. Paul ran five more trials, and Skana continued to score zero. Paul noted that she vocalized throughout the fifteen trials.

On the next day Skana got all wrong answers on twenty more trials at two and a half inches. For four days Skana had been getting wrong answers. Paul felt as if he were back where he had started three months earlier, that his experiment was a flop. The visual-acuity experiments had been his idea. The aquarium and the university had hired him on the basis of his proposal to complete the visual study, to provide the scientific community with this new piece of knowledge about whales. It now seemed as though he had nothing to offer.

On the fifth day since Skana's sudden regression, Paul set up the experimental apparatus without much enthusiasm. He decided to try Skana one more time at two and a half inches. Maybe she had forgotten. She had learned it once, so she could learn it again. But this time Skana refused even to push the lever. She swam around the pool, refusing to respond to Paul's bell. Paul found himself losing his temper. At one point he yelled at Skana from the edge of the pool. Suddenly self-conscious, he could see heads turning through the gift-shop windows. Skana seemed to ignore him.

He was angry when he left that day. He stopped at the Cecil for a beer, but talked to no one. At home he slouched on the sofa, feeling low.

"I'm going to give Skana a break," he told Linda. "There's just no sense in going back out there for a while."

At the university he told Pat McGeer and Jim Tyhurst that Skana's response had become somewhat erratic, and that the visual-acuity experiment was going to take a little longer than he had originally thought. Daily he drove out to the university lab, catching up on his work there.

Two weeks passed, during which he avoided Skana and the aquarium altogether. On a Sunday in early August, Paul and Linda took Yashi to the beach, but rain began to fall, forcing them back home. That evening, while Yashi slept, Linda played the violin and Paul sat quietly at the kitchen table drinking coffee. Rain spattered on the roof. Paul's thoughts kept returning to Skana. He felt stuck. It seemed ridiculous to go back and run another series of trials, but he couldn't just stop. Maybe he should forget about Skana and try to start again with Tung Jen. It would go quickly—he was all set up. Maybe Skana had suffered some brain damage or something; maybe she wasn't such a healthy specimen after all.

Paul stared out at the bleak night. He thought of Skana and Tung Jen sleeping and breathing in the downpour. He thought of what it must be like having to wake up for every breath. He closed his eyes and tried to imagine sleeping and waking every two minutes. Listening to the violin and the rain, he dozed off. When he awoke, Linda was sitting beside him.

Paul thought for a moment. Then he looked up. "Linda?"

"Yes," she replied.

"Something's going on with Skana. This may sound weird, but—well, I think she . . . I don't quite know how to put it. I *know* that she knows how to work the levers, and I know that she can see the cards and differentiate between two lines and one line. Before this regression, or whatever it is, she was scoring almost one hundred percent with the two-and-a-half-inch gap and with the one-sixteenth gap she got over ninety percent. Now all of a sudden she gets—" Paul stopped to calculate in his head. "Now all of a sudden she gets eighty-three trials in a row wrong! Even if she was just guessing, she'd get fifty percent." Paul's pensive mood suddenly vanished. He smiled. "I know this sounds strange, Linda, but I think that Skana is getting those wrong answers on purpose."

"Maybe she wants to stay back a grade," Linda offered, smiling.

"Yeah," said Paul. "She's flunking out of this school."

"Do you really think she's trying to get wrong answers?"

"She got the exact wrong answer eighty-three times in a row. Now, I just can't imagine that's a coincidence. That would be like flipping a coin and getting eighty-three heads in a row. She knew the right answer, but she gave the wrong answer. She didn't seem to care at all about the reward. What would you make of that?"

"She probably thinks your experiments are boring."

"Hmmmm." Paul pondered. He cupped his chin in his hands and looked at Linda for a few moments. He recalled their first meeting. He had come home to his apartment in Venice Beach and found her there with some friends of his. They swam together in the surf at midnight, and it was classic love at first sight for both of them. "Well," said Paul, "I'm going to go back to the aquarium tomorrow, but I don't think I'll attempt any more trials for a while. Linda, I think this experiment may be more interesting than any of us suspected."

Paul drove into the aquarium parking lot early, before any of the other employees arrived. It had been two weeks since he had seen Skana. He went through the back entrance, out through the glass front to the open-air pool. Skana was resting near the surface, breathing slowly. Paul put down his shoulder bag and walked up to the edge of the pool. Skana breathed out heavily, "Whoooooo," took in a massive breath, "Uhhhhh," and dove below the surface. Under water, she circled the pool and then broke the surface again, taking another breath: "Whoooooo! Uhhhhh." Gulls fluttered about in the yellow light above the pool, hoping, perhaps, for a free meal from the lone human.

Paul took off his shoes and sat down on the edge of the pool with his feet in the water. Far off in the distance he could hear the early-morning traffic on the Lions Gate Bridge. As the rising sun warmed the air, moist from the night's rain, a low fog crept through the park. Crows squawked and squirrels nattered in the trees. Skana approached Paul slowly; he took his feet out of the pool and leaned over on his knees. Skana stuck her head out of the water, pointing her rostrum and lower jaw directly into Paul's face.

"Hi, Skana," said Paul quietly. He looked around; the gulls were still, standing on the railing and on the empty benches. "Listen, Skana," he said, "I think I understand. I wish you could understand me. We're not going to do that silly test anymore, okay?" Paul laughed out loud. Some of the gulls stirred, but Skana moved closer. Paul reached out gently and touched Skana with his fingertips. She held still in the water as he rubbed her immense head.

Skana slipped back into the water, swam around, and returned to the edge of the pool. Paul lay down on his belly, leaned into the pool, and stroked Skana as she slowly rose above the surface. Her skin was slick and rubbery to the touch. She turned her head to the side and moved her eye close to Paul. He found himself staring into an attentive and curious gaze. He cocked his head, squinted one eye, and looked at Skana with the other. He moved his head closer until their two eyes were about ten inches apart. Skana's large eye was a filmy, black, bowl-bottom-shaped surface wherein Paul could see his ghostly reflection as if in a carnival funhouse mirror.

Paul began to whistle a simple tune. Skana turned her eye away, until the tip of her jaw pointed directly toward his face. He tried to mimic sounds he had heard her make, issuing shrill, modulating whistles. Skana remained motionless, her jaw a few inches from Paul's lips. Then she slipped back into the pool and nimbly glided through the water; she rolled like a barrel under the water, sending a stream of bubbles from the blowhole at the top of her head.

Paul felt more tranquil than he had in months. He silently marveled at Skana's aquatic ballet. The morning was growing bright; Paul could hear automobiles pulling into the parking lot at the back of the aquarium building. He knew that he was going to have to talk to someone soon about his discoveries with Skana.

Jim Tyhurst was in his office when Paul arrived at the university. The door was open, but Paul knocked anyway. "Come on in," said Tyhurst, waving Paul forward. Paul sat down.

"Jim," he started right in, "things are going much better than I thought. I think the results that we have for the visual-acuity tests are pretty accurate. I got a little thrown off by something that happened, but I think this might open up a whole new series of studies with the whale." Paul paused, waiting for some sign that he should continue.

"Well, what happened?" asked Tyhurst.

"Once Skana learned what we were doing, she performed well, at the ninety- to one-hundred-percent level until the gap got down to one thirty-second of an inch. I think this was the threshold of her ability to see the gap because her performance became erratic. The interesting thing is, though, Jim, when I went *back* to the one sixteenth, Skana refused to do the test anymore. She made eighty-three wrong responses in a row, even at two and a half inches. Now I can't be absolutely certain, of course, but . . . I'm only hypothesizing at this point, Jim, but I think she gave those wrong responses on purpose. I've never seen a lab animal do that before. I don't think anyone has."

"Hmm." Dr. Tyhurst thought about it.

"Jim," Paul continued, "we were investigating the vision of an acoustically oriented animal. I want to do some more studies. I think acoustic information is much more important to these animals than visual information. It could be that sound stimuli would be more enticing to Skana than, say, food. She sure snubbed her nose at half a dead herring."

"It sounds interesting, Paul," Dr. Tyhurst said, leaning back comfortably in his chair. "So what did you find out about her vision?"

"Well, she sees underwater about as well as a cat sees in the air. Similar to the dolphin we tested earlier. The visual threshold is in the vicinity of one twenty-fourth to one thirty-second of an inch when viewed from eighteen inches: six minutes of arc."

Paul and Jim Tyhurst talked for about half an hour. Paul was well ahead of his work at the university lab, so he spent the afternoon in the library. He searched the animal-behavior literature for some mention of the phenomenon he had witnessed with Skana. He found nothing. He phoned a colleague at UCLA, and he asked around the zoology department as well as the psychology department. No one had ever heard of a lab animal purposefully giving wrong answers.

"This may have happened before," Paul told Linda later, "but no one noticed. It certainly isn't in any of the literature."

"So what would you call it? Is there a Latin phrase for animal rebellion against scientists?" Linda laughed.

"Maybe." Paul smiled. "It's like she just said, 'No! I'm not doing this anymore.' She would vocalize, press the wrong lever, then vocalize again. It seems so much like a straightforward communication. 'No!' If you look at the data, the phenomenon is like an instant turnaround. I don't know. . . . We'll call it 'instant reversal'—no, 'spontaneous reversal.' How's that? Spontaneous reversal. That's what the data show."

Paul spent the next few days at the aquarium, where he spent most of his time with Skana; he hardly went into his lab. When no one was around, he would sit barefooted on the little training platform at the edge of the pool with his feet in the water. Skana would entice him to rub her head. Like a house cat, she would nudge his feet to get a scratch. Paul would rub her head with his feet as she hung motionless in the water.

Once again Paul began to stay late at the aquarium. He even tried getting into the pool with Skana one evening, but he got anxious when she nudged him with her nose and he climbed out. Skana had forty-eight four-inch teeth; her jaws were big enough to eat him whole. Paul felt familiar with Skana, but he didn't trust her playfulness. Even if it was just by mistake, he didn't want to end up in Skana's mouth.

One morning in late August, Paul sat on the training platform dangling his bare feet in the water. He had relaxed his pressing experimental pace, and had taken to simply watching Skana, letting her come to him. The sun was just coming up as Skana swam lazily about in the center of the pool. The trees in Stanley Park were swaying in a light breeze; the gulls and crows chattered at the garbage cans along the walkway, looking for breakfast.

As she often did, Skana approached Paul slowly until she was only a few inches from his feet. Suddenly, without warning, she slashed her open mouth across Paul's feet. He felt her teeth drag across both the tops and the soles of his feet. Stunned, he jerked his feet from the water and gulped incredulously, as he watched Skana swim serenely away and across the pool. He sat there on the platform for a few moments and then gingerly lowered his feet back into the water.

Skana circled leisurely, approaching Paul once again. Guardedly, he left his feet in the water. Exactly as she had just done, Skana glided to within a few inches of Paul's feet, then suddenly raked her teeth across them again. Paul jerked his feet from the water.

Paul's curiosity overcame his caution. He put his feet back into the water for a third time to see what Skana would do. Once again she approached slowly and then quickly slashed her mouth over his feet, brushing the skin with her four-inch teeth. And again Paul jerked his feet from the water, but put them back in as Skana swam her circle.

Eight more times, eleven times in all, Skana approached Paul and raked her teeth across his feet, touching both the tops and soles. Each time Paul automatically responded by pulling his feet from the water. Then, on the twelfth time, Paul sat relatively calmly with his feet in the water, controlling the urge to flinch as Skana's teeth touched his feet. Immediately Skana stopped.

"Zweeeeeeeeep! Aaaaaaauuup," Skana called from the center of the pool. Paul laughed to himself. "AaaaaAAAAaaaaaa," he tried to mimic Skana's vocalizations. Suddenly Paul realized, with a sense of astonishment and wonder, that he was no longer afraid of Skana. Her little game had exposed his anxiety and somehow dissolved it. As the sun warmed the cool morning air, Paul felt his last drop of fear vanish.

"Why did she do that?" Paul thought to himself. "Was she trying to frighten me? Was she just playing a game? Why did she stop when I left my feet in the water?" And then Paul realized that he was no longer thinking of Skana as an experimental subject, as a lab animal. It was as if there were someone there. He realized that his entire approach to Skana had been clouded by a view that was perhaps not only incorrect but ignorant and insensitive. He felt humbled.

He realized also that Linda had probably been right about Skana's being bored with the experiments. Why had it taken him so long to see the obvious? Paul shook his head, a little amused at his own plodding mind.

The gulls and crows, joined now by the squirrels, continued their morning chatter. Paul could feel the warm sun on his face, but he could also feel a coolness in the breeze. Summer was almost over. Skana swam and splashed in the pool. Paul shook his head as he watched her. "So you're the scientist now, eh, Skana?" He chuckled. "Who's experimenting with whom?" Skana was swimming belly-up, plowing through the water with the back of her head, powered by the graceful strokes of her great flukes.

2
Eye to Eye

It was warm in the house, though walking through quiet Kitsilano neighborhoods in the low autumn sun, Paul had been cold. Pastel roses still blossomed in shadowy gardens, though the bustling summer pace of Vancouver had begun to give way to the lulling rhythms of November. Paul sat by the fireplace. He shook three Chinese coins and dropped them clinking onto the rug.

At UCLA an Asian colleague had introduced him to the *I Ching,* the Chinese "Book of Changes," an ancient text of sage advice intended by its authors—the legendary Taoist Fu Hsi, King Wen Wang, the Duke of Chou, and Confucius—as a practical guide on the journey through life's great questions. In his university days Paul had completely memorized the *I Ching*'s sixty-four hexagrams, around which the dualities and dilemmas of life were woven. Since then, whenever Paul was stuck on a question he would consult the *I Ching,* which seemed to have an uncanny way of coming up with useful advice.

To keep the research ball rolling at the aquarium, Paul was under some pressure to formulate the next battery of tests for Skana and Tung Jen. But Skana had shaken his basic scientific belief about what he was doing. Skana was not just a specimen upon which he could run his experiments; she had forced him to take another look at her. What he was beginning to see was an extremely sensitive being who seemed to have some conscious control over her actions beyond the manipulations of the scientist's behavior-modification techniques. What, he pondered, was he to do?

He dropped the coins on the carpet six times to determine the hexagram, the one in sixty-four that would help guide him. The first line was a yang line, representing the strong, active, creative principle of heaven. His next toss of the coins gave a yin line, the receptive, dark, yielding power of earth. Four more yin lines gave him the twenty-fourth hexagram, *Fu,* or "Return." Paul knew the Confucian commentary well.

The yang line represents the return of the light, a turning point. "The old is discarded, and the new is introduced," says Confucius. There is change, but it is not brought about by force; rather, it is a spontaneous change that is in accord with the nature of things. "It is not necessary to hasten anything artificially," comments Confucius. "Everything comes of itself at the appointed time."

Paul lay down before the fire, listening to the rush of air and the crack of burning embers. He realized that he had known all along what it was he had to do. The university wanted publishable science, and the aquarium wanted a trained whale that could perform for the tourists. Those agendas seemed secondary to Paul now that he had come eye to eye with Skana. "A change in accord with the nature of things," Paul thought. He wanted to know what he was dealing with, who Skana was, how intelligent she was. Was Skana really trying to communicate something of herself to him, or was that just his imagination? He wanted the truth. Wasn't that what science was all about—the search for truth? He'd been looking at the whale through a tiny window. Now he wanted to *know*.

Through the autumn days that followed, Paul began to play experimentally with Skana, developing techniques of participatory observation. He quickly found himself learning much more about her than he had during the vision experiments. On one sunny day, as an amusement as much as an experiment, Paul decided that he was going to paint Skana a picture of herself to see what response she might have to her own image. He spent the early hours of the morning sitting by the pool, painting a color portrait of Skana.

He carefully painted her distinctive dorsal fin, her white eye markings, her gray-white saddle patch, and her flukes. When he was finished he admired the painting, then held it up for Skana to view. From the far end of the pool Skana rolled on her side, lifted her left pectoral fin, waved it around, and then gave the water a mighty slap. Paul looked back at his painting, surprised to realize he had forgotten to include a pectoral fin. Paul dutifully added it and then displayed the painting to Skana, who showed no interest.

"Okay, Skana," said Paul. "Here." And he floated the painting out on the water. As the painting drifted toward the center of the pool, Skana, from the far end, gave one sharp stroke of her tail, and the painting was sucked in a vortex to the bottom of the pool.

"Skana!" Paul cried plaintively. "I just spent two hours making that painting." Skana showed no response to Paul's outburst. "Look, Skana," Paul continued. "That's not nice. Skannaaaa!" Paul continued to rail. Then Skana gave another single stroke with her tail; the painting, caught in the turbulence, fluttered up through the water to the surface and floated over to the edge of the pool in front of Paul. He picked the disintegrating cardboard painting from the water.

"Okay, Skana." Paul was astounded by Skana's aquatic dexterity. "I guess you're not so interested in my art."

Paul soon found that sounds attracted Skana's attention much more than anything else. He began to provide her with a variety of new sounds. He rang bells, sang, played his flute, and created a range of other sounds for Skana's enjoyment. Paul noted her reactions, observing how she oriented toward the various sound sources. Often she would swim around in the center of the pool, rolling over on her back as she listened and approaching close to the source of the sound.

When Paul lowered an electric sound generator into the pool, Skana came right up to it and rested the very tip of her lower jaw on the generator. Paul noticed that Skana's initial orientation to these sound sources was auditory; then she would inspect the source visually, and then she would return to listening.

One day, after listening to the sound generator for a while, Skana swam away, over to the gateway to the holding pool, poked her head inside, and stayed there. As soon as Paul stopped the generator, Skana returned to him. Paul then presented her with a new sound source, a set of earphones, which he hung over the water. Skana circled below and then raised her head up until the tip of her upper jaw rested against the earphones. She stayed there quite still, listening. Then she repeated her pattern of briefly investigating the sound source visually before continuing a period of protracted listening. Finally, as she had done before, she left the earphones, swam over to the holding pool, and stuck her head inside. She stayed there, refusing to come back.

Paul turned off the earphones, but he did not have another sound source immediately available. Then he remembered a bell that was in his bag, one that he had been playing for Yashi the night before. When he rang it, Skana immediately removed her head from the holding pool, swam to where Paul was leaning over the pool, and held her jaw about six inches away from the ringing bell. As before, Skana pulled back, looked at the bell, then returned to her listening posture with her jaw a few inches from the bell. After a while she returned to the gateway of the holding pool and stuck her head inside again.

This ritual of lodging her head inside the holding-pool gateway seemed to Paul to be another of her creative ways of saying no, a sort of whale's version of sticking her fingers in her ears. When Skana tired of a certain sound, as she had tired of the vision experiment, she let Paul know that she had had enough.

Paul sat on the training platform one evening after everyone had left the aquarium and played his flute to Skana. As she usually did whenever she heard a new sound, Skana came up close and pointed her lower jaw toward the flute. Then she dropped back into the water. She swam around, belly-up, with her jaw protruding from the surface of the water. Paul continued to play as she swam about, pumping herself along with her pectoral fins.

When Paul stopped playing, Skana came up along the edge of the training platform and nudged Paul with the side of her head. Paul put his bare feet on the top of Skana's head and began to massage her. As she lifted her head higher, Paul's feet were carried up, and he tipped over on his back. Skana then dropped back into the water, circled, and came up again by the platform.

Paul wondered if he could step out onto Skana's back as she raised up; certainly his weight would be no burden to the three-thousand-pound whale. He rolled his trousers up to his knees. As Skana bore against his feet, Paul tested his plan, transferring his weight slowly from the platform to the back of Skana's head. When she felt his weight, she stopped rising and held steady in the water. Paul began to ease away from the platform; Skana did not move. Soon Paul was standing on the back of Skana's head, bent over, holding on to the rail with one hand. Then he let go. Balance was delicate on Skana's slippery back, but he had the sense that she was as aware of the balance as he was. Agilely she moved about, dipping down until Paul's ankles were underwater, then rising again.

Paul soon realized that they had moved out of reach of the rail, and he began to feel a bit nervous. "Okay, Skana," he said out loud, "let's go back." Skana didn't respond. Skana again began to dip below, this time deeper until Paul's pants began to get wet; then she rose again gently. Paul tried to guide Skana with his toes, but she would not return to the edge of the pool. In his jittery excitement, Paul almost lost his balance; Skana held still while he recovered. He began to lose his concern as he became aware of Skana's steadfastness, and he soon forgot about trying to get back to the platform.

For several minutes Skana swam slowly on the surface with Paul standing on her back; then, as if she had tired of the game, she returned to the training platform. In awe of her control and gentleness, Paul stepped from her back to the platform. Skana dove and cut sharp loops below the surface of the water, bending and twisting her great body. Paul stood and watched for

some time before he realized that he was shivering; the evening
air was cold, and his trousers were wet. He went into the lab
and wrote a brief account in his notebook, sitting on a stool
next to a heater.

Paul contemplated how cooperative and resourceful Skana
was, how playful; more and more he felt an equal, if not a
pupil. When he approached Skana as a manipulative investiga-
tor, she refused to play along, but whenever he approached her
as a friend, she played openly. She seemed to coax him into
play. "But doesn't a cat coax you into play?" Paul thought.
Something, however, was different from anything he'd ever
seen before; cats—and even people—were more predictable, it
seemed, than Skana.

Over fried eggs and toast the next morning, Paul told Linda,
"Skana loves to play, but only if she can play as an equal.
She's changed my mind about her. As a scientist, I posed a
question and tried to answer it; in the lab everything was so
automatic. Sometimes I feel like it was a juvenile thing I was
doing with Skana, as if I was sort of looking through this little
pinhole at her. In a way I was almost blind. Sometimes I even
feel embarrassed when I'm around her, like I should make up
for treating her the way I did."

"I'm sure she'll forgive you," said Linda kindly, meaning it in
all seriousness.

"Yes," said Paul. "I think she has."

"What about that other whale?" asked Linda.

"Oh, Tung Jen," said Paul. "I don't know; I haven't really
done anything with him. I was saving him so he would be naive, his behavior not manipulated. He's been in that holding
pool all summer. . . ." Paul trailed off, thought for a minute,
and then—as if on another track—said to Linda, "You should
come out to the aquarium this afternoon. You have to meet
Skana. Why don't you bring Yashi out at about four; when everyone goes home, I'll introduce you."

"Okay," Linda agreed.

When she walked into the aquarium office with Yashi in a
backpack, it was almost five o'clock. After making introduc-

tions to the people in the office, Paul led her back into the lab, where he held Yashi as Linda stood at the window looking out at Tung Jen.

Soon the aquarium was quiet, the lights turned off. "I brought some sandwiches," said Linda. The two of them ate the picnic supper on the workbench, taking turns holding Yashi. Paul took a Chinese wind chime from a shelf in the lab. "This is a new one," he told Linda. "Skana hasn't heard this yet. She loves to hear new sounds."

The sun had gone down; Linda stood at the pool rail. Paul stood beside her, holding Yashi. Skana approached and raised her head from the water. Then she moved closer to Linda, turned her head, and looked at her from the side. "Skana," said Paul, "this is Linda. And this is Yashi." Skana held still. "Why don't you say something, Linda?" Paul whispered.

"Oh—hi, Skana," said Linda. Skana dropped back into the water and swam rapidly around the pool, upside down. Linda and Paul leaned against the pool rail. Then Paul put Yashi into his backpack and propped it up beside the pool, picking up the wind chime to play to Skana. After a while, Linda meandered back to the lab. She found the ladder leading to Tung Jen's pool and climbed down to where the baby whale bobbed in the water. The moon was full, appearing and disappearing as the scattered clouds were blown slowly across the sky. Linda could hear the ringing of the chime from Skana's pool. She walked over to the small pool and looked down at Tung Jen, who had moved up close to the pool's edge.

The young whale sat quietly in the water, steam rising from the surface of his skin around the rostrum and near his blowhole. Linda called out softly, "Hello. Are you lonely in there?" Tung Jen moved slowly to the edge of the pool and stuck his head out of the water.

Suddenly Linda felt a strange sadness come over her. Tung Jen was just a baby; he was about half as long as Skana and about a third her overall size. He seemed lethargic and unhappy compared to the bigger whale. Tung Jen had been captured in April, just before Yashi was born, and he had spent the last seven months alone in the little pool. Linda sang in a soft

voice as Tung Jen moved his head back and forth in the water.
She sat with the whale for almost half an hour while Paul was
busy with Skana. The moonlight would flood over the pool,
then fade away, and in the dark Linda sang quiet little songs to
the young whale.

Paul came up beside her, holding Yashi, and they sat there
silently for a long time. At last Linda said, "He's lonely."

"Yes," said Paul. "I really haven't paid much attention to
him. He was very vocal and quite active when he first came
here, and now he scarcely does anything anymore. I need to do
something for him."

"Can't Skana and Tung Jen be together?" asked Linda.

"Well," said Paul, "that's up to Vince Penfold, but it would
probably be nice for Tung Jen."

"Yes, I think he would like that."

There was snow on the ground the day Paul sat in Jim
Tyhurst's office at the university and told him about his plans
to do studies of vocal behavior with Tung Jen.

"Given the variety and flexibility of *Orcinus orca* vocal behavior," Paul told Dr. Tyhurst, "I plan to try using vocalizations
as a response, which might eliminate much of the tedious start-
stop-start-stop character of most behavioral investigations in
which a reward is presented following correct behavior."

"That sounds great, Paul," Dr. Tyhurst said. "How are things
going in general for you at the aquarium?"

"Good," said Paul. "I *would* like to put Tung Jen and Skana
together, but Vince Penfold and Murray don't think it's such a
good idea. They're afraid the whales might attack each other,
but I don't think so. I think they would keep each other entertained. I really think they get bored in those pools."

"Well, the whales belong to the aquarium, not to the university, so I guess there's nothing we can do about that, Paul. Oh,
by the way, Pat McGeer wants to see you. He's in his office."

Paul left Tyhurst's office in the psychiatry department and
walked over to Pat McGeer's office in the neurological laboratory. Paul was heading toward the secretary when McGeer
called from his desk, "Dr. Spong, come in." Paul walked in

through the open door and stood in the middle of the office. "Come with me, Dr. Spong," McGeer said as he walked around from behind his desk. "I have something for you."

Paul followed McGeer along the hallway and into the specimen cooler in the lab. McGeer walked inside and brought out a large, frozen package, which he set on the lab bench. "I hear you are getting quite interested in those whales, Dr. Spong," he said to Paul. "I'm going to be leaving. I just can't be in two places at once, and politics seems to be calling me. Dr. Louis Woolf will be taking over for me. Perhaps I can do more good in Victoria than I can as a scientist. Anyway, Dr. Spong, I want you to have this. It's Moby Doll's brain."

As McGeer opened the package, Paul looked at the enormous, highly convoluted brain. It was certainly the largest brain he had ever seen, the size of a man's whole head, looking as if it weighed about twelve or fourteen pounds. The two hemispheres were distinct, and the neocortex was large and bulging. "Thanks," said Paul. "I'm sorry you're leaving. Thank you; I'll look after this."

"You're doing very respectable work, Dr. Spong. Keep it up. Well, I have to run," said McGeer, shaking Paul's hand. "When Moby Doll died I kept that, thinking it would be useful someday. Don't let it thaw out until you're ready to so something with it."

"Okay," Paul said, and then turned back to look at the brain on the bench. He had heard stories of Moby Doll, but she had been captured before his time at UBC.

In 1964, Moby Doll became the first *Orcinus orca* to be held alive in captivity so that scientists could investigate it. Previously, in 1961, Frank Brocato and Boots Calandrino, from Marineland of the Pacific in Los Angeles, had captured a four-thousand-pound female in Newport Harbor. They loaded the whale onto a flatbed truck with a sling and drove it to Marineland. However, as they were hoisting the whale from the truck to the tank, she was smashed head-on into the wall. The next morning she seemed to be completely disoriented, swimming wildly and smashing her body into the walls of the tank, until she shook with violent convulsions and died.

A year later Brocato and Calandrino came north to Puget Sound in Washington State to try again. In Haro Strait, near San Juan Island, they managed to get a lasso around a female; but she pulled the nylon rope under their boat, catching it in the propeller and bringing the boat to a halt. The whale then surfaced and began to emit a high-pitched scream. Soon a male approached the boat, dove underneath, and whacked the hull with his flukes. Brocato fired a bullet from his .375 magnum rifle into the male, which then disappeared. He fired ten more shots into the lassoed female, who died on the spot. The whale was butchered with a chain saw and sold for pet food.

Stories of killer whale ferocity circulated among would-be captors. The hunt to capture a live killer whale took on an epic aura of daring and danger.

Then, in May 1964, Dr. Murray Newman of the Vancouver Aquarium commissioned artist Samuel Burich to sculpt a life-size model of a killer whale for the aquarium's new foyer. Burich and his assistant Joe Bauer rigged up a harpoon gun on a rocky outcropping on Saturna Island, in the tide-swept Gulf Islands of British Columbia, where pods of killer whales had been seen. They planned to shoot a whale so they could take underwater photographs of it and bring it back as a model for the sculpture.

They stood watch for two and a half months. During July a pod of thirteen killer whales was seen passing near Saturna every day for several days. On July 16 a single young whale left the pod and swam near the rocky bluff. Burich fired the harpoon, striking the whale in the back just behind the head. The whale thrashed about in the water, issuing a series of shrill whistles so loud the two men could hear them from the bluff. Immediately the other members of the pod came to the aid of the injured youngster, helping to keep it at the surface so it could breathe. Eventually the pod left, and the captors tried to winch their prize aboard a fishing vessel. The whale resisted mightily for three hours, leaping from the water repeatedly and plunging beneath the surface, trying to shake off the harpoon, all to no avail.

Burich fired his rifle at the young whale, hitting it at least twice, but the whale did not die. When Murray Newman at the Vancouver Aquarium got word that the whale was alive, he flew immediately by float plane to the site on Saturna Island. The three of them—Newman, Burich, and Bauer—conceived of a plan to tow the whale forty miles northeast across the Strait of Georgia to Vancouver Harbor. Burich spliced a rubber tire in the harpoon line to act as a shock absorber. They towed the whale, by then nicknamed Hound Dog for its puppylike docility, by the harpoon stuck in its back for twenty-six hours through whitecaps and squalling winds. The whale was towed into a makeshift pen at Burrard Drydocks and a week later moved to another pen at Jericho Beach near the university. Immediately the capture sparked controversy. The SPCA and other animal protection groups denounced the capture as cruel, and a leading Canadian international marine mammal expert, Dr. Gordon Pike, called on the captors to free the whale.

Murray Newman solicited Dr. Pat McGeer to oversee a scientific study of the whale. Thinking the whale was a female, they named it Moby Doll. Moby Doll was understandably in ill health, and took no food for fifty-five days. When the whale did start eating salmon, it lived for only thirty more days, drowning in its pen in October. During the autopsy, the scientists discovered that Moby Doll was a male. The story of docile Moby Doll, the friendly killer whale, received global media attention, and when he died, it was news from the local press to the London *Times*. Vancouver was saddened by the death.

"I worry about this sentimentalizing," Newman told the Vancouver *Province*. "It was a nice whale, but it was still a predatory, carnivorous creature. It could swallow you alive." Moby Doll's body was sold as pet food, and Dr. McGeer saved the brain in the neurological lab freezer.

On-February 15, 1967, Skana and fourteen other members of her pod were captured at Yukon Harbor, in Puget Sound, north of Seattle. Three of the whales died during the capture; three were shipped to Sea World aquariums in Florida and California, where all eventually died, and a young female was kept alive for three months in the Seattle aquarium. The seven remaining whales were released. Skana, a little over fourteen feet long and weighing 1.5 tons, refused to eat and was force-fed seventy-five pounds of ground fish and hamburger daily. On March 8 she was brought to Vancouver—a four-hour journey by truck from Seattle—and exhibited at the boat show. Her feeding schedule was reduced to once every four days in an attempt to stimulate appetite, and then, on March 13, she was offered live fish, which she accepted. She ate seventy-five pounds of live cod, salmon, herring, and flounder in the next few days, and an unsightly skin condition began to clear up.

Murray Newman saw the whale on arrival and bought her for twenty-five thousand dollars. She was moved to the Vancouver Aquarium on March 20, where it was discovered that she was not a male. Her boat-show name, Walter, was changed to Skana, the Haida name for the species, after a province-wide naming contest that was won by a six-year-old boy.

It was soon learned at these various oceanariums that the so-called killer whale was not as ferocious as legend maintained, and was in fact quite gentle. Trainers at Sea World and at the Vancouver Aquarium found that *Orcinus orca* could learn tricks, as dolphins did, for the entertainment of paying visitors. Orcas, as they became popularly known, were destined to become the world's leading aquarium attraction.

Six months after Paul Spong began working with Skana, in February 1968, a single male orca, named Hyak, was captured at Garden Bay in Pender Harbor, along the Sechelt Peninsula north of Vancouver. Paul went to Garden Bay with the intention of establishing a research facility that could possibly monitor orca behavior in the whales' natural habitat.

For two months Hyak was held alone in a net pen, but his family, or pod, stayed in the area. Paul noticed the whales often seemed to exchange vocalizations across the net barrier, and he taped these sounds. In April, seven members of Hyak's family swam into Garden Bay from the open water and were themselves captured by the nets and held in pens.

The largest of the eight whales held at Garden Bay was an eighteen-foot-long, eight-thousand-pound male named Skookum Cecil. Paul spent several days setting up his recording equipment on the floating dock that linked the makeshift pens.

On the day he was finally ready to record, Skookum Cecil leaped full-body from the water, thundering back down with a colossal splash that completely soaked all the equipment with corroding salt brine. Later, after four months in captivity, Skookum Cecil tore a hole in the net and escaped.

A six-thousand-pound female was sent to Marine World in California, and later to Shirahama, Japan, surviving for twelve years in captivity. A mature, pregnant female dubbed Bonnie was flown to Marine World Africa USA in California, where two months later she delivered a stillborn calf and then died herself. A male and female named Orky and Corky were sent to Marineland in California, where Corky died two years later. The aquarium would later capture another female to replace Corky, giving this new orca the same name. Orky and Corky II eventually conceived five babies in captivity, all of which died soon after birth. Orky was taught to entertain the Los Angeles tourists, and even appeared on television wearing huge sunglasses; as a local used-car dealer Ralph Williams quipped, "Orky says you'll get a whale of a deal." The ferocious killer whale, predator of the deep, had been tamed.

Two other whales were held in Pender Harbor—a large adult female named Natsidalia and her young calf, who clung to her side night and day. Paul took a particular interest in Natsidalia and her calf and noticed that the calf swam just above or behind his mother's pectoral fin. They breathed together on every breath, a phenomenon that fascinated Paul. When deciding on a name for the calf he consulted his trusty *I Ching*. He got hexagram number 13, *Tung Jen*, or "Fellowship with Men," which said that "clear, convincing, and inspiring aims" would bring about this fellowship. *Tung Jen* (pronounced *Toong Ren*) became the young calf's name. Later, he would also be called Hyak.

In July 1968 the Vancouver Public Aquarium decided to bring Tung Jen to the small pool in Stanley Park. Newborn orcas are seven or eight feet long and weigh around four hundred pounds. They probably begin life gaining up to forty pounds a day on their mother's milk, and ordinarily nurse for about two years. Tung Jen was only about a year old and weighed nine hundred pounds when the crane hoisted him from the water and onto a truck for shipment to Vancouver. During the entire procedure, Paul recorded Tung Jen's vocalizations, a constant high-pitched scream emitted in short bursts: "Eeeeeeee. Eeeeeee." Paul rode on the truck with Tung Jen, and through the entire ride to Vancouver the whale cried out with the same sound.

For the first two weeks in the Vancouver Aquarium holding pool, Tung Jen continued his call. "Eeeeee. Eeeeeee. Eeeeeee." In the interest of his planned experiments, Paul kept the whale isolated from human contact except for feeding. As the weeks passed, Tung Jen vocalized less and less, until he eventually stopped completely except for an occasional call while asleep. He floated stationary in a corner of the tiny pool, breathing slowly and quietly, day after day after day.

In November, Vancouver Aquarium biologists, under the supervision of Vince Penfold, performed a medical examination on Tung Jen's mother, Natsidalia. To get a blood sample from Natsidalia's fluke, they tied a rope around her body close to the flukes and hooked the end of the rope to a winch on a seine boat. When the flukes were winched from the water, Natsidalia's head and blowhole were forced underwater. She thrashed about, then went into a violent seizure. Suddenly Natsidalia stopped moving altogether, dead in the water. Her heart had failed. Tung Jen was orphaned.

It was January 1969, and Paul sat in the office of Vancouver Aquarium biologist Gil Hewlett, talking with Hewlett and Vince Penfold, aquarium curator, about his planned experiments with Tung Jen.

"Vocal behavior is very important in *Orcinus orca,*" he told them. "I think what we can learn from Pender Harbor is that these whales live in very tight-knit family groups, and that they rely heavily on vocalizations for certain communications among themselves. Tung Jen has been cut off from his family members; I think he is very depressed."

"What do you mean?" asked Penfold.

"When the large male, Hyak, was first captured at Pender

Harbor, he exchanged vocalizations for several weeks with the other whales in his pod," explained Paul, "and these whales eventually came into the pen area themselves and were captured. They showed none of the fear-escape behavior one would expect from a terrestrial mammal about to be captured. In view of the vocal exchanges with Hyak, the whales must have been aware of at least some of the danger, but they seemed quite unperturbed by their capture."

"Are you saying the whales were talking to each other about the nets?" Penfold asked, giving Paul a questioning sideways glance.

"I'm not making any assumptions about the level of complexity of the information exchanges involved," Paul assured him, "but only noticing the frequent and apparently meaningful vocalizations."

"What do you mean by 'meaningful'?" Gil Hewlett asked, seeming genuinely interested. "What's an example?"

"During separation and transport of the whales," Paul continued, "vocalizations were the most frequent and the most excited. When two of the whales were being prepared for transportation to Marineland, their pen was moved across Pender Harbor, so that they were separated from the other whales by more than a mile. I recorded continual exchanges between the two groups of whales. During the final stages of removing the whales from the water, the vocalizations became increasingly stereotyped and seemed frantic.

"The vocalizations I observed seemed to be most often associated with trauma and emotion. When Natsidalia was separated from Tung Jen, she would occasionally turn in his direction and emit a series of, say, ten or twelve distinct, loud clicks. The calf would respond with one of two separate vocalizations, and then Natsidalia would turn back away.

"Tung Jen," Paul went on, "emitted a single plaintive cry again and again after he was separated from his mother, while he was being transported to Vancouver and for the first two weeks that he was here. Now he has become silent and lethargic. I feel like I've made a mistake keeping him in isolation so that he would be a naive specimen. I'm guessing that they are very social animals in the wild and that isolation in a concrete pool is psychologically damaging. I plan to use sounds, especially music, as a reward to get Tung Jen to swim around and vocalize again." Paul looked at Gil Hewlett. "His behavior has already been modified by the trauma of isolation. So I think it would also help Tung Jen to put him in with Skana."

"It all sounds very interesting, Paul," said Hewlett.

"I just don't think we can put the whales together," said Penfold. "We still don't know what they would do to each other. You go ahead and do the sound experiments, but we shouldn't try putting the whales together yet."

Paul, with the help of Don White, spent the next two weeks setting up the apparatus for the experiments with Tung Jen. Their plan was to reward Tung Jen with music every time he swam around or vocalized. They used two differently pitched tones, one at 5 kHz and one at 500 Hz, to signal to Tung Jen that he was being asked to swim or to vocalize. Paul made a primitive underwater loudspeaker by fastening a six-inch stereo speaker inside a paint can, which was lowered into the water.

Soon thereafter, Paul and Don White began the trials with the young whale. Paul would sound the tone signaling the beginning of a trial. If Tung Jen moved out from the corner where he usually stayed, Paul would play him recorded music. The first time Paul played music through the speaker, Tung Jen swam directly over to it, upside down, and hovered with the tip of his lower jaw a few inches from the bottom of the paint can. If, during the music, Tung Jen stopped and went back to his corner, Paul would turn the music off.

After several days of trials, Tung Jen was moving easily out of his corner and swimming around the small pool, upon cue, for music reward. At first Paul rewarded Tung Jen with music simply for swimming around the pool. Soon he began to reward Tung Jen for any physical behavior. Paul did not dictate which behavior Tung Jen had to perform to get the sound reward; the whale could do anything he wanted, other than sit motionless in his corner, and Paul would play the music. Day by day Tung Jen's behavior became more active and creative; he began to swim and loop and dive through the water as Paul played him classical music, jazz, Ravi Shankar sitar ragas, Bob Dylan, and the Beatles.

When Paul would play the tone signaling the beginning of a trial, Tung Jen would arch his head up, bend his body, give a flick with his pectoral fins, and slide backward in the water. One day when Paul played the Beethoven Violin Concerto in D, Tung Jen turned onto his side, slapped the water with his pectoral fins, and squirted fountains of water from his mouth in time with the music. His flukes waved gracefully back and forth in the air, and to Paul it all seemed like an incredible dance.

Tung Jen seemed to enjoy all styles of music, though Paul wondered if he preferred classical violin. He seemed, furthermore, to demand a change if Paul played the same music too often. In one session Paul was playing East Indian music by Bismilla Khan and Tung Jen swam zestfully about the pool. Paul played the tape three times, eliciting an enthusiastic response each time. On the following day Paul used the same music to start the session. Upon hearing the signal tone, Tung Jen moved into the center of the pool, but when the Bismilla Khan tape began to play he stopped immediately and returned to his corner. Three times Paul repeated the procedure, and three times Tung Jen returned to his corner upon hearing the familiar tape. When Paul switched the reward tape to a modern jazz recording by flutist Paul Horn, Tung Jen enthusiastically responded by swimming and splashing about the pool. Again, as with Skana, Paul felt as if the whale were programming him as much as he was programming the whale. Tung Jen had communicated his desire for a change in music. It also seemed to Paul that Tung Jen's behavior reflected a considerable acoustic memory.

Although Tung Jen responded well to these tests, Paul had difficulty getting him to vocalize. The young whale had become almost totally silent during his nine months in virtual isolation. Paul tried to encourage him by playing a tape recording of Tung Jen's own sounds recorded at the aquarium, but Tung Jen did not respond. However, when Paul played tapes of Natsidalia and other whales from Tung Jen's pod, he immediately began to vocalize, and from that time on he continued to respond to the

500-Hz vocalization signal with a variety of sounds, for which he would get a musical reward.

When Paul played rhythmic, energetic music, Tung Jen's behavior would become exuberant. One day in the early spring of 1969, as Paul was playing currently popular rock music for Tung Jen, the whale began to charge along the side of the pool, do astounding full-body spins, dive down, and come up on the other side of the pool making back flips and splashing water up on the deck. Paul, eager to share the excitement, ran into the aquarium office and up to Gil Hewlett's door. "Gil!" he shouted. "You've got to come see this!" Paul led the biologist out to the pool, but by the time they got back, Tung Jen had quieted down and was swimming lazily in the pool.

"What?" said Hewlett.

"Uh, you should have seen what Tung Jen was doing." Paul looked disappointedly at the whale. "Oh, never mind. He's starting to get quite active with the music playing." Gil Hewlett cocked an ear at the music and smiled. Paul felt a little silly.

After Hewlett left, Paul walked down by the pool. "You really blew it for me, Tung Jen," he said. "They're going to start thinking I'm crazy." The incident made Paul wonder if perhaps a human presence was a significant part of the reinforcement for Tung Jen's behavior. He sat in his lab late that evening thinking about it. He decided to run an experiment to see if Tung Jen would respond to the reward of human presence, companionship. He thought long about how he might do it. As the night grew dark, his tiny desk lamp was the only light on in the building. He remembered the sensation he had had the first night that he saw Skana and Tung Jen breathing together as they slept; he had felt then that perhaps Skana somehow sensed his presence and wanted him to stay. But how could he test it?

Paul turned off his light and started for the door. He heard Tung Jen make a high, modulating sound: "ReeeeEEEEeeee!" He turned the light back on, and the whale continued the vocalization. "Okay," Paul thought, "we'll try something." Paul decided that he would leave his light on as long as Tung Jen vocalized. If he stopped for thirty seconds, Paul would turn the light off, but if he started again within two minutes, Paul would turn the light back on. If Tung Jen failed to vocalize for more than two minutes, Paul would go home.

When Tung Jen stopped vocalizing, Paul switched the light off and stood at the window of his lab. Within a minute, Tung Jen started up again—"ReeeeeeEEE, waaaaup"—and Paul turned the light back on. When Tung Jen stopped, Paul timed thirty seconds and switched the light off again. They repeated this pattern for about fifteen minutes before Tung Jen failed to make any sound for a full two minutes, at which point Paul left the lab. "Good night, Tung Jen," Paul said. "See you tomorrow."

The following evening, Paul again commenced the experiment. When it got dark, after everyone else had left the aquarium, Paul put his lab light on and stood inside, out of sight of Tung Jen. He made the vocalization signal, and Tung Jen responded. Thereafter, the only reward the whale received for vocalizing was the presence of the lab light. It was Paul's way of saying, "Here I am, and I will stay here as long as you make sounds."

When Tung Jen stopped, Paul turned the light off, and the whale started again. Three hours later, at midnight, Paul and the whale were still at it. Tung Jen would emit long, drawn-out sounds that would go on for several minutes at a time: "Unnn-noooooooooooooooo . . ." If he stopped for more than thirty seconds, Paul turned the light out, but the whale would always start up again right away. Not once was Tung Jen silent for a full two minutes, so Paul stayed on to see what would happen.

The sky had been growing light for some time before Paul noticed. Once when he turned off his lab light, he saw the soft blue light of the morning sky fall on his windowsill, and then he became aware of the birds chirping in the park. Tung Jen had kept him up all night.

He climbed from his lab down to Tung Jen's pool, and the young whale stuck his head up out of the water. "Nice, Tung Jen," Paul said, reaching over to caress the whale. Paul began to wonder exactly how Tung Jen made some of the sounds that he produced during the night. "How do you do that?" he said, then began to mimic the sounds he had heard, shrieking "Ahh-hooooooo," sounding more like a coyote than a whale.

He heard Skana vocalizing from her pool in the main public area, and he wandered out to see her. Paul leaned over the edge of Skana's pool, mimicking her sounds. Skana showed interest by moving closer, positioning her eye a few inches from Paul's open mouth. Paul wondered if Skana would be interested in how he made sounds. He turned to Skana with his mouth open, exposing his throat, going "Ahhhhhhhh" as loudly as he could manage. Skana peered into his mouth, and Paul bent over farther, putting his open mouth as close as he could to Skana's head and continuing a long, guttural series of *ahs*.

"Paul?" he heard from behind him. Turning and looking toward the glass doors of the aquarium, he saw Murray Newman and Vince Penfold.

"Oh, uh, hello, Murray; hi, Vince," he said as he walked toward them. "Just showing Skana and Tung Jen how humans make sounds. You wouldn't believe what Tung Jen did last night."

"Have you been here all night?" Murray Newman asked.

"Yes," said Paul, realizing how disheveled he looked. "I was doing some vocalization experiments with Tung Jen. He's feeling a lot better; he's really recovered from his depression. Last night—"

"You look like you need some sleep," Newman interrupted.

"Well, yes," said Paul. "I guess I do."

After the two men went inside, Paul sat by the edge of the pool for a while in silence, watching Skana swim. He longed to talk about what he was witnessing, but his bosses at the aquarium did not seem interested. He went home, and there he took a short nap. When he woke up in the afternoon he told Linda, "I'm going to work late for a few nights. I really think I'm onto something with Tung Jen; he kept me there all night. I think it's pretty obvious that he is craving contact. They like people! And Linda, something really clicked for me when I saw Moby Doll's brain. I knew that orcas weren't stupid, but it never really dawned on me until I saw that brain next to a human brain: They're very intelligent. I don't know how to say this to Murray or those guys, but the whales we have there in those pools are probably as intelligent as we are. It's just a *different kind* of intelligence."

"But they're so big; isn't it natural that they would have a big brain?" Linda asked.

"The part of the brain that drives the motor functions of the body is small," explained Paul, recalling his basic neurological training. "That part of the brain—the 'old brain' it's called—is about the same size in all large mammals: dogs, monkeys, humans, and whales. The part of the brain that is more highly developed in humans is the cerebral cortex," Paul said, clasping the top of his head with both hands. "It's the part of the brain that houses our conceptual thinking, abstraction, language. Well, the whale's brain is like the human brain, with a huge cerebral cortex, only bigger, and with more convolutions. Throughout the course of their evolution, the whales, for a reason that is certainly a mystery to me, responded to some opportunity or need by developing that huge brain. Everything that evolves, evolves for a reason. If they weren't using that brain for some purpose, it wouldn't have evolved. The question is, What are they using it for?"

"Well, they're not designing nuclear bombs," remarked Linda.

"No," said Paul. "They're not."

Through the spring of 1969 Paul found that both Skana and Tung Jen would do almost anything for human contact. He spent as much as forty-eight hours without leaving the aquarium, catnapping with his head on the lab bench. At times he would sit for hours at the edge of one or the other pool, playing his flute for Skana and Tung Jen.

One day, while talking with Don White, he said, "Don, Skana and Tung Jen both love music, and they love people; I have a feeling that they particularly like *live* music." Don agreed to bring his guitar the next day and try it out.

When Don played his guitar for Tung Jen, the whale moved in close, positioning the front of his head just a fraction of an inch from the sound box. He hovered near the guitar for a long time, apparently entranced by the sound. Paul wanted to try other live musicians with the whales, so he invited a friend who played the zither, and others who were willing to play for the whales. Skana and Tung Jen showed great enthusiasm, as did the musicians.

One morning, after spending all night at the lab, Paul looked up from his lab workbench to see Murray Newman standing in the doorway. It was early; Paul could hear the staff just arriving in the office. "Oh hi, Murray," said Paul cheerfully. "I'm glad you stopped by. I wanted to ask you about something."

"What is it?"

"Well, Murray, I was thinking that if we could rig up some sort of canopy over Skana's holding pool, we could do some more specific visual and sound experiments. I think we are just seeing the tip of the iceberg with these creatures."

"Paul?" said Dr. Newman in a quiet voice.

"Yes?"

"What's going on with all these people who are coming in here?"

"Oh, the musicians. We're learning some interesting things, Murray. Skana and Tung Jen are very attentive to music, and by watching them I'm beginning to learn how they listen, how their auditory systems work. Furthermore, the orcas are very communicative, more so than any animal we know of. Because of the complexity of their vocalizations, I feel that their vocal behavior may serve useful communicative functions. I'm not making any assumptions yet, but I think we are on a very interesting track here."

"You mean the whales are trying to talk to you?"

"Well . . ." Paul faltered. He felt more than just skepticism in the aquarium director's voice; he felt that he was being humored. "All I know, Murray, is that they are very intelligent, and we are only beginning to understand the complexity of their minds."

"I'm sure they're quite intelligent," Dr. Newman said. "They're very good performers. They're probably something quite like aquatic dogs."

Paul experienced a sinking feeling. He wanted to explain

what he had been learning, but was afraid he would not be understood. "Well, what about the canopy?" Paul managed to say, though he felt agitated. "Can we get it in the budget?"

"I'll see, Paul. But I'd rather not have these musicians parading through here. We are a public facility."

"Okay," said Paul, somewhat despondently.

Later, at home, Linda tried to cheer Paul up. "Come on, Paul," she urged. "Don't be so glum. It'll all work out."

"I don't know," said Paul. "I get the feeling that I'm losing them. I mean, I try to tell them stories about what is happening, but they don't even have a spark of enthusiasm. I can't communicate to them the opportunity we have here." Paul sat, drinking a glass of wine. When he finished, he circled his finger around the top edge of the goblet and began to produce the eerie sound of vibrating crystal. He looked up at Linda and smiled. "Skana will love this," he said with an elfish grin.

The next day Paul worked all day in the university lab, and in the evening he went back to the aquarium, taking his wine goblet for Skana. He performed some vocalization trials with Tung Jen, then took the goblet down to Skana's pool. He crouched on Skana's training platform and began to make the goblet vibrate. Skana showed immediate interest. She came over to where Paul sat and put her jaw near the glass. When Paul stopped, she nudged him, and he began again, leaning out over the water. But as Skana came up to him he lost his balance, and while reaching for the railing he dropped the goblet. He watched it float to the bottom, hit the tiles, and break.

The next morning from the university, Paul phoned aquarium assistant Chris Whiting and mentioned the broken glass on the bottom of Skana's pool, asking him to get it out if he could. Chris told him that someone had already noticed the glass, and that Murray Newman was pretty upset about it.

After that phone call Paul went to see Dr. Louis Woolf, Pat McGeer's successor as head of the neurological lab. Paul explained to Dr. Woolf what he was doing at the university with sensory input in mammal brains, and preparing for the brainwave monitoring of human meditators. Then he explained his experiments at the aquarium, being careful to sound scientific and rational. He did mention at the end of his conversation, "I'm not speculating as to the eventual results, Dr. Woolf, but we may be on the doorstep of some interesting discoveries about cetacean intelligence. They are quite fascinating creatures."

Dr. Woolf reminded Paul that his turn in the faculty lecture series was coming up, and that perhaps he could formulate some of his conclusions for that lecture. "I'd be very interested in what you are finding out, Dr. Spong," said Dr. Woolf, genuinely. Paul felt encouraged; he left Dr. Woolf's office in high spirits in spite of his nagging concern about the trouble he might be in at the aquarium because of the broken glass.

Paul spent the next month preparing for his lecture. His enthusiasm became almost manic. He rose early in the morning, often working at the kitchen table over coffee. He spent most of his days in his office at the university, pulling together his research data, searching through the published literature on the subject of cetaceans, and formulating his conclusions. No lab animal in the history of behavioral science had ever done what Skana did when she refused to perform the visual-acuity test and apparently got wrong answers on purpose. Paul was certain that Skana's "spontaneous reversal" would pique the curiosity of the scientific community.

As the day approached for Paul's lecture, he was working at a hectic pace, night and day, at home, at the university, and at the aquarium. Sleeping only three or four hours a night, Paul continued his tests and observations of Skana and Tung Jen as he compiled his data and organized his presentation. His plan was to give an outline of the physiological discoveries about *Orcinus orca* and then introduce the more sublime and far-reaching discoveries concerning orca communication and intelligence. He wanted to word things just right, so that he would not offend the conservative sensibilities of the university and the aquarium; at the same time, he felt he had some important new insights into the nature of orca intelligence, social interactions, and communication, and that the upcoming lecture would give him the opportunity to clarify his ideas for the academic community.

One question, however, continued to plague Paul. His observations of Skana, Tung Jen, and the pod of whales at Pender Harbor had led him to the conclusion that these highly evolved and social creatures could not be studied adequately in small oceanarium pools.

"These are acoustic animals," Paul explained to Linda one night a week before his lecture. "In the wild, they locate themselves and other pod members, find food, and communicate among themselves with sound. Sound is as important to them as vision is to us. These aquarium pools are like sensory-deprivation tanks to the whales. They are cut off from their families, to which they have strong bonds, and the environment of concrete and tile walls would be like being in an acoustic hall of mirrors. It must be very confusing and disrupting. We're not getting a completely accurate picture of the orcas, because we aren't seeing what an orca is really like. By keeping them isolated in these little pools we're probably driving them insane, literally. That's the truth of it, but should I say so in my lecture?"

"Well, why not?" asked Linda.

"It's not going to be received very well by some people."

"The university wouldn't fire you for saying what you think; that's your job."

"Yes," said Paul, "but the aquarium isn't the university. They own the whales, and they call the shots. They aren't so interested in science over there as they are in teaching Skana and Tung Jen to entertain the visitors. They're interested in science as long as it doesn't disrupt their business. They want safe, polite science. Skana would have to walk into the office and make a phone call before they'd believe that she can communicate."

Linda laughed. "I don't know, Paul," she said encouragingly. "I'm sure you can find a way to say it without offending anyone."

"Maybe," said Paul.

During the week before his lecture, Paul hardly slept. He avoided his colleagues at the university and at the aquarium, staying to himself in his office or lab. He felt confident about

his upcoming presentation, but he still had not decided
whether he should mention his conclusions about aquarium
pools. The dilemma occupied his mind night and day.

On the evening before his lecture, Linda talked him into relaxing, convincing him that rest would do more for his mind
than thought.

"Okay," said Paul, leaning back on a pillow by the fire and
closing his eyes.

When he woke up, he could tell that more than just a few
minutes had passed. Bright orange embers glowed where the
fire had been burning. Linda sat nearby, reading.

"Oh." Paul propped himself up on his elbows sleepily. "How
long have I been asleep?"

"About an hour. I made some tea; I think it's still warm."

They sat up late, drinking tea and talking. Yashi woke up,
and Paul brought him out by the fire for a while. Linda fed him
and then went into the bedroom to lie down with him as he
went back to sleep. When Paul went in a few minutes later,
both Yashi and Linda were asleep on the bed. He covered them
up and went back out to the fire.

He took his *I Ching* from the bookshelf. "Okay," he thought.
"I need some advice." Concentrating on the question, he asked,
"Tomorrow, at my lecture, should I mention how I feel about
aquarium pools?"

Paul cast his coins as usual, and this time got hexagram number forty-seven, "Oppression." He read carefully in the book.
"When one has something to say, it is not believed." Paul was
startled by the message of the ancient verse, and he read on in
the Confucian commentary. "Superior men are oppressed and
held in restraint by inferior men," the commentary said. "It is
important to be strong within and sparing of words."

"Well," thought Paul, "I guess that settles it. 'Sparing of
words.' Maybe I should be careful, just present my data." He
mused on this for some time, then went back to reading the
text.

The commentary on the top line read, "He fears that he may
have cause for regret if he makes a move. But as soon as he

grasps the situation, changes this mental attitude, and makes a firm decision, he masters the oppression."

Paul was intrigued at how these words, written twenty-five hundred years before, could seem so appropriate. He decided then and there to say exactly what he thought in the lecture and to accept whatever consequences his words might engender among the academic and professional communities.

Paul was steadfast the next day at the university. Maybe it was the encouragement of Confucius, or perhaps his own inner resolve, but he somehow felt absolutely certain that he was doing the right thing. He waited anxiously in the hallway as students and professors filed into the lecture hall. He was not surprised to see Murray Newman there, but he was surprised to see Vince Penfold with him.

Paul was pleased that the lecture hall was full; students were standing in the doorway and sitting around the edges of the room. He began with some known physiological data about *Orcinus orca:* "The largest known *Orcinus orca* was observed in Scotland, and measured to be thirty-one feet long, weighing nine tons, with flukes nine feet wide tip to tip." Paul carried on about the gestation period, estimated to be twelve to sixteen months, and talked about the close and extended nursing relationship between mothers and calves.

Then he talked about the experiments. "Our studies of the visual acuity of *Orcinus orca* have established that their vision underwater is sufficient for use in guidance of much short-range behavior; they see underwater about as well as a cat sees in air.

"However," he continued, "vision serves only local, specialized functions. Audition, passive listening and echolocation, guides general orienting behavior; they are acoustic animals. The relative significance of audition and vision in the killer whale and in humans is roughly reversed. We have even found that we can use sound itself, especially music, as a reward; music actually worked better than food to motivate behavior.

"They have no ears, however, as land mammals do; the external ear is just a pinhole, and the canal is blocked. The anterior regions of the lower jaw and rostrum seem to function as the principal input channels for acoustic signals.

"*Orcinus orca* produces an impressive array of sounds, including echolocation clicks, burst-tones, pure tones, whistles, hornblows, frequency-modulated screams, and sounds that I cannot really find any human words for. Orca vocal behavior displays sufficient variability, complexity, and capacity for modification and elaboration, that it seems likely to serve useful communicative functions. Their capacity to send, detect, attend to, derive information from, and otherwise process and store auditory information is by any standards quite remarkable.

"*Orcinus orca* has an enormous brain, with more convolutions per surface area than the human brain. The highly developed cerebral cortex leads me to conclude that the orca has evolved this brain through using it, just as primates did. *Orcinus orca* occupies a place in the oceans equivalent to the one which humans occupy on land: at the top of the food chain with no predators. Although they eat mostly fish, they can eat anything they want, from a sea lion to other whales. Yet—and I found this quite interesting—these whales are extremely docile, even, if I may say so, friendly toward people. I've been in the water with Skana, she has rubbed my feet with her teeth, carried me on her back, and not once threatened to harm me.

"It is too early in my research to make any assumptions as to the exact nature of *Orcinus orca* intelligence, but I am quite excited about the possibilities. Among themselves they are highly social animals, they communicate with unknown complexity, and they appear to have strong family ties. Let me tell you about one of the more startling exhibitions of a conscious intelligence I witnessed with Skana."

Paul described to the audience the "spontaneous reversal," Skana's purposeful refusal to answer the test questions correctly. "This is the first time in the history of behavioral science that a lab animal so obviously refused to do something it knew how to do. And not only did Skana refuse, she gave the *exact wrong* response eighty-three times in a row. I do not make any conclusions yet, but I feel that we are heading toward some fascinating discoveries about their intelligence.

"My respect for this animal has sometimes verged on awe. *Orcinus orca* is an incredibly powerful and capable creature, exquisitely self-controlled and aware of the world around it, a being possessed of a zest for life and healthy sense of humor and, moreover, a remarkable fondness for and interest in humans." Paul sensed a division in his audience. He saw a few professorial eyes roll, but most of the audience seemed genuinely interested. He felt a surge of confidence.

"It has been my feeling," Paul began slowly, looking around the room, "since observing the semicaptive whales at Pender Harbor, that *Orcinus orca* in the wild, in the company of family, is a decidedly different creature than the *Orcinus orca* that we observe in the aquarium. Whales maintained in captivity are probably typically deprived of opportunities to experience and express many basic elements of normal auditory behavior and are probably subject to substantial levels of sensory deprivation. It is important, therefore, to assess the extent and significance of changes in the acoustic environment associated with captivity, and if possible identify and provide effective substitutes.

"*Orcinus orca*, being a highly evolved and complex animal, may be so different from us in the functional organization of its nervous system and the physical construction of its body that, despite our common mammalian ancestry, our capacity to understand even its more elementary characteristics is severely limited. I am not convinced that we get a full or completely accurate picture of *Orcinus orca* in an aquarium setting. Perhaps an alternative would be to work in semicaptive situations like the one at Pender Harbor, where it might be possible to train whales for release and recall. The feasibility of releasing trained cetaceans into the ocean and having them return upon command, has been well established in studies with dolphins conducted by the U.S. Navy.

"In any event," Paul said in conclusion, "my experiences with Skana and Tung Jen at the Vancouver Aquarium have led me to conclude that holding them there is not going to further

our true knowledge of them. The captive environment, aside
from being a sensory-deprivation experience, is also socially
depriving. While in isolation in the small holding pool, Tung Jen
was severely damaged psychologically, and I share in the responsibility for that insensitivity. I believe now, however, that
these whales should probably be freed, and that we should
continue our studies with free or semicaptive *Orcinus orca* in
its natural habitat.

"We have just begun to glimpse the magnificence of *Orcinus
orca*. Thank you very much."

The room was filled with a polite applause and much chatter.
Most of the audience began to file out into the hallway, led by a
hurried reporter who stopped at the first pay phone in the
building. Several graduate students gathered around the po-
dium to ask questions. Paul fielded a host of academic questions while peering over the students' heads to see if Murray
Newman, Dr. Tyhurst, and Dr. Woolf were still in the room. He
could not see them.

But the political fallout from Paul's lecture was obvious
enough when he showed up at the aquarium the next day. The
headlines in the Vancouver *Sun* that day were FRIEND WANTS
SKANA FREED, and LET THE WHALE GO, and the reaction was
mixed. On the one hand, there was a note for him from celebrated Vancouver newspaper columnist Jack Wasserman asking for an interview. On the other hand, however, Murray Newman was incensed. Dr. Newman escorted Paul to the aquarium
library and summoned Vince Penfold. The three of them sat
around a large table.

"Paul," said Newman, "we are not at all pleased with the
research program. I've already mentioned the musicians or
whatever they are. Vince feels that the broken glass we found
in the pool showed carelessness and endangered the animals.
We're going to have to take a whole new look at this. According to your speech yesterday, I get the feeling you are not too
interested in continuing. I think you should prepare another
proposal for us to look at; until then, let's just consider the
research on hold."

Paul argued briefly, but soon realized he was not going to

convince the two men that his line of inquiry was legitimate.
"This stuff about the whales talking to you sounds a bit
wacky," Vince Penfold told him.

Paul left the meeting quite frantic and walked down to the
pool, where he sat on the edge. His hands were trembling from
anger and exhaustion. Skana swam by, circled, and swam by
again. She stuck her head up out of the water and turned her
eye to Paul, who was compulsively beating his fist into his
palm.

"They're making a joke out of it, Skana!" Paul said angrily. "I
don't care if they do think it's wacky! Damn it!" His thoughts
were completely confused and frustrated. "They haven't heard
anything yet, Skana." Skana nudged him, but Paul hardly noticed, and continued to pound his fist on the poolside. Suddenly
Skana took Paul's hand in her mouth. He tried to jerk it away,
but she had a firm grip with her teeth on the back and palm of
his hand. She held on tightly. "Let go, Skana!" Paul shrieked,
but she remained motionless in the water, gripping his hand
firmly, though without hurting him.

Paul looked at Skana tenderly and took several deep
breaths. Slowly his body stopped shaking, and he relaxed his
hand in Skana's mouth. Skana gently let up on the pressure,
and Paul carefully pulled his hand back. Tears started to roll
down his face. He wiped them with his shirt sleeve. In the
corner of his foggy vision he saw Vince Penfold standing at the
rail on the far side of the pool. Paul instinctively averted his
gaze and just sat there for several minutes. Shaking his head,
Vince Penfold walked away. Paul looked at Skana and smiled.
The knowledge that he knew what he knew swept over him
like a great wave of solace.

Paul felt that he had to begin repairing his relationships, and
decided to start at the university. He went to see Dr. Woolf,
who was officially his boss.

Paul's lack of sleep was telling. The fatigue was visible in his
already deep-set eyes, although his enthusiasm almost covered
up his exhaustion.

"I think we should move our whale study to Pender Harbor,"

he said, looking straight ahead and sitting on the edge of his chair. "Or perhaps some other location. Everything tells me that *that* is where we will really begin to get a look at these animals. This work is just beginning with cetaceans, in a few places, but this will be unique. No one is doing this work with *Orcinus orca,* and we have a perfect spot here in the Georgia Strait or farther north."

"Paul," said Dr. Woolf, "I think that you need to slow down a bit. Let's take a long look at it, and who knows?" He shrugged his shoulders. Both men were silent for a while, then Dr. Woolf told Paul that his job at the aquarium was in jeopardy and that the aquarium people were upset at his suggestion that Skana be released.

"Maybe I shouldn't have said anything." Paul spoke fast and gestured energetically. "I didn't want to offend them. Murray Newman has been very patient with me, and I didn't want to upset him. I wasn't even going to mention it, but I got this *I Ching* reading—"

"What?" asked Dr. Woolf.

Paul went into a long, rambling explanation of the *I Ching,* which was a disaster. He sounded blundering and incoherent. Very kindly, Dr. Woolf suggested to Paul that he needed a rest, and Paul agreed. Dr. Woolf then told Paul that Jim Tyhurst wanted to see him, and Paul thanked him and left.

Jim Tyhurst was very blunt: "Paul, you are a little bit out of control. We're going to ask you to check in downstairs. We're concerned about you, Paul, and we want to know that you are all right."

"Downstairs" was the university psychiatric ward. Paul stared at Tyhurst in shock, his hands shaking. "I'm just tired, Jim. I'm not communicating. I just need to sleep for a few days. I'll just go home and sleep."

"You should just check in downstairs, Paul."

"No, really, I'll just go home and sleep."

"You can check in voluntarily or not," Tyhurst said.

"Are you saying I'm crazy, too?"

"I'm just saying you need more than rest, Paul; you need to calm down, and you need some observation."

Paul voluntarily checked into the university psychiatric ward. He had a room to himself, with a bed, a desk, a carpet, and a window that looked out onto the lawns and trees of the UBC campus. Paul was wide awake and talkative when Linda arrived with Yashi and some supper. He asked her to please phone Jack Wasserman and set up a time for the interview with the columnist. Linda left at about ten, when the doctor in charge put Paul on sedatives to help him sleep.

After three days of rest, Paul asked to go home, but the doctor told him that he had to stay for a while longer. He became agitated, which only reinforced the opinion that he was manic and out of control. Linda brought the bad news that Jack Wasserman had canceled the interview. Paul phoned the newspaper office and left several messages, none of which was ever answered. Jim Tyhurst brought him the news that his job at the aquarium had been terminated; his contract, which was due to expire soon, would not be renewed. The official reason, Tyhurst said, was that Paul's methods were endangering the whales, and the broken glass on the bottom of Skana's pool had been cited as evidence.

Several weeks passed as the rosebushes on the campus lawns blossomed outside his window. At first Paul was quiet and stayed to himself, but he soon made friends among the other patients. He could slip out and go up to his lab, and he would detour to pick up books and other gifts for the patients. Paul was popular inside, and although he wasn't aware of it, he was slowly becoming quite popular on the outside. Whereas the daily columnist had shied away, the student papers and the underground press, the weeklies and the small magazines thought Paul's conclusions were very interesting, and reporters were already on the prowl for the story.

On the day that Paul was discharged, Jim Tyhurst informed him that the university liked the idea of a field station and that there would probably be a budget for the project. Paul, "as a matter of formality," was to make a proposal, but the university was convinced of the importance of the research with free whales that Paul had touched on in his lecture.

Once out of the psychiatric ward, Paul went to work writing

up the report of his research and trying to get local reporters to tell his side of the story. Paul's picture was in several of the small papers, as was Skana's. "I'm sorry," Paul told his friends over dinner one night, "that it's coming out like the aquarium is my enemy; it gets distorted. It's just that Skana and Tung Jen became my friends. I know Murray and those guys are just doing their job, and I'm not surprised they fired me. Murray is actually a very nice man. It takes a lot to upset him."

"Where will you go to set up the field station?" a university colleague asked.

"I don't know, mate," said Paul. "We should find out where the orcas hang out and go there, I guess."

"When will you leave?"

Paul and Linda looked at each other and shrugged. "Maybe we'll look around this winter, and move next spring," guessed Linda. "Too bad we can't take Skana and Tung Jen with us."

"I'll miss them," Paul said quietly.

"We'll get to see them," Linda encouraged.

"It won't be the same," Paul smiled as if he accepted the painful fate of having to end his work with Skana and Tung Jen.

"They'll miss you, too, Paul," said Linda, "and they're the ones still in captivity. At least you got out."

3

Blackfish Sound

Paul was something of a minor celebrity in the intelligentsia corner of the Cecil pub during the fall of 1969. The fact that he'd been fired from his job endeared him to most of the regular clientele, and the fact that he had been publicly called a madman by his former employers endeared him to almost everybody. His picture had appeared in enough newspapers that strangers would sit down at his table and say things like "I'm right with you, man," or "Hey, Paul, I dig what you're doing; if I could help you in any way . . ."

Paul quickly learned the first lesson of fame: It can be a nuisance. He could no longer have a quiet beer in his favorite corner of his favorite pub; there was always a crowd. Nevertheless, he was good-humored and friendly and, for the most part, enjoyed the attention. One day in August, Paul sat in the corner of the pub telling a group of avid listeners about his experiences.

"I did an absolute flip in my mind," he said earnestly. "I was an intent student in university, and I was trained to be a scientist, not emotionally involved at all with my subject. I was a data collector and a behavior manipulator. But it was blind science. Skana forced me to interact with her more closely, more openly, and more emotionally. I don't even know when

the exact moment was—maybe it wasn't until right near the
end when I really let go of my remote scientist role—and I
became something else, more of a participant-observer."

"Do you need any help setting up the research station? I've
got a boat," someone offered.

"I don't know, mate," said Paul. "I don't even know exactly
where I'm going. Pender Harbor is too tied up with the aquariums. They want to capture the whales for shipment to pools all
over the world. I'll need to find another place, but I don't even
know where to start looking."

Paul's old pub friend Walt was there, and he piped up, "Go to
Alert Bay, Paul, and ask the Nimpkish Indians. They'll know
exactly where to go."

"Where's Alert Bay?"

"It's the town on Cormorant Island, near the north end of
Vancouver Island. You take a ferry from Kelsey Bay to Beaver
Cove, from one log dump to another, you might say, and then
on to Alert Bay. That's all heavy logging country up there; I've
been tree planting there. You don't drive your car off the ferry
in Alert Bay; they winch it off. Then you see this fantastic
painting of a killer whale and a sign that reads, ALERT BAY,
HOME OF THE KILLER WHALE. The Nimpkish band is centered in
Alert Bay, and a lot of its people are fishermen. I'd go there
first; they'd be able to tell you where to look for killer whales."

"Orcas!" said Paul. "Let's call them orcas. I'm beginning to
resent that word, 'killer.' But sure, Walt, Alert Bay. Alert Bay it
is."

Paul and Linda immediately began to make plans to go to
Alert Bay. Their life, which had slowed down at the beginning
of the summer, began to pick up speed again.

Linda, Paul, and some friends organized the Pacific Killer
Whale *(Orcinus orca)* Foundation, which rented a mailbox and
started collecting a mailing list. Their first campaign was to get
people to learn to call killer whales "orcas." "You may as well
call us 'killer apes,' " Paul told the reporter from the *Georgia
Strait,* Vancouver's underground tabloid newspaper. The organization became known affectionately as KWOOF—which, if

pronounced correctly, sounded like an orca blowing at the surface of the water.

For their trip to the islands of the northern inside passage, Paul and Linda sold their Volkswagen van and bought a well-used red Long Land-Rover, which became known as the KWOOFmobile. Paul was still working at the university lab as an assistant professor of psychiatry, screening applicants to be meditators in his brain-wave studies. The KWOOFmobile was a common sight as it raced between the wooded grounds of UBC, the flowered neighborhoods of Kitsilano, and the electric buzz of downtown Vancouver.

Before leaving for Alert Bay, Paul wanted to return to the aquarium to see Skana. On a fine autumn day, Paul, Linda, Yashi, Walt and Roy Bonin, the zither player, went to Stanley Park. They walked through the zoo, stopping to look at the polar bears, the seals, and the monkeys. They paid, like every other visitor at the aquarium gate, and went in to see the whale show.

The five of them sat high in the bleachers as Skana went through her routine of fluke slaps, leaps, and splashes for the crowd, all on cue from the trainer's whistle. Skana leaped straight up until her entire body was out of the water, slammed back down with a tremendous splash, and then opened her mouth for a bucket of herring.

"On this next one," said the young hostess, in a blue, white, and red aquarium outfit, "some of the kids in the first row might get wet." The kids huddled together and squealed excitedly in anticipation of getting sprayed with water by the whale. The trainer blew his whistle, and Skana looped around the pool twice under the water. On her second pass in front of the gallery she leaped and came down in such a manner that a perfect rainbow of water curled over the low Plexiglas shield, showering a few drops on each child. The children's shrill voices shrieked in unison. Skana came up in front of the children and vocalized loudly, shaking her head. Paul and Linda laughed, letting out orcoid shrieks.

After the show, Paul and Linda took Walt, Roy, and Yashi down to see Skana. Paul opened the door on the railing and stepped into the pool area. His friend Don White was there, and they talked for a while. Then Paul knelt down by the pool. Skana recognized him immediately and swam up to see him. Paul stroked Skana on the head; he crooned as quietly as he could so as not to attract attention, and Skana nudged him. "Well, Skana, this has to be quick, girl. I'm going up north to see your friends. Sorry to be leaving. Somehow I'll find a way to get you out of here." Paul laughed as Skana bobbed up and down in the water.

A storm was rattling the windows of Paul and Linda's house on a night in December 1969. The house sat on pilings at the end of a long boardwalk stretching across a North Vancouver tidal marshland known as the Maplewood Mudflats. They had bought the house from an old squatter who had brought it there to one of the few remaining natural settings in the city. They were planning to go to Alert Bay after the New Year, and had organized themselves to be gone for a month or more. Rain was beating against the windows when they heard a knock on the door. A neighbor had come to call Paul to the phone. Paul put on his coat and went next door.

"Yes," Paul answered.

"Paul, this is Wendy; you met me in Irvine's Landing when those whales were caught up there."

"Oh, yes, sure. What's going on?"

"Well, those same fishermen have caught four more. They're holding them in nets. Everyone is saying there's a bunch more hanging around outside the nets, but it's dark now, so it's hard to tell. There's gale-force winds out there, and they're having a hard time keeping it together. The boats are blowing all over the place, and Garden Bay is crisscrossed with fishnet."

Without hesitating, Paul said, "We'll be up there as soon as we can. We were already organized to go to Alert Bay, so we'll just come on up."

Irvine's Landing and Pender Harbor are small fishing and logging towns ninety kilometers northwest of Vancouver along the mainland coast, looking west across Georgia Strait to Vancouver Island. The Pacific Ocean tides sweep into the inland passage between Vancouver Island and the mainland through the Strait of Juan de Fuca, which lies between British Columbia and Washington State, 180 kilometers to the south. From there the tides flow south into Puget Sound and north into Georgia Strait and then into the countless fjords, inlets, and waterways that make up British Columbia's twenty-five thousand kilometers of rocky coastline. Irvine's Landing sits near the mouth of Jervis Inlet, which twists seventy-five kilometers into the coastal mountain range.

When Paul, Linda, and Yashi arrived in the KWOOFmobile, they got the rest of the story about the whale capture. On the morning after the storm, the fishermen had captured the rest of the pod, which had stayed with the four whales already in the nets. Altogether, twelve whales had been captured in the bay, but one bull had torn through the nets and escaped, leaving eleven.

A fisherman told Paul, "That one bull tore right through the nets, like nuthin' to it. It seemed like he was trying to show the others how to get out, 'cause he kept tearing back in, and then back out. Some killer whales know all about fishnets. I've heard of 'em going inside a set, eating salmon, and getting out before the net is closed. And I heard a story about a gill-netter in Alaska who saw three killer whales approaching his net after he'd set it. They dove, and he didn't even see the corkline ripple, but when he pulled the net in, it had three holes in it. Believe me, that whale knows what nets are all about."

Paul photographed the captured whales and recorded their vocalizations. Graeme Ellis from Sealand in Victoria was there, and other scientists showed up. Bids were coming in from all over Europe and North America; Bill Cameron, the fisherman who had caught the whales, stood to make a lot of money. Four large whales, a mature male and three adult females, were released because they were too big to ship. Another female escaped while the captors were trying to corral her into a sling. After being released, one of the females gave birth, and the four adults and the newborn swam away. Paul conjectured that the whales may have come into Pender Har-

bor for the purpose of giving birth. He did not know it then, but
he would meet up with these same whales later.

Two adolescent whales, a male and a female, were shipped
to Marine World in San Francisco. A two-ton female was
shipped to England and later to France, where she died after a
year. An infant female, an adolescent female, and an adolescent male were delivered to Marineland of the Pacific in Los
Angeles, where the infant died the following year, and the
young male a year later. The other female was named Corky,
and she was mated with Orky, who had been captured in the
same spot eight months earlier. Corky would be the first whale
to conceive and give birth in captivity, although the baby—and
four others that later followed—would die shortly after birth.
Corky and the other whales that were caught there in Pender
Harbor were far from their normal home. They were, in fact,
members of an orca family that made its home in Johnstone
Straits, where Linda and Paul were heading. Paul would one
day know this family well, and eventually he would gain an
even deeper understanding of the tragedy he had witnessed as
Corky was hoisted from the water. His fate, however—and he
did sense this—was intimately linked with hers.

"Healthy orcas in the wild probably live about as long as
people do, fifty to eighty years, and maybe longer," Paul told
his friends at Irvine's Landing. "You saw how tight-knit they
are, the way they stay together. I was thinking of studying here,
but these captures are for aquariums, not for observation;
Linda and I plan to look for a spot farther north. Anyway," he
added, "with these captures last year and this year I doubt the
whales will be back here." Paul was correct; orcas did not
return to Pender Harbor after 1969.

After the Irvine's Landing New Year's Eve party, Paul, Linda,
and Yashi rode on the ferry to Vancouver Island and drove
north along the Island Highway on a blustery-cold January
day. They passed through the town of Campbell River at the
north end of Georgia Strait and then turned inland through the
forested foothills of the island range. They returned to the
coast at Kelsey Bay, a logging camp at the southern end of
Johnstone Strait. The twenty-foot tides that sweep around both

ends of Vancouver Island meet here among the rocky passages
such as Surge Narrows and the Uclatas, creating massive currents and great whirlpools that even the most experienced fishermen negotiate with considerable respect. The orcas, Paul
would learn later, were divided into two main groups: those
that normally stayed north of these tidal rapids and those that
normally remained south.

A sleeting rain beat against the windows of the Land-Rover
as the three travelers drove onto the ferry that would take them
north to Beaver Cove and then to Alert Bay on Cormorant Island. As the ferry chugged through the icy wind, Paul stood at
the rail, gazing over the gray water. Rocks, islands, and snow-
peaked mountains rose up all around; the choppy sea looked
vast, and disappeared into a mist.

Paul sat in a comfortable wooden chair in the Nimpkish Hotel pub, looking out of a huge window at the whitecaps of
Broughton Strait, beyond which rose the mountain peaks of
Karmutsen and Hoy on Vancouver Island. A trim, dark-haired
young man in gumboots and a plaid wool shirt sat down at his
table. "Jimmy'll be here in a minute," he said, smiling.

"Oh, fine. Hi, I'm Paul Spong." Paul reached out over the
table with his hand.

"I figured," said the native fisherman. "Not too many new
people around here to choose from." He laughed and shook
Paul's hand. "I'm Gilbert. You guys got a place to stay?"

"Well, no," said Paul. "I guess we could stay in the hotel
here."

"No problem. You can stay with us."

Gilbert Cook had a friendly smile; he was from a long line of
local fishermen, and operated a seiner named the *Cape Cook*
out of Alert Bay. Following various leads from Vancouver and
Irvine's Landing, Paul had tracked down Gilbert and chief
Jimmy Sewid of the Nimpkish band, a legendary fisherman
known all along the coast. When Jimmy arrived, Paul noticed
right away that he carried an aura of authority and knowledge.
He nodded to almost everyone in the pub as he made his way
to the table. Paul instinctively stood up to shake his hand.

Jimmy Sewid sat down and rolled a well-used marine navigational chart out on the table, holding the corners down with ashtrays and beer glasses. His thick finger, covered with years of calluses, pointed to Alert Bay. "Here we are. This is Broughton Strait." Jimmy pointed out the window and then back to the chart. "And on the other side of the island is Cormorant Channel." He pointed with his thumb back over his shoulder, and then his finger followed a huge circle. "This is Johnstone Strait; here's Robson Bight. Lots of blackfish hang out around there for some reason, in the shallows. They come up here through Blackney Passage, around Hanson Island, and up into Blackfish Sound. We call killer whales blackfish. They pass through here, between the White Cliff Islets and Donegal Head, and out into Queen Charlotte Strait. I don't see 'em too much in the wintertime; they go out to sea, I guess, or somewhere; who knows. In the summer they're all over the place. Some fishermen shoot at them, 'cause they think the whales are competing for fish, and I guess they are, in a way; but I would never shoot at a blackfish and no one on my boat would ever shoot at one—and I catch plenty of fish." Jimmy Sewid laughed, Gilbert started to laugh, and Paul nodded his head, sipping his beer.

"One of the stories I heard from a long time ago," Jimmy Sewid told Paul, "was that one of our young men shot a blackfish but only wounded him. He drove a lance into the whale and beached it. Then the next day he towed the carcass back to his village, thinking he had done some great deed. But the old men told him he was a fool; they all came down and prayed by the body and asked the spirit of the whale to forgive them, that it was only one foolish man who didn't know.

"But from my own time, when I was a kid, maybe fifty years ago at Village Island, I remember a whole herd of blackfish coming to our beach. We had a nice settlement there: tide flats, a clam beach, sheltered from the wind, and getting nice sun. One day there was a commotion in the village and we all ran down to the beach, and the whales—there must have been fifty of them—were right in the shallows, right up to the beach, looking at the village. The people were talking about how the whales were going to get caught by the tide and stranded on the beach. They sent us boys after the oldest man in the village —he was maybe a hundred years old—and he was an old friend of the Max'inux. He knew about them."

Jimmy was leaning across the chart on the table, looking right at Paul as he told his story. "This old man came down to the beach and stood at the edge of the water looking right at the whales, and he hollered at them: 'My friends, you are making a big mistake! If you stay in here the tide will go out and you'll dry up and die. Go on! Go away from here!' The old man screamed at them, and they backed up as the tide was dropping, and they left; they swam away. To this day, many of our people believe that if you speak to a blackfish it will understand what you say."

Indians ranged along this coast, from the Aleut and the Chukchi in the Bering Sea to the Salish around Puget Sound. The Chukchi never hunted the orca, which was a sacred animal to them. The Tlingit, along what is now the Alaskan panhandle, and the Haida on the Queen Charlotte Islands also revered and never harmed the orca, the blackfish, or *Skana,* supernatural one. The Tsimsyan people of the B.C. coast say that the spirits of all great hunters on the sea become *pte'naerhl,* blackfish, when they die; thus, no one would ever harm one of these creatures.

The Kwakwala-speaking peoples, Kwakw*aka'*wakw or Kwakiutl, live in the center of this northern coast along the north end of Vancouver Island, on the adjacent mainland coast, and on the islands between. Alert Bay, 320 kilometers north of the U.S.–Canadian border, is one of the major settlements, bringing together members of numerous bands, including the Nimpkish. The Indians share the town with about a thousand other people, fishermen and their families, a few shopkeepers, some ferry workers, schoolteachers, and a contingent of the Royal Canadian Mounted Police. The Indians call the whites "Mammaclas."

In the center of town, along the street from the Nimpkish Hotel, is a graveyard with a mixture of wooden crosses and totem poles. The poles depict important elements of the natural and mystical life of the people, and include images of the wolf, eagle, salmon, bear, thunderbird, D'Sonoqua the wild woman of the woods, and Max'inux the blackfish. The Indians tell of a game their ancestors used to play in the days when these waterways were teeming with far more blackfish than the hundred or so known still to inhabit the area: The fishermen would paddle up to a sleeping whale, taking care not to lift their paddles from the water, lest the sound of dripping water awaken the great animal. One of the braver fishermen would get out of the canoe and, gathering his courage, walk along the back of the sleeping whale, then jump back into the canoe before the whale awoke and paddle silently away.

There is an old story of a young man who was crossing what is now Queen Charlotte Sound, near Hope Island, with his brother. He tried to stop his brother from shooting at a blackfish, but the brother shot anyway, wounding the whale. The boat capsized in a gale, and the brother who had shot at the whale drowned. The other brother was washed ashore, and when he regained consciousness he found himself singing a song that he had not heard before. In the water he saw the whale, and the whale told him, "Thank you for trying to help me; you are my friend. I am Max'inux, and that song you were singing is the song I have given you. I have given you my powers, and now you will be able to benefit your people by healing them. You will be the *pahala,* medicine man."

The whale sang to the man, "Alive I make you,/You will find spiritual treasure,/You will find spiritual treasure."

The man sang back, "I was carried on the water by Long-life-giver with your supernatural power,/Flitting about on the water, poor I, with Long-life-giver with supernatural power."

The story is reenacted in dance to this day at the Big House in Alert Bay.

"The first boats our people used around here were hollowed-out cedar logs," Jimmy Sewid told Paul. The three men sat at the window for most of the afternoon, drinking beer and talking about orca lore and possible sites for Paul's field station. Paul felt at home with the native people, who seemed to accept and even honor his obsession with orcas.

"I need a spot," said Paul, "that is not only on the orca routes that run close to shore, but that also has a protected landing with a sharp drop off where I could tie up a boat. I would like it to be remote, so that it is private; I'd like a tall bluff for viewing a wide range, fresh water, a beach, and shelter from the wind."

Jimmy and Gilbert laughed and shook their heads. "Who wouldn't?" said Gilbert, rocking back in his chair.

"There's an old site here," he went on, pointing to the chart, "on Parson Island, where Blackfish Sound runs through Blackney Passage into Johnstone Strait. There's an old well back in the woods there."

Paul set his beer down and looked closely at the chart. Blackfish Sound was surrounded by islands: Swanson Island, Compton Island, Harbledown, Parson, Cracroft, Hanson, the Plumper Islands, and countless rocks, shoals, reefs, inlets, and tricky passageways. Paul saw Indian Channel, Village Island, where the old man spoke to the whales, Midsummer Island— and as his eyes wandered over the chart, they scanned hundreds of coves, bays, mudflats, and mysterious-looking, unnamed inlets. One of those coves, he thought, was going to be his new home.

Paul and his family stayed in Alert Bay for nearly two weeks, visiting the Big House, walking along the beach, and listening to whale stories from Indians and fishermen. Amateur naturalist Ken Fairwell, at the government dock in Alert Bay, told Paul that some fishermen had seen orcas digging for clams on a sandy beach in two fathoms of water, flukes in the air, heads in the sand. He also told Paul about a lone sei whale that made its home in Blackfish Sound. Ken knew the distinctive mark on the dorsal fin, and said he'd seen it in the area for nearly fifteen years. Brian Lewis, a fisherman, took Paul out on his boat for a spin around the southeast point of Cormorant Island on one of the few calm days during late January. Paul stood at the bow for the entire ride scanning the water for black fins, but he did not see a single one.

Back in Vancouver, Paul and Linda prepared for the expedition that would land them at their new home, somewhere among the island waterways of Blackfish Sound. They collected such items as buckets, paddles, blankets, video and camera equipment, tape recorders, an oscilloscope, axes, food staples, an outboard motor, a tent and tarpaulin, an electric generator, binoculars, a chain saw, and an assortment of other tools that might prove useful in the struggle to stay warm, dry, fed, and alive at some rugged, isolated outpost.

Paul received a package in the mail from Moscow from Professor A. G. Tomlin, containing a copy of Tomlin's collection of Russian cetacean research studies. Paul wrote back, explaining his plan to do research with free *Orcinus orca*. Although Paul did not know it at the time, it was to be the beginning of a long relationship with Soviet whale scientists.

Paul and Linda expected to return to Alert Bay in the early summer, but their plans were again disrupted by the capture of a pod of orcas, this time at Pedder Bay, on the southeast tip of Vancouver Island along the Strait of Juan de Fuca.

Out on a Sunday-afternoon pleasure cruise on the first of March, Bob Wright, owner of the Sealand aquarium in Victoria, saw the sun reflect from the body of what looked like a white whale. As he and his crew approached, they could see a pod of orcas that indeed included an albino. Like a modern Captain Ahab, Wright had long been obsessed with capturing a white whale to display in his pool. He radioed his aquarium capture boat, the *Lakewood,* which quickly arrived on the scene with a single gill net. When the whales swam into Pedder Bay, the gill-netter cut across the half-mile-wide entrance, trapping the whales behind the net.

Don White, Paul's assistant from the Vancouver Aquarium, was there, and once the whales were corralled, he felt sorry for them. He wanted to let them go, but the whales "belonged" to Bob Wright, who was frantically trying to keep them in makeshift pens. Fearing the whales would break through the nets, Wright had his crew stay up all night dropping seal bombs—equal to about a quarter of a stick of dynamite—into the water to scare the orcas away from the flimsy net. Don White later told Paul, "One diver nearly got hit with a seal bomb. It was a real macho scene, and it was a miracle that no one got killed. The whales must have been freaked!"

By the time Paul arrived at Pedder Bay a few weeks later, there were five whales securely held in net pens. Don White told Paul that before the heavy nets came in, the white whale had broken free and then returned to be with the other whales. The white whale, a female that Bob Wright named Chimo, was transported to the Sealand aquarium along with another female named Nootka. Nootka was later transferred to California, then Texas, and then Ontario. A California aquarium offered a million dollars for the white Chimo, but Bob Wright kept her as a mate for his male orca, Haida.

All the whales at Pedder Bay had refused food, but when Nootka and Chimo were first put into Haida's pool, Haida took one of his herring to each of the new whales, pushing the fish through the net that separated them. He pressed the herring right against Chimo's mouth, through the net. Both new whales began eating.

Back at Pedder Bay, seventy-five days passed, and the three remaining whales—two females sold to the Seven Seas aquarium in Texas and an eight-thousand-pound male slated to be released—still had not eaten. The orcas were so emaciated that their skin was stretched tightly over their rib cages, making them look like hungry stray dogs. The male was called Charlie Chin because of his protruding lower jaw; the two females were identified as Scar Jaw and Pointed Nose from their physical characteristics.

After seventy-five days without food, Scar Jaw began crashing into the logs around the pen. She seemed to be desperately looking for a way out, and at one point she got entangled in the net. Don White noticed that she was gulping sea water and sputtering as if she was having difficulty breathing. Sealand Director Bob Wright sent Graeme Ellis over to assist Don White. Graeme phoned back to Sealand for a vet, but Bob Wright did not send the vet out. After a few hours, Scar Jaw began vocalizing with Charlie Chin. The two whales went on for a while; then Scar Jaw opened her mouth and sank to the bottom of the bay, dead. Charlie Chin immediately began to

tear at the netting with his teeth, pulling and thrashing his head
with what was left of his waning strength.

Word came from Sealand to the men at Pedder Bay: "Don't
tell anyone it died." Whale captors had received some bad
publicity after a Seattle Marine Aquarium capture, when dead
orcas washed up on Puget Sound with slit bellies and anchors
tied to their flukes. The orders from Bob Wright were to haul
Scar Jaw's carcass from the bottom of the bay and tow it out to
sea. They were not to slit its belly to make it sink or attach
weights to it, so there would be no evidence that it was one of
their whales. The aquarium denied that the whale had ever
been captured, saying that there were only the two remaining
whales, not three. Don White and Graeme Ellis were both disgusted; Don stayed on to see if he could help Charlie Chin and
Pointed Nose, but Graeme quit the aquarium staff, saying that
he no longer wanted to have anything to do with capturing
whales.

Three days after Scar Jaw died, Don tried feeding the two
remaining whales some fresh salmon. For the first time since he
had been captured, Charlie Chin came over and took a salmon
in his mouth. He swam over to Pointed Nose and started vocalizing; the two whales exchanged calls. Charlie Chin placed the
salmon in front of the emaciated female, who took it in her
mouth and swam around the pen vocalizing. Then Charlie Chin
came up to her, took the head of the salmon in his mouth as she
held the tail, and the two of them continued vocalizing and
swimming while carrying the fish between them. Then they
tore the fish into two pieces and each ate half. It was the first
food they had taken in seventy-eight days. Charlie Chin went
back for more and brought the female another salmon, which
she ate; then Charlie returned to the edge of the pen and ate
one himself. In the days that followed, they each ate up to 450
pounds of fish per day.

Paul was outraged when he and Linda left Pedder Bay on
their way north to find their research site. In contrast to the
gentleness and kindness expressed by the whales, the whale
captors seemed to be ruthless and greedy. Capturing orcas was
big business and had nothing to do with science, Paul realized;

whales were tossed away like so many used soda cans. As he drove north along the Island Highway in June of 1970, Paul quietly vowed to himself never again to support the capture of orcas, even for ostensibly scientific reasons. He knew in his heart that it was a sham, and he would have to find a way to study free orcas, whales that could come and go as they pleased.

Paul and Linda rented a house in Alert Bay, from which they organized a small expedition crew that would locate and establish a camp. With them were Yashi, Nettle the cat, and their Afghan puppy, Yo. Frank Baker, a native Indian who knew the local waters, offered to go along as a guide. Naren Carter was a friend and a newly converted orca enthusiast. University student Lindi De Vault had offered to help, and handyman Michael McLean provided a boat and survival skills essential to life in the isolated northern rain forest.

Gilbert Cook marked out some possible sites on a chart, and Paul, with some of the crew, began to explore the area on the twelfth of June. Departing from Alert Bay, they moved southeast along Johnstone Strait on a sunny day, Michael McLean skippering his small boat. "Whales!" Linda yelled at one point, upon seeing fins in the water. They turned out to be a family of Dall's porpoises cutting little arcs in the blue water.

During several excursions, the party poked into inlets and bays, looking for the one that would be just right. On the third day out, they saw their first free orcas. "Whooo! Uhhh," they heard, and looked up to see three black dorsal fins moving slowly toward them in the distance.

"It looks like a bull, a female, and a baby," said Paul. The three whales surfaced in unison, exhaled in rapid succession—"Whooo! Whooo! Whooo!"—inhaled, and dove together. When the whales surfaced again, they were nearer the boat; Paul let out a howl. The whales breathed and dove, slipping silently into the water. As the whales passed the boat, they continued to rise, breathe, and dive in unison, their black dorsal fins cutting effortlessly through the bright, rippling water.

Paul watched them disappear into the distance without ever

breaking the steady rhythm of their travel. "Imagine," Paul said
to Linda, "taking every breath together as we walked down the
street."

On the morning of June 16, the party investigated the camp-
site that Gilbert Cook had suggested on Parson Island in the
swirling waters of Blackney Passage, where the swift tides
flow to and from Blackfish Sound. Motoring along with the flow
of the tide, the rising sun coming up, Paul gazed across
Blackney Passage. Turning to Michael he asked, pointing,
"What's that island there?"

Michael checked the chart. "It must be Hanson Island."

"I can see a nice bluff from here, and what looks like a little
bay," said Paul. "Shall we check it out?"

"Why not?" said Michael.

The group motored across Blackney Passage toward the
bluff. Paul studied the chart closely; the little bay was marked,
but unnamed, and as they approached, Paul could see that
there was a gentle beach at the back of the bay and a rock
outcropping on both ends. Immense red cedar, spruce, and
Douglas fir trees came right down to the high-tide line, and the
bluff rose about a hundred feet to a rock cliff that overlooked
Blackney Passage and Blackfish Sound.

Paul, barefooted, jumped into the knee-deep water and
pulled the boat to shore. Michael, Lindi, and Frank all wandered through the dense forest, along the mossy banks, and up
the rock cliffs. Paul, Linda, and Yashi made their own way into
the forest. A little stream crossed their path, and they followed
it up a course that was thick with ferns, huckleberry bushes,
and mosses of every color. They came upon a little clearing lit
by the sunlight diffused through the trees so that the white,
orange, maroon, and gray-blue lichen radiated an electric bril-
liance. Paul and Linda looked at each other with wide eyes.

"Jimmy and Gilbert laughed at me," said Paul, "when I told
them what I was looking for, but here it is, everything we
wanted. I knew those orcas were a good sign yesterday." Paul
reached into his shoulder bag and pulled out his *I Ching*. "Let's
just check it out, eh?"

Paul and Linda sat down on the mossy carpet, and Paul took

out his coins. He got the forty-ninth hexagram, "Revolution," the reverse hexagram of the one he got the night before his university lecture. The verse read, "On your own day/You are believed./Supreme success,/Furthering through perseverance./ Remorse disappears."

Linda and Paul smiled at each other and lay back on the soft cushion of lichen and moss with Yashi snuggled between them. As they looked up through the treetops, a bald eagle flew high above, gliding on the wind, cocking its head back and forth. "Neighbors," said Paul. "I hope we don't disturb them." The eagle caught a draft of wind and was gone in an instant.

As they sat by the fire that night, they heard whales blowing from the darkness. Excited and shivering, they stood on the rocks, looking out over the black expanse, but they saw nothing. Several times again they heard the whales blowing near the shore.

"This spot is perfect," Frank told them. "There's lots of clean fresh water in that stream up there, and from the bluff you can look straight down into the water. If the whales go by here close to shore, you'll get a good look at them."

Paul had a three-stage plan. Initially he wanted to remain in a single spot and simply observe the whales that passed by without disturbing them or interfering with them in any way. After gaining some insight into their natural movements, Paul planned to repeat some of the sound experiments that he had started at the aquarium, to see what reaction free whales might have to various sounds, such as music. Finally he planned to track and monitor the activities of the whales. The first item of business was to set up a camp that would keep his little party warm and dry on shore.

Over the next several weeks, Michael and Naren built a two-story tree house with driftwood from the beach and planks that they salvaged from long-abandoned shacks on nearby islands. They rigged up plastic to keep the wind and rain out and installed a wood-burning stove inside. Paul, Linda, and Yashi bunked on the first floor, and Paul used the second floor for a sound lab.

On the fourth day a pod of ten or twelve whales came by

close to the rocky bluff. Naren Carter stood on the rocks playing his flute, and Paul climbed the bluff to watch them go by.
The joyful human settlers called out as the family of orcas
paused in their travels, diving and circling below the bluff.

Paul and Linda were inexperienced at living in the woods.
Michael McLean and Frank Baker, fortunately, were not, and
the two men put the camp into excellent shape, building a
heater out of a fifty-five-gallon drum and scrounging materials
from the beaches to build a crude kitchen. During his excursions into the woods, Frank Baker discovered numerous Indian
middens, sites of ancient camps, and he found evidence of a
fire that had burned the woods a hundred years before.

Paul spent the time rigging his hydrophones in the water and
hooking up his oscilloscope and recording equipment. Michael
helped him get his generator and electrical systems functioning. On July 17, 1970, Paul made his first recordings of free
orcas. Whenever orcas would pass, the campers would all stop
working to watch from the beach. Paul recorded each passing,
the number of whales and their direction. One day Michael
took Frank, Lindi, and Naren back to Alert Bay and returned
with a heavy wooden seine skiff towed behind his boat. Gilbert
Cook had loaned them the skiff, telling Michael, "Those whale
people better have a good boat, or we'll be fishing them out of
the drink one of these days."

About every two or three days whales would come by in
groups ranging in size from three to twenty or so. Paul rigged
speakers to the hydrophone and amplifier so that they could
monitor the whales' underwater vocalizations from their camp.
At various times of the night or day they would hear the haunting calls of orcas. Paul heard sounds unlike anything he had
heard before: long, modulating cries that he transcribed in his
notebook as "Whaaaaaa-eeeee-aaaaa-eeeee-aaaaa," and other
inhuman and mystifying screeches and calls.

Sometimes the whales would pass by in complete silence,
slipping through the water like phantoms, their windy breaths
mixing with the breeze in the forest and their firm dorsal fins
cutting the water like great black knives. The orcas seemed
purposeful and self-contained in their travels, neither fearful

nor particularly interested in the antics of the little band of humans on Hanson Island. Paul felt small and insignificant in this tiny unnamed cove surrounded by green rain forest and by flushing, ever-moving tides. The wind would come up out of nowhere and bend the huge trees in great arcs and speed the clouds across the sky, over the receding blue mountains.

Paul and Linda took long walks in the woods, finding wild-flowers, strange rain-forest growths on the sides of trees, and little forest glens so perfect and delicate that they paused and moved carefully so as not to disturb the wild order of things. Paul and Linda found a "cathedral grove" that included three giant spruce trees Michael guessed to be more than three hundred years old and an immense cedar tree twelve to fourteen feet in diameter that was possibly a thousand years old and looked like the grandmother of the forest. Daily they watched a great blue heron as it fished in the shallows of the cove. Yashi, two years old, loved the forest. He entertained himself much of the day, with sticks, seashells, rocks, and sand. The young Afghan puppy, Yo, also loved the forest, scurrying about after squirrels and sniffing every leaf. Nettle, the calico cat, settled in by the fire or stretched out in the sun during most of the day and made occasional forays after mice and birds. The settlers grew into a comfortable routine, eating simple meals and sleeping huddled against the cool breezes at night.

Orcas.

The sleepers hardly knew if the breaths they heard at night were real or just dreams. They would match stories in the morning to find out who had heard what. They came to know the Ping-Ponging call of the screech owl, the high modulating whistle of the eagles, the whooshing wings of the ravens, the distant howl of wolves, as well as the breaths and calls of the orcas.

Paul heard Yo barking at 3 A.M. on July 1; he got up and walked barefooted to the rocky outcropping, where he heard a pod of ten whales go by in the high tide, close to the rocks.

The whales moved slowly and together, from right to left, heading northwest through Blackney Passage. As they disappeared into the blackness, Paul could hear their massive breaths. After about fifteen minutes the orcas reappeared, dipping in and out of darkness at the edge of sight. Paul saw two whales rise close to the rocks, then dive and vanish. When he went back to bed after an hour, he could still hear distant breaths as he dropped off to sleep.

By the end of July, Paul had underwater speakers below the low tide line as well as huge speakers sitting on the shore, so he could play music to the whales as they passed by the camp. He played the human music that Tung Jen and Skana had liked most, including Ravi Shankar's *Improvisations* and various classical pieces. He would watch from the rocks, but if the whales responded, they made no obvious sign.

While returning from a supply run to Alert Bay, Paul, Linda, Yashi, and Michael motored slowly as a light chop slapped against their loaded boat. As they entered Weynton Passage heading for the Plumper Islands and Blackfish Sound, they noticed a line of black dots in the distance, toward Johnstone Strait; orcas were coming toward them.

Michael stopped the engine, drifting forward along the shore of Hanson Island with the flooding tide. The orcas came toward them against the tide, but moving swiftly. They counted about thirty whales moving in groups of two to seven, and Paul noticed that each small whale was with at least one adult. One immense bull momentarily towered over the boat as his huge dorsal fin cut the water only a few feet away, followed by the rising of his great body. The whales passed on both sides of the boat, moving north toward Queen Charlotte Strait.

Whales could be seen from the camp almost every day for two weeks, sometimes several times a day. Then the whales seemed to leave the region; days passed, and no orcas were seen or heard. Then, on August 8, Paul went out in the skiff by himself, to Parson Island across Blackney Passage, to be by himself and jig cod for supper.

As he rowed home, the sun was setting behind Hanson Island and the whole sky was lit, salmon color at the horizon, then light blue, becoming deep blue above and behind him. In the middle of the passage, the stars were beginning to become visible, and soon Paul could pick out the North Star off his starboard, high above Blackfish Sound. He checked his compass and noticed that true north was about twenty-three degrees to the west of magnetic north. The tide was ebbing and taking him home, so he drifted, tired of rowing.

The blows seemed deep inside him before he was completely conscious of them, but when he did become aware, he turned and sat motionless. The glassy surface of the water reflected the stars behind him, and he could not help seeing himself in outer space, nothing but stars above and below, floating as an astronaut would, free of the earth. The whales were like approaching aliens: unreachable presences passing through the void on their own mission. Unconsciously Paul held his breath and heard the soft staccato puffs, barely above the threshold of imagining. Then there was only silence, then the cadence again. He counted the blows: One, two, three, four, five, six, seven, eight, nine, ten? Eleven? Twelve? Then again silence, and again the blows. Eleven.

Before he saw anything, he could feel the sharp echolocation pulses through the bottom of the skiff. When he first saw the fins, they were like flickering shadows in the dance of starlight on the black, silken sea. Then, looking over the side of the skiff, Paul saw the blue phosphorescent trails of two massive shapes cut directly below him. The two fins emerged powerfully from the water in front of him, controlled thrusts bursting through the surface of the ocean accompanied by explosive exhalations and quick, instant inhalations, ending in a fast, rising whistle that stopped suddenly. The breath washed over Paul, a fine mist descended around him, and there was silence again. In the distance, Paul saw a line of fins rise and disappear against the thin band of light on the horizon, and then he was alone, rocking in the little wake left by the passing whales.

The tide was about to carry Paul past his camp as he rowed quickly toward the shore. The moon rose up behind him as his skiff glided into the cove and scraped the rocky bottom of the beach. Paul tied the skiff to a secure log. He told Linda about his encounter; she had heard the same whales on the hydrophone speakers.

Linda and Paul ate fried cod and chips by the fire and listened to the owl in the moonlight. Then, with Yashi they all huddled together on the bed inside their little shack. Paul awoke, later during the night, heard wolves howling somewhere in the distance, and went back to sleep.

On August 15, Paul saw the gray-black speckled back of a sei whale in the channel near the camp. This was the lone sei whale that Ken Fairwell had told him about. Paul named her Sol, short for "solo." He wondered if Sol's family had fallen victim to whalers in the North Pacific.

Paul had invited some of the musicians who had played for Skana to visit him on Hanson Island and to play music for free orcas. On August 18, a forty-eight-foot, concrete-hulled, unrigged sailing vessel, the *D'Sonoqua,* arrived at the camp on its maiden voyage, skippered by Vancouver owner Jim Bates. The crew of thirteen comprised more musicians than sailors, including the Vancouver bluegrass-rock bank Fireweed, led by Danny McGuinness.

As the musicians tuned up on the deck of the *D'Sonoqua,* anchored about a hundred feet from Paul and Linda's camp, a pod of ten orcas came around the corner from Blackfish Sound. The band immediately began to pump out electric bluegrass music amplified through stacks of speakers. The whales, passing slowly on the surface, made no audible sounds themselves, but they paused nearby.

Several of the orcas stopped and poked their heads out of the water in a gesture known as "spyhopping," while other whales waved their pectoral fins in the air and slapped the water. Paul saw two whales raise their heads symmetrically from the water on either side of a stationary whale that floated between them. The whales stayed around for about twenty minutes, then suddenly departed all together, heading south toward Johnstone Strait.

Later that evening the whales returned. Paul noticed that sometimes the whales' movements seemed to coincide with the tides: They would pass about an hour before either high or low tide. He assumed that perhaps these movements also coincided with the salmon runs described to him by fishermen.

Paul wanted to see if the whales would eat salmon fed to them from the boats, as an initial phase in a plan to eventually feed them salmon laced with monitoring equipment. To do his net fishing legally, Paul obtained a special permit with the help of Federal Fisheries Minister Jack Davis. He set the net out from shore and caught some salmon, but it was difficult to tell if any of the salmon they threw overboard were actually taken by the orcas. "I sort of doubt," offered Linda, "that the orcas need us to catch fish for them."

On the night of August 20, however, orcas apparently came and took fish from the net, as all the salmon that had been there the night before had disappeared by morning. The whales took only the salmon, leaving the dogfish and cod.

On Saturday night, August 22, Paul, Linda, and the *D'Sonoqua* crew went into Alert Bay to play at a dance for the local people. The band boogied into the early hours, and it was a sleepy crew that headed back for Hanson Island on Sunday afternoon. When they came upon whales in Johnstone Strait, the band began playing music from the deck. Paul counted about thirty whales and thought he recognized a few groups by the shapes and markings of their fins. He guessed that it was the same large pod that he and Linda had seen in Blackfish Sound earlier in the summer.

At one point Paul stood at the stern, transfixed by the sight of more than a dozen orcas, with a huge male in the middle, swimming in a line abreast on the surface of the water, about fifty feet behind the *D'Sonoqua*. Later he told Danny McGuinness, "There is no doubt that the whales like your live music better than all the recorded music I've played for them. Live music! That's the thing that gets them interested. Maybe it's the presence of the musicians that makes the difference. It was the same at the aquarium."

Paul rigged up a hydrophone for the boat so that the musicians could hear the whales just as the whales could hear them. With wah-wah pedals and electric reverb boxes, the band created orca imitations on their instruments. Singing violins and howling guitars echoed from the steep cliff walls and filled the air as the boat drifted at anchor in Blackney Passage.

It was hard to tell if the whales were enjoying the show, but the musicians were in ecstasy, wailing away as if they were playing before an audience as important as any they would ever meet.

Paul recognized one of the whales that swam around the boat that day, a mature female with a deep notch just below the top of her dorsal fin. He made a note of this female and thereafter began to record the physical characteristics of the whales that he saw, with the intention of identifying the groups and individuals. To remember her, Paul named this whale Nicola.

Soon after the *D'Sonoqua* and her crew departed, Paul, with Linda and Yashi, made a quick trip to Vancouver to help quell a brewing controversy over the squatters at the Maplewood Mudflats and to encourage a film company to visit Blackfish Sound. The crew, from Fortune Films, arrived soon after Paul returned to Hanson Island, but were largely unsuccessful in their efforts to film the orcas. Early in September, Michael, Naren, and Lindi departed for Vancouver, leaving Paul and his family alone on Hanson Island.

By the end of September, they were feeling like experienced settlers and were pleased with their first observations and contacts with free orcas. Once Paul had sat for hours on the bluff, watching the windswept, gray waters of Blackfish Sound. When the whales passed, he looked right down on top of them and saw their whole bodies in the water, almost touching as they surfaced and dove together. Paul was spellbound by their exquisite beauty and strength. Their passage seemed so effortless, so calm.

Overall, Paul was most impressed by the orcas' social organization; it seemed so efficient and harmonious. He had not witnessed a single incident of aggressive or frantic behavior among the orcas. Their pursuit and harvesting of the abundant salmon seemed effortless. Paul reflected on how insignificant his own presence was in their scheme of things, in their orderly orca existence.

The orcas were as active at night as they were during the day. Paul was awed by the apparent coordination of the family groups and the larger congregations of orcas as they made their calm, watery rounds. They did not seem to Paul like vicious, wild hunters of the sea, but rather like a benign intelligence gently and purposefully fulfilling its destiny as certainly as was humankind.

As Paul mused over these observations, he realized that his one regret was that he had perhaps been too preoccupied with equipment and recordings and other technical aspects of his work. He felt that he had paid too little attention to the whales themselves, and he resolved that when he returned the following year he would spend more time on the water with the whales, close to them, in their time and in their rhythm.

During the entire first ten days of October, a light rain fell steadily; the wind blew up from the southeast, then turned and blew directly into them from the northeast. On the first clear day after the rain, Paul stood out on the rocks watching a pod of orcas pass in the distance. Gulls filled the air with their own busy chatter, looping and diving after herring that glinted on the surface of the water. A heron stood motionless in a tidal pool, its image reflected in the water. Blackfish Sound was painted in gray and silver with only a hint of blue, giving the landscape a pewter color. Clouds blew overhead like white, gray and black continents, drifting in the gray sea of the sky. A small pod of Dall's porpoises huddled close to the shore as the orcas passed.

"Listen!" Paul heard Linda call.

"What?" Paul turned and looked over his shoulder.

"Listen," she said from the woods as she pointed up. Paul held his breath. Just barely audible came the first sounds from the sky: "Ah-lonk, ah-lonk, ah-lonk, ah-lonk, ah-lonk, ah-lonk . . ."

Paul bent his head back in the direction of the sound, but he saw nothing. Then from behind the trees he could see the wavy lines of geese undulating in several fanning V shapes, a few stragglers poking into line and then falling back and poking in again. The sound grew louder and more distinct. The geese were high, looking like tiny vibrating dots while their lines swayed like the tentacles of a jellyfish.

"Well," said Paul, "I guess the summer is officially over; time for anyone to leave who isn't prepared for winter."

The little family broke camp over the next few days. They secured their shelter against the winds and loaded their gear into a seine boat that carried them back to Alert Bay. Five orcas escorted them along Blackfish Sound and then continued north toward the White Cliff Islets as the boat turned southwest. Linda and Paul called a long "Good-BYEeeeeeeeeeee" as they left the whales and motored toward Alert Bay.

In town they heard from friends that someone had released Charlie Chin and Pointed Nose from the pens at Pedder Bay. On the night of October 27 someone had thrown weights over one corner of the net, sinking it and allowing the whales to go free.

4

A Meeting of Minds

Paul sat up in bed. He could hear Linda and Yashi by the fire, and he could feel the warmth of the air rising. It was August 11, 1971.

Paul and Linda had spent the previous winter at their home at the Maplewood Mudflats, while Paul continued his brain-wave experiments at UBC. Their little squatters' community had come under pressure because of a proposal to build a shopping center over the mudflats, a development that would have displaced their home and destroyed the natural estuary that surrounded it. In the spring, Paul, with Linda and Yashi, traveled to Europe and spent a month cycling through the rural south of England and the Netherlands. On Yashi's third birth-day, in April, they were in Amsterdam. The central city streets were closed to traffic, and a big party was going on. Paul and Linda wandered through the crowds, Yashi riding high on Paul's shoulders, agog because he believed the party was for his birthday, which happened to be the same day as that of the Dutch monarch.

After returning to Hanson Island in June, this time with a kayak, Paul and Linda moved back into their tree house, sleeping with Yashi on the ground floor, near the kitchen stove. Paul's lab still occupied the second floor. By August they had settled into a pleasant routine of monitoring and recording the whales' vocalizations and observing families and pods from the shore and from the kayak. Paul had been thrilled by his first excursions in the kayak, marveling at his immediate and easy acceptance among the orcas.

As Paul sat on his bed, he heard blows close to shore. He got up and went outside, walking the few meters to the rocks. From there he saw several Dall's porpoises directly off the shore, diving in a small circle at the edge of a dense fog. Dall's porpoises are black and white, with markings similar to those of orcas; they travel in family groups like orcas, and grow to about seven feet in length. Paul had often observed the porpoises coming in close to the shore when orcas passed.

The fog obscured the view into Blackfish Sound as Paul listened quietly. The porpoises had disappeared, and he heard nothing more but the lap of water on the rocks. He went back into the house and picked up his flute.

"I'm going out for a bit," Paul told Linda.

"In the fog?"

"No problem, I won't go far."

"Are there whales?"

"I don't think so, but I just saw some Dall's porpoises," said Paul.

Paul went down to the beach and carried the kayak to the edge of the water. Yashi was dragging huge strands of kelp across the beach with a determined and purposeful expression on his face.

"What are you doing?" Paul asked.

"I'm carrying my equipment," said Yashi.

"Where to?"

"To my lab."

Paul rolled up his pants and waded out into the cool ocean water, pulling the kayak along by the bowline and carrying his flute in one hand. Little wavelets lapped against his shins as he pulled the kayak up beside him. He held the kayak steady in the water, stepped in, and paddled out into the mist.

Paul heard Linda's violin and turned around to see her playing on the rocks, looking ghostly through the haze. The Dall's porpoises moved away and Paul followed, but they disappeared into the fog. After a minute paddling in the damp air, Paul could just barely make out the shoreline when he turned around to look. Then he heard louder blows from farther away and realized that orcas were coming. He turned toward them and floated quietly, listening. All hints of land gradually closed from sight, and he was surrounded by the white mist.

The blows came closer, although Paul could see no sign of life. Faintly, he could still hear Linda's violin, but it was distant. Drifting with the tide, he picked up his flute and began to play. He kept his eyes closed as he played, and occasionally in the darkness he heard blows. After a few minutes he opened his eyes, to see six orcas sitting on the surface about a hundred feet from the kayak, just barely visible, dreamy apparitions in the gray wash of misty air and water. The whales were not diving and swimming, but were floating on the surface, breathing slowly.

Paul closed his eyes again and continued to play his flute; when he opened his eyes again, he saw three whales surfacing about fifty feet in front of the kayak, moving away from him. He recognized the female with the deep notch at the top of her dorsal fin. "Oh, it's Nicola," he thought. Beside her was a huge male, whose towering dorsal fin had distinctive waves in its trailing edge. "Wavy!" Paul shouted. A smaller whale swam beside the two adults, and Paul wondered if perhaps this was their child and if together they formed an orca nuclear family.

Paul paddled quietly after the whales, which were moving slowly forward in the water. The three whales surfaced every thirty seconds or so, staying about fifty feet in front of him; then, after several minutes, they disappeared. Paul stopped paddling and began to play his flute again, this time with his eyes open. Within a few minutes he was surrounded by whales drifting at the surface in the fringes of the fog; they seemed to be in distinct groups of three to six, and he recognized them as a pod or perhaps several pods that he had seen many times. Paul guessed that there were about fifty whales in all. He stopped playing his flute and paddled after them as they began to move slowly away.

He paddled his kayak next to a group that included several youngsters, and he found it easy to keep up with their gentle pace. Feeling quite secure, Paul tagged along through the fog, occasionally moving from one group to another. He moved right in among one group so that whales were on both sides of him. He could see them rising through the water, their huge black and white bodies moving effortlessly though powerfully. The whales would break the surface, exhale with a loud "Whoooo!" and then breathe in and dive below. He felt surrounded by the blows.

As Paul paddled, a group of whales came up in a line abreast, three on either side of the kayak, swimming continuously on the surface of the water. Gradually they increased their speed, and Paul paddled faster and faster to keep up; it seemed as if he was in a race with them. Paul's excitement swelled as the huge bodies of the whales huffed along side, two of them almost within touching distance. For a moment he completely forgot where he was and impulsively leaned out of the kayak, reaching toward the whale on his right, almost losing his balance, and having to jerk back quickly to avoid tipping over. In the confusion that followed, the kayak almost ran into the whale, and the six orcas in the group simultaneously disappeared. Paul felt rather embarrassed, thinking that he had carelessly scared off his new friends as soon as they trusted him. He paddled for a while, but the whales were gone. He stopped and drifted with the tide again, playing his flute. Within a few minutes the whales were back, making passes within ten feet of the kayak.

Paul followed the whales at a leisurely pace until it seemed as if the pod was splitting up into three groups that began to travel in different directions. Because of the fog, it was unclear exactly what was happening, or where he was, so Paul picked out one group and followed it. For a while they continued to travel slowly enough to make it possible to keep up with them. Then the whales suddenly sounded and did not return to the surface within sight.

Paul waited a few minutes and then played his flute again, but the whales did not return. He realized that he had no idea where he was; he assumed that he had been traveling with the flooding tide and must be somewhere in Johnstone Strait, but he could not be certain where. He decided to look for some land and wait until the fog cleared, and paddled in the direction that he thought would bring him to Cracroft Island on the north coast of the passage. He was quite tired when he finally saw an outcropping of rocks.

When the haze began to clear, at about one o'clock, Paul saw that he was on a small island with several other islands nearby, but he did not at first recognize them. Paul didn't remember any such islands in Johnstone Strait, and for a brief moment he had the feeling that he was in some sort of a dream. As the fog vanished, he paddled out from the shore, and looking back he saw the chalky bluffs that gave the White Cliff Islets their name. To the west he could see Donegal Head, and he realized that he was at the entrance to Queen Charlotte Strait, eight or nine ki'ometers from home, in the opposite direction from where he thought he was.

Apparently the tide had actually been ebbing for the almost four hours that he'd been following the whales. By now the tide was turning to the flood, so it would carry him home.

On his way back, Paul paddled evenly over a glassy sea, still exhilarated from his long morning with the whales. He had been so close to them as they traveled, and they had been so accepting of his presence, that he felt almost as if he were a member of their pod, and he was filled with the wonder of his new relationship with the whales. As he moved along Blackfish Sound, helped by the tide, he reminisced about the female he'd come to know as Nicola. She had come close to him in the kayak several times during his outing in the fog, and he had felt especially reassured by her presence. He also made mental notes about several other whales that he recognized; in Nicola's group were Wavy and an old adult female with a broad back and a stubby dorsal fin that must have been badly damaged in some long-ago accident, leaving it looking like the opening petals of a lily tulip. At first Paul called her Tulip, later Stubb. In another group was a huge male with a hooked dorsal fin that curved forward, almost making it seem as if he were swimming backward; Paul named him Hooker. Paul felt he was getting to know the orcas as individuals.

Paul arrived back at his cove at four o'clock, about half an hour before high tide, tired but happy. While Yashi, Yo, and Nettle slept nearby, Paul and Linda talked by the fire. "It's as if they have no fear," said Paul thoughtfully. "Try to get close to any animal in the wild, and it will either flee in fear or, if cornered, fight fiercely. But the orcas exhibit no fear, and no aggression toward a human presence."

"Did you ever feel afraid?"

"No. I felt foolish once when I nearly tipped the kayak over trying to touch one and they all split, but I never felt afraid. I haven't really been afraid of an orca since Skana did that trick with her teeth on my feet."

"At first I worried," said Linda, "because you had disappeared into the fog, but then I realized that you were with the whales, and somehow I felt relieved; it occurred to me that they wouldn't let you come to any harm."

"It was just like that first time; they went so slowly when I was with them, as if they realized that I couldn't go as fast as they could. Who knows? Maybe they thought I'd get lost, and I was, too. They just seemed to take me in, to accept me. I can't think of any other wild animal that would immediately let a human come in so close among their young. They're a very confident gang."

They sat quietly by the fire, occasionally stirring it with a stick. Paul continued reflectively, "Their ancestors were land mammals, right? And it seems they went back into the sea forty or fifty million years ago. They've come so far that they've had no real enemies for millions of years of evolution."

Linda nodded.

"They're at the top of the food chain in the ocean, they have no problem getting enough food, and they don't need houses and wool clothes to keep them warm," Paul continued. "We haven't witnessed a single aggressive act by an orca in two years, except when they eat," he said, smiling, "which might seem aggressive if you're a salmon.

"And after all the stories of people shooting orcas, there isn't a single account of an orca striking back at a boat."

"Maybe they know that if they start attacking people, the humans will wipe them out."

"Maybe. They've watched humans from their origins on land as they moved out over the water. They must have seen us light our first fires. They've seen all our wars and powerful bombs. The federal Fisheries Department used to encourage people to shoot the orcas up here, and drop dynamite on them from the air because they thought the orcas were too much competition."

"And still, they're so gentle," Linda said. "I wonder why."

"Maybe they understand power better than humans do," said Paul. "They know when to use it and when not to use it.

"Forty million years of evolution! By the time *Homo erectus* started walking around, the whales had already evolved complex social systems, and huge brains, and probably an intricate language."

Linda continued. "I've heard that when whale babies are born, some of the females act as midwives and help deliver the calf. They help it to the surface for its first breath of air and then teach it to breathe with the rest of the group," she said, looking up from the fire to Paul. "Remember that group of whales we saw all breathing together? And what you said about imagining always breathing together with our family as we went through our day? Well, the whales have been doing that for tens of millions of years! You know those meditators you're studying at UBC? Talk about breath control! Whales are conscious of every breath they take for their entire lives! I think that must have a lot to do with the way they act, the way they move so gently and control their power."

Paul shrugged. "Sometimes I imagine what we would do if we were in outer space and we came upon an alien creature with a complicated language, a huge brain, and a peaceful society. Would we kill them for their meat and oil? Here we have an alien intelligence right here, and what are we doing? It's sad." Paul looked up at the stars. "We *are* in the middle of space. We *have* met an alien intelligence."

Two mornings later, Paul took the kayak into Alert Bay for supplies. As he set out from the cove, he saw a large group of orcas moving against the beginning ebb tide through Blackney Passage, south toward Johnstone Strait. As he followed the whales, Paul recognized Wavy. "It's Wavy's pod," he thought. He also saw Nicola and Tulip. The two females each appeared to be leading a group of whales that included several young-sters.

As Paul approached, two of the whales thrust the upper part of their bodies from the water in a characteristic spyhop ges-ture, rising vertically with their pectoral fins held out to the side. In this pose they could visually survey the surface of the water. There seemed to be five separate groups, although Paul had difficulty counting the exact number of whales as they dove and moved around. Wavy and Nicola swam together. Tu-lip swam off to the side nearby with another younger female, and two other females could be seen with young whales at their side. Perhaps, thought Paul, this was an orca extended family. Later he made notes about their physical characteris-tics and apparent relationships. With Nicola in the lead, the whales moved south into Johnstone Strait as Paul turned to-ward Alert Bay.

Paul spent the night in Alert Bay and headed back toward Hanson Island in the morning. As he moved around the point of Cormorant Island, a light rain began to fall. Paul looked up to the white and gray clouds moving across the sun; ahead he could see patches of blue sky. Two Dall's porpoises swam across his bow as he moved slowly into Weynton Passage; he could see a shaft of sunlight falling on Hanson Island in the distance, and he wondered if the weather would hold.

On his way into the passage, he stopped at the Stephenson Islets for a rest. As he sat on the beach, he saw Sol, the lone sei whale, so he followed her across Weynton Passage. He fol-lowed the whale as it meandered around the Plumper Islands and disappeared at the north end of Blackfish Sound. Paul stayed close to the southern shore of the sound and discovered several new passages through the rocks off Hanson Island. The rain came again in a sudden downpour and then just as suddenly stopped, and Paul could see Blackfish Sound flooded in sunlight.

The surface of the water became glassy calm, and a rainbow stretched from Swanson Island on the north shore of Blackfish Sound over Hanson Island, disappearing into Johnstone Strait on the other side. Paul moved slowly along the shoreline, paddling as close as he could to the herons and seabirds in the tidal shallows. Several bald eagles circled overhead, diving after fish and lighting on the tops of giant fir trees along the shore.

As Paul watched, a mature eagle dove into the water and grabbed a fish, presumably a salmon. The adult bird took the fish high into the air and dropped it into a shallow bay. The fish hit the water with a smack and remained on the surface, twitching. The adult eagle returned to the tree, and a young eagle with speckled, furry feathers swooped down toward the stunned fish, locking its talons into it. The young bird struggled to fly, but the fish was too heavy and the bird's grip unsure. Several times the young eagle dropped the fish, picked it up, and tried to fly away. Paul watched for about fifteen minutes before the young eagle managed to carry the fish to the shore, though not to the top of the tree.

By the time Paul reached home, the summer sky was growing dark; the rain was falling again, and he was happy to see the glow of the fire through the trees as he approached the cove. He was beginning to gain greater respect for the immensity and power of the wilderness.

On August 15, Bob Wright from Sealand in Victoria, the man who had captured the whales in Pedder Bay, showed up on Hanson Island in his thirty-foot cruiser. Paul and Linda served him lunch and sat on the rocks talking with him. Paul felt uncomfortable, sensing that Wright was in the area to survey the possibilities of capturing orcas, but he decided not to confront the fast-talking entrepreneur directly.

"This is a unique place," Paul said. "The whales are undisturbed here, so we're able to observe their natural behavior. It's slow work, because we are on the whales' time, not our own schedule, but I am learning things that I couldn't possibly learn anywhere else."

Wright nodded as if he understood. "I think we're interested in the same things, Paul. I want people to learn to love the whales as much as you do. We just have different ways of doing it."

Paul did not completely trust the businessman's earnest gaze, which moved from out over Blackfish Sound directly into Paul's eyes. "Well," said Paul, "the whales seem to live without fear, and I think the peace of mind that gives them makes for a certain gentleness and kindness. So maybe that is a good lesson for us, eh?"

Bob Wright smiled. "Don't worry, Paul," he said. "I'm not going to capture whales here." Paul returned the smile, holding inside his distrust of the man's designs. The two men traded whale stories on the rocks as the sun beat down over Blackfish Sound. No orcas passed by, and Paul was glad of that.

The next afternoon, as Paul paddled home from an outing with the whales, he noticed that the fishing boats that had been absent for more than a week were back in Blackfish Sound. Fisheries patrolman Ross Hickling, whom Linda and Paul had met the previous summer in Alert Bay, stopped by one evening on his boat, the thirty-eight-foot *Port Alice*. "I was up in Thompson Sound," Ross told them, "and I saw seven killer whales herding fish. They're pretty good fishermen. There were lots of springs up there, and the whales were going after them as fast as the trollers were. I saw 'em make a loop around the salmon, herd them toward the beach, and then, when they had them all corralled, they ate quickly and left."

Ross suggested to Paul that the orcas seemed to follow the salmon, and that perhaps the whales' arrival in the area coincided with the spring salmon run. Paul and Ross agreed to collaborate on the hypothesis by sharing data. Perhaps, Paul thought, the orcas might come to be seen as an asset by the Fisheries Department, rather than competition.

After Ross left, Paul sat by the stove making notes. He could hear Linda playing her violin, the music wafting through the trees. Yashi was drawing on a large tablet. "What's that?" Paul said, pointing to the picture.

"A whale," said Yashi.

Paul turned it around and looked at the pencil drawing. The shape looked very much like an orca, with a dorsal fin, eye, and mouth. "Nice, Yashi," Paul said. "Nice whale."

On the following day the winds grew steadily, until by the middle of the afternoon Paul and Linda were looking out at the whitecaps. Rain pelted against their windows and walls, blowing in almost horizontally from the northeast, across Blackfish Sound. Through the evening Yashi snuggled with Paul and Linda in their bed, as the three of them stayed awake listening to the fiercest storm they had yet experienced on Hanson Island. Tree limbs crashed down on their roof and all over the ground. Waves slammed against the rocks, and the wind whistled in the forest.

Paul's firewood pile was soaked in the rain, and it took him a long time to get a fire going in the morning as the rain still poured down. With much huffing and puffing on his part, the fire began to blaze, and Paul made some ginseng tea. After hanging out everybody's clothes to dry, he made hotcakes in the skillet and called for Linda and Yashi to come. They ate breakfast and passed the day reading stories by the fire; twice they heard orcas through the speaker system, but they remained nestled by the fire as the rain pelted the windows.

The sun rose brilliantly colored on the following morning, and the day was calm. Seven orcas came by, and Paul followed them in the kayak through the kelp beds along the shore of Hanson Island and across to the point of Cracroft Island, then returned. He noted a whale he had not seen before, a female with two notches in her dorsal fin. In the afternoon, Chris Whiting and Liz Jackson, Paul's friends from the Vancouver Aquarium, showed up at Hanson Island for a visit. Paul's little outpost was becoming something of a mecca for whale enthusiasts.

On August 22, Paul was awakened by blows at 5 A.M. A half hour later he paddled his kayak out to more than forty whales that had gathered in Blackney Passage. As he moved toward them, Paul saw they were moving back and forth, as though trying to make up their minds which way to go. One pod was Nicola, Tulip, and Wavy's group, and another group was also familiar, but Paul did not know a third group of about ten whales. He elected to follow Wavy's pod as they moved into the middle of Blackfish Sound and then headed toward the Swanson Island shore, only to turn and move back to the middle of the sound again. As he followed, Paul noticed a second group of about a dozen orcas heading up the Hanson Island side of Blackfish Sound, also following a zigzag course. The whales seemed to be in constant communication, because they would change direction in unison, although they were scattered across the two-kilometer width of the passage. The whales continued their zigzag patterns as they traveled the length of the sound.

At the north end of Blackfish Sound, Nicola's group moved to the shore of Hanson Island, and the other group moved to the opposite shore, near Swanson Island. Then Paul noticed an additional group of about ten orcas beyond, toward Donegal Head. They seemed like the same unfamiliar group he'd seen in Blackney Passage, and he wondered if these whales had traveled around Hanson Island on the Johnstone Strait side and were reuniting with the others. All the whales formed a huge circle, two kilometers in diameter, reaching from Hanson Island, along the Plumper Islands toward Donegal Head, across the entrance of Queen Charlotte Strait to Bold Head on Swanson Island, and then back across Blackfish Sound to Hanson Island. As the circle began to close toward the center, Paul realized with sudden insight that the orcas were herding salmon. He could see little swirls in the water where the fish approached the surface, and occasionally a salmon would leap from the water. There was definitely a school of salmon inside the closing ring of orcas.

Paul noticed that small groups of the whales would suddenly disappear, leaving whirlpools in the water, presumably to move into the center of the circle, feed on the salmon, and return to the outside. Then a few more whales would go into the center and feed. This went on for about an hour before the whales broke up into several groups. Paul followed Nicola and Wavy as they moved into the shallows near the Plumper Islands.

As before, there were about twenty whales in the group. Nicola swam just ahead of Wavy, and off to her side were two impetuous calves puffing vigorously at the surface. Paul wondered if perhaps she was "babysitting" for the other adults. Two other adult females followed a short distance behind Nicola and Wavy. Although he could not be certain, Paul at first assumed that Nicola and Wavy were mates, but he knew that he had much more observing to do before he would be able to feel confident about the orcas' social structure. Nicola and Tulip seemed to be older, so perhaps the babies in this group were their grandchildren. Paul could only conjecture.

The other groups looked similar: Older males, whose tall, erect dorsal fins were unmistakable, and older females, who were a bit smaller and whose dorsal fins tended to be shorter and more curved. Traveling with them were young orcas—a newborn and a few others, perhaps two or three years old. The calves swam at the side of an adult, most often their mother, and would often nudge up against the adult or even swim up on the adult's back and slide back into the water playfully.

In a sheltered indentation of the Plumper Islands, out of the current, eight whales stopped on the surface. Paul was startled to see them forming a perfect line, breathing exactly together. He had seen Skana and Tung Jen do something similar in the aquarium pools, and he associated the behavior with sleeping or resting. Sitting quietly in his kayak, Paul watched as the group of whales continued to breathe together in precise synchronization, a meter or two apart. Then, in perfect unison, they sank below the surface together, remained underwater for about thirty seconds, to rise together and breathe as one again. The cycle was repeated, over and over. Paul assumed this was some sort of group resting behavior. The whales continued the pattern for about ten minutes, then moved through a small channel out into Weynton Passage and proceeded toward Johnstone Strait. They lingered in Weynton Passage until slack tide as Paul watched from a distance.

When they moved into Johnstone Strait, Paul followed in the kayak, huddled against the cool wind, his woolen cap pulled down over his ears. He watched the whales as they traveled in groups that stretched out across the strait in a formation that looked like a chorus line, but which Paul guessed was more like a fishnet. Paul followed the thirty or forty orcas until they reached Blackney Passage, and then he turned north and back home, having circumnavigated Hanson Island for the first time.

By the end of his second summer on Hanson Island, Paul had come to recognize three pods of whales. What he first identified as "Wavy's pod" seemed upon closer observation to be more appropriately called "Nicola and Tulip's pod." Female orcas may live longer than males, and perhaps maintain the social continuity. Hooker's pod was smaller, with just eight members, and was easily recognizable because it included several large males. The third pod that Paul identified was made up of whales he had actually first seen in December 1969, when their pod of twelve was captured at Pender Harbor. There were now only six adult whales, accompanied by three youngsters. The larger male of the pod had a little notch at the very top of his dorsal fin and later became known as Top Notch and then as A5. Five adult females traveled with him, one named Saddle because of the unusual shape of the gray saddle patch behind her dorsal fin on the left side. Another had deep gouges along her back, and she often swam near to A5. It was supposed that Saddle was the female who gave birth shortly after her release from Pender Harbor. The original group had lost most of its young members, a whole generation. The pod had only partially recovered. The large bull that had escaped at Pender Harbor must have died in the meantime, as he also was no longer with the pod.

Paul was only beginning to rough in the outlines of the orca population in the area, and he was not certain that his social interpretations were accurate, but he was sure that the whales had a coordinated social web consisting at least of families, pods, and occasionally multi-pod feeding parties. Paul noted the new calves born since the previous summer. He estimated that there were about fifty whales in the three pods he could identify, and perhaps another fifty whales in other pods he had also seen passing through the area, for a total population of about one hundred orcas that frequented the Johnstone Strait and Blackfish Sound area in the summer.

As the autumn storms came, the whales were seldom seen, and Paul, Linda, Yashi, Yo, and Nettle returned to Vancouver in the KWOOFmobile, loaded with household effects, lab equipment, tapes, and journals. Paul felt that his research was going well; he realized that what he wanted to know was going to take many seasons of careful observation. He imagined that to really understand the orcas he patiently would have to monitor the lives of the young just born that year. "If I could follow one whale through its life cycle," Paul told Linda on the ferry between Beaver Cove and Kelsey Bay, "I would think maybe I had done something worthwhile."

The whales, Paul felt, had shown him trust and had begun to reveal something of themselves to him. His only concern was that the aquariums might take advantage of this place where orcas trusted humans. Orcas had not returned to Pedder Bay or to Pender Harbor since the captures there, and the buying price for a live orca in North America had risen to a hundred thousand dollars.

When they returned to Vancouver, Paul and Linda immediately became embroiled in the expanding conflict over the Maplewood Mudflats. A year earlier, Paul had leaned on a bulldozer blade as it started toward one of the squatters' buildings, halting the demolition. Now, armed with a court order, the district municipality was determined to evict Paul and the other residents, among them an eighty-year-old man, Michael Bozer, who had spent fifty years building his ordered and simple, free little world. When the end came, Paul was in Ottawa, attempting to seek the intervention of Canadian Prime Minister Pierre Trudeau. Without warning, the District of North Vancouver moved to evict the squatters and burn their houses. Paul was saddened and outraged to hear that his wife and child had had to move their possessions from their home and then stand and watch it burn to the ground while he was thousands of miles away. It was four days before Christmas 1971.

Eventually the mudflats estuary itself would be safe, as the municipality decided not to proceed with the development. Old Michael was allowed to live out his days at his home, the last remnant of a way of life in the city. So it was a victory in the end. But meanwhile, Paul, with Linda and Yashi, retreated into the interior of British Columbia, renting an old house at Pilot Bay on Kootenay Lake for the winter. Once a week they trekked in and out, along several miles of narrow snowy trail winding through woods, pulling a sled loaded with Yashi and supplies. Paul continued to run his experiments at UBC by remote control, but mostly this was a time of healing for his family, which had been badly traumatized by the violent change in their life.

In April of 1972 Paul received a phone call from Canadian National Film Board director Tom Shandel, who wanted to make a film based on Paul's work. They met in the Cecil on a beautiful spring day and outlined a script. Paul wanted to present to the film audience a picture of the whales that he had come to know, a picture of their gentleness, their playfulness, their grace, their mutual devotion, their magnificent control of power. Tom was taken by the vision as Paul told him stories of whales.

Tom wanted to shoot the film at the Vancouver Aquarium with Skana, but because Paul was officially barred from working with Skana they decided to ask Bob Wright if they could shoot the film at Sealand with Haida and Chimo. Wright was enthusiastic, and Tom then called flutist Paul Horn to ask if he was willing to play music to the whales for the film. Tom, Paul, Bob Wright, and Paul Horn were joined by producer Werner Aellen, three cameramen, two sound technicians, and three assistants. They met at Sealand in Victoria on May 29. The day before, Paul had shaved his beard.

For three days, Haida and Chimo astounded the film crew with their repertoire of tricks, leaps, coordinated spyhops, and general dexterity in the water. Paul Spong led Haida through a series of the sound tests that he had conducted with Skana and Tung Jen. Haida particularly liked the ringing wine goblet, and the photographers went wild filming Haida's reactions to Paul, who even swam with the whale, much to the film crew's delight.

When Paul Horn played his flute, the whales were obviously ecstatic, and Chimo became much more active than she had been. As if they were the last couple on the dance floor at an all-night jazz club, Haida and Chimo kept the musician playing and the spectators enthralled as they swam to the music. Both whales issued their unearthly cries, as Paul Horn played, and the musician followed along with their unique modulations. The members of the film crew, who had been holding their breath in silence during the filming, broke out in applause when the cameras stopped rolling.

The National Film Board's working title for the film was *A Whale of a Sound*. Paul, however, wanted the film to break out of old stereotypes of whales and to present a new image. He wanted to title the film *We Call Them Killers*. Tom Shandel agreed to the new title, taped an interview with Paul to explain his work with orcas, and retreated with Werner Aellen to edit the footage. Later, the film was released as a theatrical short, playing in movie houses in Canada, the United States, and elsewhere. Years later, Paul's mother, Tui, wrote from New Zealand to tell Paul that she had seen him in the film when it played with *Gandhi* in Paul's native Whakatane.

Paul's work in town was over for the year. He and Linda hurried to put together their supplies and gear so that they could continue their work on Hanson Island. Paul wanted to get some data on the orcas' annual return to Blackfish Sound and see if the information would corroborate Ross Hickling's theory that the return coincided with the arrival of the spring salmon in the area. They had no time to waste.

Yashi, who had just turned four in April, was also ready to leave. "I don't think I want to live in Vancouver anymore," he announced.

"Why?" asked Paul.

"It's boring," said Yashi bluntly.

"Well, where do you want to live?" Linda asked.

"I want to go back to Hanson Island. I have *big* friends there."

"Who are your big friends?" asked Paul.

Yashi gestured with his fingers as he counted: "The whales are my friends, the trees are my friends, and the slugs are my friends," he said.

"The slugs are your friends, too?" Paul asked.

"Yes," said Yashi seriously, with a nod of his head. As Paul and Linda stood smiling, the phone rang. Paul left the room to answer it. When he came back into the room, he was grinning and shaking his head.

"What happened?" Linda asked.

"Haida and Chimo have become lovers," said Paul. "Maybe they fell in love to Paul Horn's flute. Anyway, Bob Wright is really happy, and says that Chimo seems to be coming out of her shell a little bit."

Two days later, Paul, Linda, and Yashi loaded the KWOOF-mobile, tying equipment onto every available square inch of the sides and top until they looked like a family of high-tech hillbillies fleeing the Dust Bowl. With Yo, Nettle, and Yashi crowded in, they brought chuckles from more than one ferry crew between Vancouver and Alert Bay as they traveled north with their load.

Paul swam in the cold, murky water, the kelp rubbing against the legs of his wet suit like slimy seacats. Overhead the gulls shrieked and glided about as if they were discussing some enormous crisis in their aerial gull world. The currents of the ebbing tide washed about his body, swirling the ocean and lapping against the hard rock shoreline.

Paul swam along the surface, breathing through a snorkel, then took a deep breath and—closing his eyes—dove through the kelp, paddling deep below. When he opened his eyes underwater, he could see nothing through the mask but the murky swirl of the tide-churned sea. Visibility was only three or four feet, restricted by the dense plankton blooms of summer. Back on the surface, he breathed through the snorkel as he hung in the water. As an experiment, he closed his eyes and sank until his ears were well below the water, listening to the sounds of the ocean world. He became aware of the vibrating engine of a passing fish boat, and then he began to pick out other distinct sounds, a splash, a swoosh, the throbbing of his own blood.

Taking a full breath, he dove deeply, swimming farther and farther toward the bottom. As he began to feel the pressure in his lungs, he stopped swimming and drifted slowly upward, letting small puffs of air out, to extend the time that he could hold his breath. When he could stand it no longer, he pumped hard with his arms and legs toward the surface. After pumping twice, he expected to break the water, but it did not happen. With a slight panic he opened his eyes. He saw nothing but kelp undulating in the tide. He stroked again and rose up through strands of kelp. Then again he pumped, and burst through the surface, letting out a huge, sighing breath and taking in the fresh, wet air.

The gulls over Blackfish Sound had quieted, resting on the water; the whole bay was still. Then a single gull squawked, and a wisp of wind caught Paul's face. He treaded water, breathing deeply, then rolled over on his back and floated there with his eyes closed.

He daydreamed the kelp into a family of whales nudging him and playing with his body like a beach ball. He wondered if someday the whales would ever feel comfortable enough to come close. He had been thinking of a new lab, a floating lab, doughnut-shaped so that the orcas could swim into the middle. The inner pool of the circular lab would be ringed with speakers. The whales were *acoustic* animals, and perhaps, he thought, they could be lured into the acoustic space created by the sound system. It seemed probable that they would come to investigate. There, thought Paul, he could enter into a relationship with whales and perhaps get to know them as he had known Skana, with one important difference: These whales would be free to come and go as they pleased. Paul had spent the past few days drawing rough sketches of his floating "OrcaLab," as he called it.

As he floated on his back, Paul heard the unmistakable

"shreeeEEE" of an orca call. He realized that his ears were below the water and that he was picking up the orcas directly, not through a hydrophone. Then again, longer: "shreeeeeee-EEEEE." And an answer: "aaaAAAAAAaaaaa."

Paul smiled to himself. Soon the rolling water world was filled with sound, whale voices calling to each other as the orcas cruised their domain. The calls grew louder as Paul floated on the surface with his eyes shut. He dove under the water and tried to make sounds by forcing the air out of his mouth; even if the whales could hear his gurgling, muffled howl, he thought they probably wouldn't be all that interested. Whales in the wild were a decidedly different phenomenon than captive whales. It was going to take a long time to convince the whales that he was worth their trouble to investigate.

A few days later, Paul heard orcas on the hydrophone, then saw them approaching from Johnstone Strait. He put on his wet suit in a hurry and swam out from shore. He stopped swimming when he saw two dorsal fins surfacing together, coming toward him along the shore of Hanson Island. Several times he saw the two small fins rise out of the water, so he assumed they were two young whales. When the whales were abreast of him, about fifty feet away, he saw them turn on the surface and dive below, coming toward him. Paul sank below the water and waited. The orcas swam into sight and stopped ten or fifteen feet away. He could see them clearly: There were not two whales but four, two on top and two below; one of the lower pair was smaller than the others. Immediately he realized something about their coordination of swimming and breathing, in pairs, alternating up and down so that four whales appear as two from the surface. The four orcas hovered there, looking at Paul for a few moments. Then they turned slowly and swam away.

Paul spent the early part of the summer of 1972 building a new house on Hanson Island and observing the whales. Soon he and Linda moved out of their tree house and into the sunnier shelter on the rocks that looked out over their bay. With a chain-saw attachment called an Alaskan Mill, designed by local homesteader Will Malloff, Paul milled planks for doors, walls, shelves, and a table. He built a two-layered bed, with a bed for Yashi below and a bed for Linda and himself above.

As Paul and Ross Hickling suspected, the orcas did indeed arrive in the area with the onset of the annual salmon run. Early in June, small groups of orcas were seen first, traveling fast, and Paul guessed they were probably scouting parties. Then in mid-June, as the salmon season opened, larger groups appeared. Paul thought that there were about ten "senior bulls" in the local population. These older males were unmistakable, over twenty feet in length and weighing up to ten or twelve thousand pounds or more. Their impressive dorsal fins, reaching over six feet in height, distinguished them within the pods. In addition to Wavy and Hooker, Paul had also named two other males, Flop Fin, after his unique dorsal fin, and Tilt, for his habit of diving at an angle.

Paul observed that while hunting, traveling, or resting, the whales would be in subgroups that often breathed in unison; he wondered if the young whales were receiving systematic instruction in techniques of breath control and coordination. If the whales were resting or simply traveling, not hunting, they would often move silently; however, while hunting, the orcas would be in constant vocal communication, calling out with their rich repertoire of sounds. Although the orcas have a reputation for attacking and eating other marine mammals such as seals or other cetaceans, Paul often saw minke whales or the lone sei passing nonchalantly through the orca pods. Although the Dall's porpoises would often hug the shoreline when the orcas passed, Paul witnessed no instances of orca attacks on anything but salmon.

In Alert Bay for supplies, Paul learned that the sei whale, Sol, was dead. Ken Fairwell had found her floating upside down in Blackfish Sound with bullet holes in her head. Unable to tow the carcass, Ken left the dead whale to drift out to sea with the tides.

"Someone was probably just using her for target practice, shooting at her for fun," Ken told Paul.

Paul felt queasy. He had heard stories from old-timers about sperm, humpback, fin, and sei whales being a common sight in local waters in earlier times, and had realized that this lone sei was surely the last of its pod, and probably one of the last sei whales on the West Coast.

Paul shook his head in a mood of helplessness. He felt sad about the death of Sol, and he also felt a sadness for the vast gap that seemed to separate people from these magnificent beings. He felt lonely himself, and he felt the larger loneliness of humankind.

Paul's depression was lifted somewhat when he went to his mailbox and found several letters from KWOOF supporters sending donations and encouragement. On his way back to Hanson Island, Paul crossed paths with Nicola, Wavy, and others, leisurely swimming down Johnstone Strait. He paddled amongst them. One juvenile whale leaped clear out of the water, its body seemingly suspended in air, then crashed down with a tremendous splash. Paul followed the whales along the coast of Vancouver Island; other whales breached, and Paul loudly applauded each leap, shouting approval.

The whales were moving with the tide, so Paul followed them past his usual turn home through Blackney Passage, knowing that the tide would turn around in about three hours and carry him home. The whales hugged the coast until they got to Robson Bight, where they stopped and milled about. Paul recalled that Jimmy Sewid had told him the whales liked to hang out in the shallows of Robson Bight. The bight is four kilometers wide at the mouth, and at its deepest recess its shoreline is formed by the Tsitika River estuary.

Paul noticed that Nicola's pod seemed to lounge and play along the rocks that dropped sharply from the shoreline into the water. At first he thought they were perhaps feeding, but he saw no sign of fish. Paul watched what seemed like relaxing play, the whales dipping along the rocky shoreline. Eventually the whales again moved as a group, heading east along the shore of Vancouver Island. After traveling about two kilometers, the whales stopped again, and Paul paddled his kayak to a rocky beach where he could climb up on a bluff looking down at the whales. Nicola, Wavy, and the others frolicked in the shallow water along the coast. From above, Paul could see their sleek black and white bodies twisting and rolling in the shallows. Whales stood on their heads with their flukes in the air, reared up until half their body stood above the water, lay on their sides, and slapped their fins in the water.

He watched the whales until the tide turned, and then he walked down the bluff to his kayak. From the beach he could see the whales only a short distance from the shoreline, twisting and arching in the water. Paul stood, fascinated by the behavior. He bent down, picking up a double handful of stones. The little pebbles were smooth and rounded. Were the whales rubbing themselves on the rocks? Paul wondered. He looked up at the whales and back at the smooth round stones. Perhaps whales had been coming here for thousands of years, rubbing themselves on the smooth pebbles of the sloping beach. Paul put several of the glistening stones in his pocket, untied his kayak, and headed home on the ebbing tide.

Later, on the rocks on Hanson Island, Paul and Linda witnessed similar activities among the orcas. They were also treated to some spectacular shows. Early one evening, before sunset, they watched as orcas streaked across the water at top speed, spraying water in all directions. And one dark night they saw two whales swimming in just a few feet of water in the little bay beside their camp, making a huge circle that phosphoresced and bubbled in the black water. They wondered if their camp shoreline was just a favorite playground, or whether the games were directed at them, the tiny band of humans.

As usual, friends and visitors stopped by Hanson Island in the warm summer weather. George Dyson, whom Paul had met aboard the *D'Sonoqua,* arrived by kayak. George was nineteen years old. He lived in a tree house on the eastern shore of Indian Arm inlet, east of Vancouver, and was a designer and builder of modified Aleutian kayaks called baidarkas. George impressed Paul with his endless practical skills and knowledge of boats and the ocean.

Paul also appreciated George's astute and ever-probing mind, as well as his quiet demeanor and gentle kindness.

Ron Keller arrived from San Francisco in July, bringing along a donated inflatable rubber boat and a good deal of expertise. Paul and Linda welcomed his skills and enthusiasm. An immediate friendship was formed. The Hanson Island outpost was evolving into a homey, comfortable encampment. Paul, Linda, and Yashi slept under plastic stretched over the pole framing of the new house, and guests slept in tents in the forest. Ron started a garden for them, building up a rock wall, hauling soil from the forest, and planting seeds. They grew radishes, squash and lettuce, kale and cabbages, and scattered flowering nasturtiums among them. In a box they planted a fragrant yellow and red rose. Paul and Linda were thrilled by their first harvest.

One evening in mid-August, the whole camp heard orcas on the speakers; they went to the rocks, where they could hear whales blowing in the darkness. Paul started to count the blows, but there were so many he couldn't keep track. He had never heard so many whales passing at one time. For more than two hours the whale blows could be heard in the night. So many whales passed that Paul wondered if they were circling Hanson Island and coming by again. He guessed that over a hundred had passed by. The next day they heard from a fisherman that someone had seen two hundred orcas in Robson Bight.

Paul set out for the bight by kayak, but if there was such a gathering he arrived too late to witness it. He did, however, spend the day in Robson Bight and at the rubbing beach to the southeast, observing the orcas that were there. He concluded that the orcas indeed used the shallow rocks for rubbing and scratching, and that the Robson Bight area was a center of activity for the local orca population.

Late in the afternoon, Nicola swam toward the kayak and dove underneath. Over the edge, Paul glimpsed Nicola's eye looking up at him as she glided past. Then she spyhopped in front of him, giving Paul a feeling of being astutely surveyed. He played his flute as Nicola swam near the kayak. Paul wondered if Nicola was getting to know him as distinct from other humans on the water.

1. *Paul Spong with captive orca, Haida, at the Victoria Aquarium, massaging the whale with a feather [Photo courtesy of Paul Spong]*

2. *Skana in her pool at the Vancouver Aquarium [Photo by the author]*

3. (Above) Skana in her pool at
the Vancouver Aquarium
[Photo by Paul Spong]

4. (Right) Paul Spong plays his
flute to Skana
at the Vancouver Aquarium
[Photo courtesy of Paul Spong]

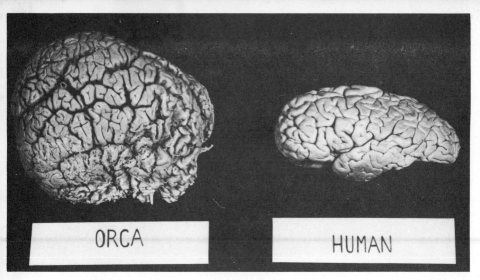

5. Orca brain and human brain [Photo by the author]

6. Visitors photographing free orcas in Blackfish Sound
[Photo courtesy of Paul Spong]

7. *Musician playing flute for orca in Johnstone Strait [Photo by the author]*

8. A family of orcas in the fog in Blackfish Sound [Photo courtesy of Paul Spong]

9. *Lone orca passing through bay in front of Orcalab [Photo by Paul Spong]*

10. *Three orcas playing in Blackfish Sound [Photo by Yashi Spong]*

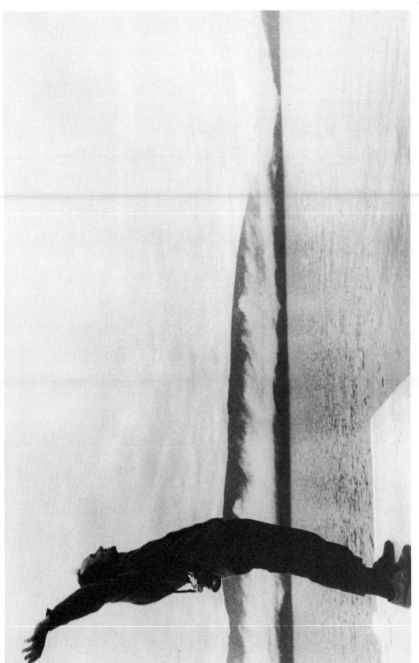

11. Paul Spong overlooking Blackfish Sound [Photo by the author]

12. Robert Hunter, Patrick Moore, and Paul Spong backstage at the Green-peace Whale Show in Vancouver, 1974, in preparation for the first Green-peace voyage to save the whales [Photo by the author]

13. Henry Payne, a mystic environmentalist who donated land to Green-peace to help finance the whale campaign [Photo by the author]

When the *D'Sonoqua* and her crew arrived for their annual visit, Paul took them to Robson Bight, where they found Top Notch's pod and Nicola's pod, more than twenty whales altogether, lounging in the shallows. As Paul was exercising on the bow of the *D'Sonoqua,* he was approached by Dr. Michael Bigg, a marine mammalogist who was conducting an orca survey for the Canadian Department of Fisheries. For the past two years, Bigg, with his colleague Dr. Ian MacAskie, had been collecting data on orcas in all British Columbia waters. In 1971 he had orchestrated a one-day census survey using spotters along the coast of B.C. and Washington State. He was now spending a month in the Johnstone Strait area, beginning a detailed photographic census of the local population.

Paul was interested and eager to help. From his research, Dr. Bigg had concluded that there were perhaps two to three hundred orcas that frequented the B.C. coast. It was only the rough beginning of an outline, but Bigg's study would eventually become the definitive orca census. Paul told him what he knew about pods, pod structure, and his guesses about the elders of the pods.

Later that day, Paul, clad in his wet suit, rowed the *D'Sonoqua*'s skiff into the shoreline near the rocks, where he put on a mask and snorkel and dove into the water. Visibility was still poor. As he turned around in a circle, surveying the underwater realm, he suddenly caught a glimpse of something too big to be a fish. It had to be an orca, he thought, and remained motionless in the water, waiting to see if the whale would come to him. After a few moments, he saw the form again, and there was no mistake. The massive black and white body was graceful under the water, but also awesomely powerful. With one almost imperceptible stroke of its flukes, the orca cruised in an arc, disappearing into the murky distance, not to be seen again.

Perhaps it was the accumulation of his own experiences, or perhaps it was the orca lore from Indians and fishermen, but Paul was beginning to expect unusual occurrences around the whales. A Nimpkish Indian in Alert Bay told Paul that the Indian people used to throw offerings to the whales, abalone shell or valuable metals, in the hope of being granted wishes or good fortune. "The whales are more human than humans," he had told Paul.

Indeed, the orcas had an aura of magic about them, and it seemed as if every friend who came to visit Hanson Island left with some story of a coincidental or mystical encounter with whales.

In late August, Michael Berry and Maureen Wright visited Hanson Island in their eighteen-foot sailboat. With them was their young German shepherd, Phoenix. Michael and the dog were constant companions, hiking and running through the woods, leaping over logs on the beach, throwing and chasing sticks.

Whenever they went sailing, leaving Yo and Phoenix on shore, Phoenix would swim as far as he could after the boat, and then return. One day, when a group of orcas went by, Paul, Michael, Maureen, Linda, Yashi, and George departed in the boat, leaving the two dogs on shore. They spent the morning following the whales northwest through Blackfish Sound and then returned to Hanson Island, where they anchored in the bay. When they got ashore, Yo greeted them but Phoenix was nowhere in sight. Michael looked around, called, whistled, and became anxious when Phoenix did not show up. Finally it dawned on Michael that Phoenix probably had tried to follow the boat and had been swept along in the tide, unable to get back to Hanson Island. "Oh, God!" Michael wailed. "We've got to go look for him. He swam after us and couldn't get back." Paul and Michael went back out, as the others stayed on Hanson Island. They motored up and down Blackfish Sound, calling and searching, but they saw nothing. Michael took the boat along the shoreline, shouting and whistling, but Phoenix was nowhere to be found.

"He'll drown," cried Michael, tears swelling in his eyes. "He's just a puppy." Paul tried to comfort him, but he could not offer much hope. As the sky grew dark, Paul and Michael returned to Hanson Island. Everyone sat around the table by the kitchen fire talking about Phoenix. Linda and Maureen had searched the beach, calling, but also returned as the day had grown dark. After supper, the party sat gloomily and quietly listening to the crackle of underwater sounds through the speakers connected to the hydrophones. Occasionally, and sadly, Paul would get up and adjust the volume on the amplifier. At one point, Michael clasped his hands together, exclaiming, "Please, whales, help him, please bring him back!"

About an hour before midnight, they heard orca calls on the speakers. Without a word they all went outside to the rocks. In the moonlight they could hear the whales passing just off the shore. Paul counted seven blows. They watched the darkness as the orcas passed and as the sound of their blows faded away, leaving the five human watchers silent on the rocks. Waves lapped below their feet.

"Phoenix!" Michael screamed. Climbing onto the rocks from the black, pulsing water was Phoenix, soaking wet and looking miserable. It had been twelve hours since he had been lost. Michael ran to Phoenix, ecstatic to see his companion. He carried the exhausted dog into the house, sat him by the fire, and dried him off. Phoenix couldn't possibly have been swimming for twelve hours, everyone agreed. Perhaps, someone suggested, he swam to shore, walked home, and then stumbled back into the water. But Michael was convinced: "The whales brought him back," he said, perfectly serious.

When Paul's friend Bruce Logan came to visit, he wanted more than anything to see a whale jump, but throughout his stay on Hanson Island the whales did not oblige him. Paul told him, with his cryptic grin, "If you ask the whales for what you want, they might help you."

Bruce laughed.

"Check it out," said Paul.

A week later, on the Kelsey Bay ferry, Bruce and Paul sat in the coffee shop looking out at the waters of Johnstone Strait, Bruce puffing on a cigarette. He'd been trying to quit smoking for several years, but nothing had worked.

"Okay," he said to Paul, half mocking in tone but completely serious in intent. "I just want to see one whale jump. If one whale jumps for me on this ferry ride, I'll quit smoking!"

As the ferryboat was nearing Kelsey Bay, Paul and Bruce

simultaneously snapped their heads around to the window. About a hundred meters from the ferry, a whale was breaching, fully out of the water. Paul broke into a laugh, such that other passengers on the ferryboat turned around to look. Bruce's jaw hung open. "But . . . but that wasn't an orca," said Bruce. "What was it?"

"It was a minke," said Paul through his laughter. "You didn't say what kind of whale."

"But I meant an orca," Bruce protested. Just at that moment the minke whale—a smaller cousin of the larger baleen whales like the fin or the blue whale, with a white bar across its small pectoral fin—leaped again from the water. Paul kept laughing, and Bruce shook his head. Again the whale leaped clear of the water as Bruce stared, and then for a fourth time. Paul was holding his sides, nearly choking on his laughter as Bruce put out his cigarette. "Okay, okay," Bruce surrendered. "That's it, I quit." That was the last cigarette he ever smoked, and the incident became his favorite whale story, retold many times in the years to come.

A mystique began to surround Hanson Island. Stories were amplified and embellished in pubs from Alert Bay to downtown Vancouver, and Paul's reputation began to take on the epic and mythic proportions that he feared.

A tourist from Washington State approached Paul on the Victoria ferry.

"Uh, excuse me," the man said. "Are you Dr. Spong?"

"Uh, oh, yes," said Paul, startled.

"I've heard about what you're doing. I'd love to come see the whales." Paul and the tourist talked for a while, and Paul returned to the KWOOFmobile looking a bit sheepish.

"What's wrong?" asked Linda.

"I hope we're doing the right thing," Paul said quietly.

"Why do you say that?"

"It's going to be tricky," he said. "I want to educate people about the whales, but I don't want to be a celebrity, and I don't want to turn Johnstone Strait into a circus. We should be careful about drawing too much attention."

"It might be too late for that, Paul."

5

The Whale Show

Paul drove slowly over the Second Narrows Bridge, which spanned Burrard Inlet east of Vancouver. Rain drummed on the roof and windows of the Land-Rover as the windshield wipers fought pathetically against the onslaught on the outside and Paul rubbed the mist from the inside. The nimbused headlights of the few approaching cars were like bodiless ghost eyes in the evening downpour.

Paul had been invited to a publishing party at the posh Georgia Hotel in the center of town. An editor from McClelland & Stewart, Canada's classy publishing house, had invited Paul to the event, which celebrated the publishing of *A Whale for the Killing* by the naturalist Farley Mowat. Paul was the most famous—or perhaps notorious—whale celebrity in Vancouver at the time, so he made the guest list.

He circled the downtown streets, looking for a parking place, too frugal to spend a dollar and a half at a hotel parking lot. He pulled his coat closed with one hand and held his wool tuque on his head with the other as he ran along the street to the hotel entrance, where a doorman, slightly taken aback at Paul's rural and wild appearance, let him in.

The lobby reverberated with stately chatter amid elegant holiday decor. The concierge at the front desk directed Paul to the second-floor suite where the cocktail party was well under way. Television crews lounged in a corner with drinks, and Paul recognized several local journalists. Nodding and smiling, he moved directly to the bar.

"Drink, sir?" the bartender said.

"Uh, yes, I'll have a scotch on the rocks, please." Paul reached for his wallet.

"There's no charge, sir."

"Uh?"

"There's no charge, sir," repeated the bartender.

"Oh well, make it a double," said Paul, grinning.

"Paul!" An energetic young woman approached. "I'm glad you could come, Paul. I want you to meet Farley." Paul assumed the woman was the editor who had invited him, but she failed to introduce herself, and he had forgotten her name. He trailed along behind her as she led him through the hum of cocktail small talk and boozy laughter.

In the far corner of the room, about a dozen or so fashionable partygoers were gathered around a small bearded man with a plain brown tie over an equally plain green shirt. Paul's hostess tapped impatiently on her empty wineglass waiting for a speaker to conclude, then pushed into the ring and spoke well above the general hum.

"Farley." He looked at her, as did the others, and she continued. "This is Paul Spong—remember my telling you about his work with killer whales?"

"Oh yes," said the beleaguered author, gazing up from his seat at Paul, who suddenly felt conspicuous and shy, holding his drink, hat, and coat, with rain droplets still clinging to his sweater. "Pleased to meet you, Dr. Spong." Farley Mowat didn't hold out his hand, but simply nodded.

The others in the circle all looked at Paul as if waiting for him to speak. Paul said nothing; he gazed back into the man's eyes, and also nodded. "We should talk before the night is over," the author said to Paul, and Paul managed a polite yes.

After an uncomfortable silence, Paul said, "I just got here. I'm going to put my things down. I'm very pleased to meet you. I'll, uh, catch you when you're free."

"Okay," Farley assented, smiling.

Paul nodded and smiled at the circle of guests, then backed out through the crowd.

Standing alone at the bar, working on his second scotch, Paul heard a soft voice at his ear. "Paul?" He turned around and found himself face to face with the smiling author.

"Oh hi," said Paul. The two shook hands. Farley gestured to the side with his head and led Paul through the crowd to a corner of the suite.

"So," said Farley emphatically. "I want to hear what you know about whales."

Farley Mowat was Paul's senior by a decade, give or take a few years. Paul, looking him in the eye, could feel his authentic curiosity and enthusiasm.

"More than any animal that I know of," Paul said, "including humans, the whales seem to live without fear and, without aggression. I mean, that's where I'm at right now. They are extremely intelligent, but I'm not sure what *kind* of intelligence they have. It's different. It's hard to say, and there's a lot I *don't* know about whales; way more than I do know."

"I understand," consoled Farley. "It sounds like whales on the West Coast are a lot like whales on the East Coast, inspiring maybe, but also confusing."

"Yes," said Paul, feeling a warm camaraderie, and he told Farley about his experiences with the orcas of Blackfish Sound and about Skana, concluding with "she even calmed me down."

"Calmed you down?"

"Well, she held my hand in her teeth and wouldn't let go until I cooled off. Like I said, Farley, I don't know; some of this stuff seems pretty far out, but all I know is that Skana forced me to treat her as an equal, and when I did she revealed a lot of herself to me."

"I had an experience like that with a fin whale. She was also captured, but accidentally. She got stuck in a little lagoon known as Aldridge's Pond in a fishing village called Burgeo on the south coast of Newfoundland. That's what my book is about."

"I'm sorry to say I haven't read it."

"I don't think you have to; it sounds like you probably already know what it has to say. But I'll get you a copy before we leave tonight."

"So what happened with this fin whale, in a nutshell?"

"A fin whale in a nutshell! Now there's a trick," Farley laughed. "Well, in a nutshell, she looked at me as I've never been looked at before, and she spoke to me as I've never been spoken to before. I felt a fragile link, but it was severed before I could follow it up. She had gotten herself stuck in this little lagoon, and several of the local hunters emptied about two hundred rounds into her as a sort of sport. We managed to call the dogs off, but it was too late; she died a few days later."

"How did she speak to you?" Paul asked.

"She beached herself, because she was too exhausted and sick from the bullet wounds to stay afloat. I had managed to get close to her in a dory while she was still swimming, and she had stuck her head out of the water and looked directly at me. She gave out this unearthly cry, and I had a strange feeling that she was talking to me, trying to reach me.

"Then, when she was lying exhausted on the beach, I ran up to her and just went crazy, pounding on her head and telling her to back off and get off the sand. It was the only thing I could think of to do. I screamed, 'Get off, back up, you crazy bitch,' and she did! She backed up and swam around, but in the end she was just too sick. She beached herself on the other side of the pond and let out the same unbelievable, sonorous moan that I had heard before. It was the most desolate cry I've ever heard, and I knew then, and I know now, that that call was meant for *me*. She tried to reach me, and in a strange way I guess she did."

"Amazing!" said Paul. "You know, I heard an Indian story about an old man who told some orcas that were in danger of stranding to go away from the beach, just like you did, straight out, and the whales left. I don't know what's going on—I guess I should tell you they fired me from my job at the aquarium for saying things like this."

"Oh really? How come?"

"I told them I thought Skana should be let free."

"Good for you. I must admit, I thought perhaps I was going a bit daft a few times. But what really did it for me was seeing how the whales related and communicated with each other. This female's mate stayed outside the pond every day, and they continuously vocalized with each other. They even breathed together! Exactly together. A fisherman watched the two whales for quite a while one day. They breathed exactly together, *every time*, while he watched.

"They are into a pretty high level of contact with each other," Farley continued. "The fin whales that I saw seem to travel in families, and from what I could see, they mate for life."

"The orcas seem to travel together that way as well," said Paul. "I've identified several family groups, and extended families, or pods. I've seen three whole pods, maybe forty whales, hunting together, surrounding the salmon, and taking turns feeding. I don't know if they mate for life, but they certainly do fool around a lot. Funny thing about that: You'd expect the ocean would be full of orcas—long life span, abundant food supply, good care of young, and no predators. . . ."

"Except humans," added Farley.

The party swirled on behind Paul and Farley, who hardly noticed, intent as they were on their conversation. "In a way," said Paul, "I'm just beginning to glimpse the depth of these orcas. They never stop surprising me. I think we're on the edge of a very profound change in the way humans see whales."

"But the sad irony is, Paul, that just as we are beginning to experience this delightfully different intelligence, we, as a species, are wiping them out."

"Yes, some fishermen and other people on the coast here shoot at the orcas."

"I'm afraid it's much bigger than that, Paul. I first began to notice it with the fin whales off the East Coast. In 1958 the Norwegians began extensive whaling off Nova Scotia, and the fin whales declined steadily. By the winter of 1965–66, only two fin families were seen off Burgeo, where hundreds of whales had once roamed. The Norwegians shoot killers as well, be-

cause they think they're hurting the herring fishery. In 1964 the
U.S. Air Force practiced strafing runs on killer whales. Japan
and Russia both have huge factory whaling fleets that are currently scouring the oceans for the last of the great whales. It's
really a wholesale slaughter, Paul. I hope there are some
whales left to study in a few years."

"Do you think it's that bad?" asked Paul.

Farley leaned forward. "Listen, Paul, there are only a few
people who have seen what you've seen, who've had the experience. Most of the world still gets its ideas about whales from
lingering images of Moby Dick and tales of vicious monsters of
the deep. The factory ships are wiping out the whales as fast as
they can. What do they care? It's all for a few dollars. When
the whales are gone, the whalers can transfer their assets to
another business. They make dog food and lipstick out of the
whales. The Russians lubricate their ICBMs with whale oil. So
do the Yankees."

Paul winced at the thought.

"I work with a group called Project Jonah," Farley went on.
"It was started by a woman in California, Joan McIntyre. You'll
meet her someday. We're trying to spread around the consciousness about whales; people just don't know. I'm working
on Canada, trying to get Canada to stop whaling and trying to
get them to vote against the whaling nations at the International Whaling Commission. It's an uphill battle, but it absolutely has to be done. The work you are doing is groundbreaking; it's way ahead of its time, Paul—or should I say right on
time? Actually, I hope it's not too late."

"What do you say to people who ask you, 'Why whales?
Why not people? There's lots of people starving; why don't you
try to save them? What's one whale in a tank?' That's what I
hear when I talk about this."

"You're always going to have people who think that humans
are God's gift to the universe, who think that humans are the
only ones who think, who love, who have compassion, who
suffer and cry over the loss of a loved one. We've been brain-
washed into thinking that humans are 'above' all other creatures. Well, I've seen more compassion and intelligence in

whales than I've seen in a lot of people, Paul, and I'm sure you have, too. This isn't a question of what's more important, whales or humans. It is a question of what is more important, life or death? A planet free to evolve with wondrous diversity, or a planet destroyed by ignorance?"

"I . . . I agree with you." Paul paused. "But I wonder if I'm not just a bit afraid to step out and say it so clearly and . . . publicly."

"You could help us, Paul."

"How?"

"It would be good to have someone on the West Coast in Canada. My head spins, really, Paul. There is so much to do, and to talk about. I wish we had a few days, but I have to go to Victoria on this book tour."

"Well, why don't I come with you. I'll introduce you to Haida and Chimo."

"Great," said Farley. "I've never seen a killer whale before."

"We call 'em orcas," said Paul. *"Orcinus orca."*

"Orca. Okay, Paul, that would give us some time to talk about all this."

"Sure," said Paul eagerly. "Where are you staying?"

"Right here. Why don't you call me in the morning. Do you know how to get to the ferry?"

"Sure, no problem," said Paul, sensing not so much that he was being drawn into a vortex against his will, but rather that this was so much bigger than his will that the choices had already been made in some other realm. This kindly, bearded author from the Canadian Maritimes was the first being since Skana to so rivet his attention.

The next morning, the sad news came from Victoria that Chimo, Sealand's albino orca, had died of a massive infection. Farley, being Canada's foremost spokesperson for whales at the time, was asked to comment. "If I had the power, I'd put an absolute embargo on putting whales on display before that inflated ape called man," said Farley, calling the holding of whales in captivity "an atrocity."

With mixed feelings, Paul, Linda, Yashi, Farley and his wife,

Claire, boarded the ferry to Victoria and stood at the rail gazing out over the choppy gray November waters of Georgia Strait.

"If you read the ship's logs of the early European sea captains," Farley told Paul, "you'll find out that the ocean was *teeming* with whales two hundred years ago. They saw whales every day, thousands of them. There are accounts of whales from horizon to horizon, for days on end. Now we consider it a rare and extraordinary event to see a whale. Where did they all go?

"The whales have been reduced from their peak populations by eighty to ninety percent. Most people have no idea what a treasure we're losing. I'm helping Joan McIntyre compile a book of whale history as a way of trying to communicate to people about the whales. Why don't you contribute something?"

"Like what?" asked Paul.

"Well, why don't you just write up what happened to you, how you met Skana, and the orcas up north."

"Well, I'm not much of a writer."

"Just tell what happened. We'll help you edit it, if it needs that."

"Okay," said Paul. "What is the book going to be called?"

"Mind in the Waters. The stories of people and whales, stories not so different from yours, go back as far as any written or oral history we know of. Like the Indian stories you've heard around here, all over the world there are stories of humans befriending whales and dolphins."

"I remember stories from New Zealand," Paul said. "I guess I never really thought much about them then, but there was a story about this dolphin named Opo who would play with the swimmers at Opononi Beach, and there was a famous dolphin that sailors called Pelorus Jack. Pelorus Jack used to guide vessels through treacherous waters."

"The ancient Greeks and Romans tell stories of young children riding on the backs of wild dolphins, and these stories are just too prevalent around the world to dismiss as some sort of collective hallucination or myth. Aristotle has several passages about dolphins, and he even mentions that their voice in the air is something like a human voice, and that they can pronounce vowels and series of vowels, but have difficulty with consonants.

"But somehow it all got turned around," Farley continued. "Melville calls the killer whale 'savage.' There was this image of brave men in tiny ships out hunting the great sea monster. Well, today the factory ships are six hundred feet long, and the killer boats are a hundred and fifty feet long, equipped with sonar and exploding harpoons. The whales haven't got a chance; the whalers take whole pods: adults, babies, everything. They're killing whales at the rate of one every twelve minutes, twenty-four hours a day, three hundred and sixty-five days a year. So who is the vicious monster of the seas?"

At the Sealand aquarium in Victoria, Paul, Farley, Linda, and Yashi were ushered into the whale pool compound. Haida floated alone in the center of the pool. Paul, who knew Haida quite well, led Farley down to the training platform. Haida had a favorite game that he liked to play, of giving kelp to visitors. He brought a piece of kelp up from the bottom of the pool and held it dangling from the front of his mouth with his jaws closed, offering it to Farley. Farley picked up the piece of kelp and waved it in the air. Haida nudged against Farley's hand, and the author let the whale take back the kelp. This game continued for a while, until when Farley leaned over to take the offering, Haida opened his mouth and dropped the kelp deep into his throat. Farley started to reach in after the kelp, but stopped short as his hand began to pass the rows of immense teeth. "No way!" he said emphatically to Haida as he pulled his hand back. Immediately Haida lifted the kelp out of his mouth with the tip of his huge pink tongue, extending it right up to Farley's face.

Paul watched silently as Farley looked Haida in the eye and gently took the gift of kelp. As Farley stood watching Haida submerge back into the pool, tears welled in the writer's eyes and rolled down his cheeks. Later, he told Paul he'd been overwhelmed by a sense of loss and loneliness.

As Farley was shown around the rest of the aquarium at a

fast pace, Paul watched Haida. He did not seem nearly so animated as usual. Paul felt concerned about Haida's health, wondering how he would fare now that he was alone in the pool and his mate was dead.

Later that day, Paul sat in a comfortable room in Victoria's Empress Hotel, thumbing through a copy of *A Whale for the Killing* that Farley had given him. He read: "As I grew older, the whale became a symbol of the ultimate secrets which have not yet been revealed to us by the 'other' animals. Whenever anything came to hand about whales, I read it avidly; but the only thing which seemed to emerge with certainty from all my reading was that the whales appeared to be doomed by human greed to disappear and to carry their secrets with them into oblivion."

Paul was lost in thought when Farley slipped into the chair beside him. After a moment's silence, Paul asked, "So what are we going to do?"

"Well, the first thing," said Farley without wasting a breath, "is to pressure Canada to stop whaling. The Canadian Government is still operating a small whaling fleet in the North Atlantic and casting its vote with Japan, Russia, Norway, and the other whaling countries at the International Whaling Commission annual meetings. The United States is voting with the whalers, too; there are people in the States working on that. The hope is that we can begin to turn the tide, to secure a moratorium against these huge whaling fleets. That will relieve the worst of the pressure on the dwindling whale populations. We can work on Canada; I on the East Coast, and you on the West Coast."

"Okay, mate, what's the strategy?"

"Petitions and letters. Make up a petition that says something to the effect of 'We the undersigned believe that whereas whales are a resource shared by all humanity, blah, blah, blah all about whales, we ask the Canadian Government to cease whaling and to vote for an international moratorium at the next Whaling Commission meeting.' Something like that. Have people sign the petition and send a letter to their Member of Parliament. We have people working in Ottawa, and we'll get Trudeau to take notice of this sentiment. Who knows? I think it might work."

"Okay, mate. We've already got a mailing list started, so we can send out a mailing. All right," said Paul. "Yes, it's a deal."

Several days later, Paul's phone rang in the early morning. A reporter known to him had called to get Paul's reaction to the news that Haida was ill and was refusing to eat. Paul had anticipated some sort of reaction, by Haida, to Chimo's death.

"He's probably heartbroken, Art," said Paul. "Haida and Chimo had become very close in the last months, so I'm sure he must miss her. I heard they did the autopsy on Chimo right beside the pool, in front of Haida. I thought that was pretty insensitive."

"What do you think will happen?" asked the reporter.

"Well, you know aquariums haven't had much luck keeping orcas alive anywhere near their natural life expectancy, so I guess deaths have to be expected. I've been advocating for years that if aquariums have to keep whales, they should periodically, say, after a few years, let them go free again. In Haida's case, he's still young, and if he were returned to his family, I think he'd stand a good chance. As it is, I don't know. It doesn't sound too good.

"Listen," said Paul, "call me in a few days. I think we'll go over to visit Haida and see what's going on."

Paul and Linda left for Victoria the next day, and when they arrived at Sealand they discovered that Haida was still refusing to eat and seemed depressed. Paul had brought along his flute, thinking maybe it would cheer Haida to hear some music. Since he had previously received permission from Bob Wright to visit the whales, he walked directly to the training platform by the pool.

Haida languished in the middle of the pool, slowly breathing on the surface. Paul played his flute, but Haida hardly moved. Linda came down onto the training platform beside Paul as he continued to play. Eventually Haida began to move slowly, and swam over in the direction of Linda and Paul. Rob Waters, the manager of Sealand, came running out.

"What are you doing?" Waters shouted, and Paul stopped playing. Haida was up against the platform, and Rob Waters was standing above on the pool deck. "You have to get off of there," he told them. "The public can't go out there. It's dangerous."

Paul started to protest, but the aquarium manager was adamant. Standing up on the deck, Paul explained to Waters that he had permission from Bob Wright to visit the whales. Waters told Paul that Bob Wright was not around, and that as far as he knew, members of the public were not allowed in the pool area. Rather than argue, Paul nodded and said, "I'm sorry. I'll talk to Bob, and we'll straighten this out. I only came here to visit Haida and help cheer him up."

"Cheer him up?" Rob Waters looked askance at Paul.

"Well, his mate just died," said Paul flatly.

Waters just shook his head and went back to his office. Paul and Linda left the aquarium and made for the nearest pay phone. Paul phoned Paul Horn, who lived nearby, and asked him if he would be willing to play some music for Haida. Then he phoned Bob Wright at home and arranged to get a message to Rob Waters that Paul Horn would be allowed to visit the aquarium and play music to Haida.

Another day passed before the first visit could be arranged, and Haida continued to refuse food. He remained still in the center of the pool, lethargic and silent. Cracks had developed around his blowhole, and he seemed to be giving up his will to live. The aquarium whale shows had been canceled, and Haida was injected with penicillin by the aquarium veterinarian, Alan Hoey, who suspected that Haida had picked up the streptococcal infection that had killed Chimo. Haida, however, showed no sign of shaking off the illness or depression, whichever it was.

When Paul Horn first played his flute, Haida showed no visible interest. After a second session during which Haida did not respond, Paul Horn stood at the edge of the pool and feigned annoyance. "Look here!" he yelled at Haida. "If you're not going to show any interest, then just forget it. I've got other things to do!" The musician left, but he returned the next day, and

Haida swam slowly over to him and drifted by the pool edge as the flutist played. Paul Horn returned daily, and Haida responded more enthusiastically each time. He swam to the side of the pool by the musician, rolled his head above the water on the third day, and began to snap out of his mourning. He would swim vigorously when Paul Horn played, and he began to vocalize with the flute music. Soon he began to eat, returning to normal health, and the whale shows at Sealand went back to the regular schedule.

The newspapers and radio talk shows carried the ongoing debate about what had cured Haida, the penicillin or the flute music. Although veterinarian Alan Hoey declared that the flute music would have no effect whatsoever on Haida, the general public tended to believe that Haida had been lifted from depression by the music.

Latching on to public sympathy for Haida, Bob Wright announced that he would stop at nothing to get the whale another mate. It would henceforth be Sealand policy, Wright announced, to keep whales in mated pairs. His whale-capturing crew began patrolling for whales among the inland waterways off Vancouver Island.

Paul and Linda plunged energetically into the campaign to end Canadian whaling. They printed fliers and petitions on a hand operated Gestetner mimeograph machine that they bought for fifty dollars in a secondhand shop. They posted them around Vancouver, mailed them to everyone who ever wrote to KWOOF, and took the petitions to supermarkets on blustery winter days. Although some people did not understand—"Wales?!" one woman shrieked at Paul outside a supermarket. "Oh my God, what's happening in Wales?"—Paul found that people were generally interested and supportive. Occasionally someone would say something like "Save the whales?! Save them for what? What are they good for?" Most people, however, signed the petition, and Paul and Linda felt encouraged.

Paul tried to reach all of his earlier media contacts and told his story to every reporter who would listen. The ensuing me-

dia attention brought a new stream of letters to KWOOF, and
Paul and Linda sent out whale information packages accompanied by a plea for funds. Financial support came in the form of
modest checks in the mail, crumpled dollar bills, even quarters
from children, and it began to add up impressively. Paul and
Linda put the money back into more mailings, and within two
months they had collected several thousand signatures themselves. In addition, other letters and petitions poured into Ottawa from the West Coast.

On December 20, Farley Mowat called Paul and told him that
the Canadian Government, in an Order in Council, had officially ended the Canadian whaling industry. Farley could not
be certain, but he had high hopes that Canada would vote with
the United States for the moratorium at the IWC meeting the
following summer. Pressure, Farley said, should be kept up.
"Fantastic!" exclaimed Paul. "What a Christmas present! Good
for Trudeau. Next, the world!"

Paul sat in a restaurant on El Camino Real in Palo Alto,
California, during an evening break of the annual Bio-sonar
Conference at Stanford Research Institute. He was having dinner with the organizer of the conference, Dr. Tom Poulter, and
cetacean researcher Ken Norris. Paul was listening to the two
men discuss their research, and he was reflecting on his own
experiences with whales. Dolphins, Norris had learned, have
two distinct voices, one for social communication and one for
navigation. Most of Paul's recordings of orcas were of communication, although occasionally he could hear the clicks of the
orcas' echolocation system. Dolphins, and presumably orcas,
could use both voices simultaneously.

Dolphins and other cetaceans also seemed to have two distinct sound receivers. At the forehead of the dolphin was a
lens-shaped cavity filled with oil, which focused incoming
sound through air passages to another oil-filled cavity in the
lower jaw, which Norris had called the "acoustic window."
The dolphins also used the forehead cavity to focus their own
outgoing sounds. The dolphins' second sound receiver was the
lower jaw, and Paul had found the same to be true with Skana,

Tung Jen, and other captive orcas. The sound that enters the lower jaw travels in oil through an ever-widening cavity that opens into the acoustic window, deep within the swelled jawbone.

Dr. Norris had discovered the cetacean "acoustic window" while walking a Mexican beach in 1959. He came upon the skeleton of a bottlenose dolphin and was examining the bones when he noticed the odd, bulging shape of the lower jaw. The lower jaw's mandibular canal, which carries blood vessels and nerves, grew wide toward the posterior section. Right near the skull, the jaw was just a thin, hollow shell of bone, so thin that light shone through. From this acoustic window, formed by the ballooned jaw of the dolphin or whale, sound travels to the cetacean's inner ear. The whales' bodies, being many times closer to the density of water than land mammals' bodies are to air, pick up the sound directly, without ears. In essence, cetaceans literally hear with their whole bodies, sound traveling through the surface of their skin directly from the water until it hits the jawbone or a forehead cavity called the melon and is then directed to the brain through the nerves of the inner ear. Sound is also delivered to the brain as a tactile message from the whole body.

In San Francisco, Paul met with Joan McIntyre and the other Project Jonah whale enthusiasts, including Ron Keller, and presented an orca slide show along with the *We Call Them Killers* film at the San Francisco Zen Center. The reception was enthusiastic. From Joan McIntyre Paul learned that the band of whale lobbyists in the United States had been successful in pressuring the U.S. delegation to the International Whaling Commission to take a conservationist stand. Joan brought back tales of the IWC infighting from the London meeting. She told Paul, "You wouldn't believe the so-called scientists over there on the Scientific Committee. Half of them are in the pocket of the whaling companies—the whole thing is a sham. The IWC Scientific Committee recommended against the ten-year moratorium proposed by the United States on the grounds that further research was necessary and that the whaling industry itself was providing that much-needed scientific knowledge through the work of biologists on the whaling boats. Whaling, they said, was necessary for the advancement of knowledge about whales. Russell Train, the U.S. commissioner, said, 'Well, I can understand the need for more whales to study, but do you really need thirty-five thousand?' Ray Gamble, the British scientist, stroked his chin diabolically, laughing himself at the absurdity of it, and said, 'Yes, and maybe more.' The British even voted in favor of the moratorium, knowing it wouldn't pass anyway, so they would look good in the press. There's some sleazy politics going on in that scene. The Japanese and the Russian delegations are unabashedly looking after the whaling interests; they don't even pretend to care about whales."

The moratorium motion had been introduced by Russell Train of the United States and ostensibly supported by Great Britain. Argentina and Mexico also voted in favor, but the motion was defeated by the votes of Russia, Japan, Norway, South Africa, and Iceland. Canada had abstained from the vote—an improved, if gutless, position.

Joan McIntyre felt that a moratorium might secure the necessary three-quarters majority vote in 1973, but Canada and the three other abstaining nations—Australia, Denmark, and France—would have to be persuaded to change their position.

When Paul arrived back in Vancouver, the lobbying campaign intensified. He appeared on virtually every radio and television station in the city, as well as the nationwide Canadian Broadcasting Corporation, calling for Canadian support of the U.S. moratorium proposal. "We should be ashamed," Paul commented over national radio, "that Canada isn't *leading* this movement to save the whales, but is dragging along behind public sentiment like an archaic dinosaur!"

Paul's conviction was magnetic. Talk-show hosts loved his animated righteousness and respected his grasp of the facts; he was a popular guest. Telephone lines would light up when he was on the radio, and public enthusiasm swelled. Paul was scheduling his days like a politician: meetings over lunch, interviews, invitations to dinner. His phone rang constantly. The vortex that he had feared being sucked into now swirled all around him; he was the center of a growing frenzy whose proportions he had not even dreamed of.

Coinciding with whale celebrations held in the United States and England on the second of June, Paul and Linda organized a "Whale Celebration" in Stanley Park, near the aquarium. The celebrations had been inspired a year earlier, in Stockholm, Sweden, when the fledgling United Nations environmental agency had adopted a resolution calling for an immediate moratorium on commercial whaling "as a matter of urgency." The Whale Celebration in Vancouver was an inspiring affair. Dozens of children painted whale pictures and were led through a whale dance. There were whale balloons, a huge pink whale float, music, and whale stories.

The celebration in London was massive, with people from all over the world gathered at the entrance to the IWC meetings, but their efforts did not turn the tide. They failed to pull the necessary three-fourths majority. Canada abstained again.

Paul fiddled with the controls of his recording equipment; Blackfish Sound was filled with the eerie calls of orcas. George Dyson stood beside him, gazing out the window. Paul, Linda, Yashi, and George had been on Hanson Island for a week, kayaking with the whales and listening to the chorus of calls that came from the hydrophones in Blackfish Sound.

"John Lilly says that dolphins communicate with sounds ranging from about one hundred hertz to eighty thousand hertz, and I suspect that orcas are rather lower than that, maybe in the high end of our audible range," Paul explained to George. "Humans communicate with sounds ranging from about three hundred hertz to maybe three thousand. So the whales have a larger potential repertoire of sounds."

"Reeeeennnaahhhhhhup! Waaaah, WAAAAAH, WeeeeEEE-eeeEEE," came the calls modulated in pitch and tone, sounding like some avant-garde jazz musicians or beings from outer space.

"The whales apparently make these sounds," said Paul, "by forcing air through their nasal sacs and other cranial cavities.

They have a cavity in their forehead which is shaped like a lens and acts as a focusing device for the sounds that they emit. It's a pretty elaborate sound-production setup."

"Who's that?" questioned George, pointing outside.

"Oh, that's Graeme Ellis and Jim Hunter," explained Paul. "They got some funding from the fisheries branch to take photographs for Mike Bigg's orca survey. We're sharing information." Ellis and Hunter were with the pod of orcas, traveling in their motorized rubber inflatable. Ellis had established a camp on Parson Island, across Blackney Passage from Paul's camp.

The roar of the outboard motor could be heard through the speakers, and Paul reached up to turn the volume down. "Sometimes I worry about all that noise in the water," Paul said to George. "And this is just the beginning of people coming up here with motorboats and chasing the whales around. It would be nice if we could learn how to study whales without changing their behavior through human intrusions."

George laughed.

"What's so funny?" Paul asked.

"Well," said George, smiling, "I didn't mean the people. I meant who are the whales?"

"Oh." Paul picked up his binoculars and looked out across the water. "There's Wavy with that other big guy. It's Nicola's group." Paul and George watched as the whales moved into Blackney Passage from Blackfish Sound, where they paused and milled about in the swift tidal currents. They waited there for perhaps half an hour before a third group of about nine whales caught up with them, and then the sixteen orcas moved around the point into Johnstone Strait.

A few days later, Paul received a message from a film crew at the University of Victoria who wanted to make a documentary film about orcas. Paul agreed to meet Erich Hoyt, one of the crew, in Alert Bay on his next trip to town.

Erich Hoyt was enthusiastic. In Alert Bay, Paul ran into Hoyt as he came out of the market. They walked down the main street, past the graveyard where Paul pointed out the whale totem. Chatting on the street, Paul briefly related his history with whales, explaining in the end that he was currently torn between the demands of his studies and the urgency he felt about saving and protecting whales.

"I fear," he told Hoyt, "that there may not be any whales left to study in a few years because of the international whaling and fishing industries. I'm also afraid that this local habitat will be destroyed by too many people and too many speedboats. Maybe I've already drawn too much attention to these whales and to this area. Now they're talking about extending the highway as far north as Port McNeill and Port Hardy. I hope I don't blow it for the whales here by giving this place too much publicity."

Hoyt was sympathetic and seemed to understand Paul's concerns. "We'll be filming and recording from a sailboat, the *Four Winds*," Erich assured Paul. "I have an electronic synthesizer with me. I want to copy the whale sounds, play them back to the whales, and see if I get any response. The synthesizer is the only instrument capable of duplicating the frequency range and complexity of the whales' sounds. If we can attract the whales' presence," Hoyt went on, "if they decide to investigate the new sounds occurring in their environment, then we'll have the cameras going and we'll be able to film them. And if we can elicit some kind of sound response, we could record it for the film's sound track."

Paul was intrigued, and offered to lend Hoyt some equipment. "I'll help in whatever way I can," Paul told Hoyt.

The *Four Winds*, skippered by Bruce Bott, pulled into Robson Bight on July 20, ducking out of a southeasterly wind. Bott had previously worked for Bob Wright, had untangled Chimo when she had been caught in the nets at Pedder Bay, and had swum in the water with Chimo and Haida at Sealand. Now he was on a mission of his own. As a diver and photographer, Bott wanted to get the first-ever underwater films of free orcas.

Erich Hoyt had been practicing his orca sounds on his synthesizer. He had three phrases down fairly well, which he had picked up from tapes of orcas. Nicola's pod was in the bight. Through the earphones that he wore, Hoyt heard a call that he believed to be Wavy's; he had recorded a very similar call eight days earlier and had learned it on the synthesizer. His version wasn't perfect, but good enough to be recognized by the orcas, he hoped.

As Hoyt played the notes of the phrase, the speaker fastened below the *Four Winds* carried the musician's sound out into the underwater world of Robson Bight. His tape recorder was picking up the entire exchange. Two seconds of silence followed his notes; then the whales answered. What Hoyt later determined to be three, maybe four, whales answered in perfect unison. Their answer was a perfect-match copy of his imperfect copy of their original call.

When Paul heard the tape, he sat quietly for a long time. Erich Hoyt broke the silence: "I suppose mimicry is neither a sign of intelligence nor of language," he said to Paul, "but I'm intrigued."

"Yes!" said Paul. "You've really got something there, Erich. Your recording shows that the whales have a tremendous capacity to process sound, to send, receive, and analyze acoustic information."

Paul told George later during a walk in the woods, "I've been thinking for a long time, trying to understand why the whales have evolved such huge brains. What, I kept asking myself, are they using them for? What struck me, after hearing the tape of Erich and Wavy's gang, was that in two seconds the whales picked up the sound, knew it was different from their call, and re-created Erich's version immediately. Erich practiced for a week to get his rather imperfect version, and the whales got his, perfectly, in two seconds!"

"So you think the whales' brains are something like huge sound-analyzing computers, eh?" said George.

"Something like that," said Paul.

"Maybe they form sound pictures instead of words," George offered.

Paul looked up at him, nodding and smiling. "Yeah," he said. "Sound pictures."

Graeme Ellis came by Hanson Island in late July, pulling into the cove in his inflatable boat. "Just saw Stubb and her pod up in Double Bay," he hollered to Paul. "They're coming down this way."

"Thanks," said Paul from the rocks. "Why don't you come in for coffee, and we'll wait for them."

George, Linda, Paul, and Graeme had fresh-baked bread and coffee and talked about the orcas. Graeme Ellis told Paul about Mike Bigg's plan to label the individual pods with a letter of the alphabet. "Nicola, Stubb, and Wavy are in 'A' pod," Graeme told Paul, "and Hooker is in 'B' pod." Tulip, or Stubb, was A1, Nicola was A2, Wavy was A3, and the others in the pod were similarly identified. Bigg planned to number every pod and individual in the local waters with his system.

"Whales!" said Yashi, as the sounds came over the speakers.

Graeme laughed. "Pretty good setup you have here, Paul."

Paul turned to Yashi. "You want to go out and see the whales, Yashi?" he asked. Yashi, now five, had not yet gone out in the kayak with the whales, but he was eager. Paul and George readied the two-person kayak, and Paul paddled out into Blackfish Sound with Yashi in the front hole of the kayak.

"That's Nicola," Paul whispered to Yashi as they approached. "See the nick in her fin." Wavy surfaced immediately beside Nicola, and then the rest of the group of six adults and four juveniles rose in a line abreast, breathing almost together, their breaths coming fast, like a round of explosive charges going off. "See the babies, Yashi." Paul paddled to within thirty feet of the whales.

"I'm scared," said Yashi.

"Okay," Paul answered, "we won't go any closer." As the kayak drifted, Paul tried to photograph Yashi and the whales with one hand as he steadied the kayak with the other. He noticed through the lens a whale surfacing near the front of the boat. As he looked up over the top of his camera, he saw Yashi with his hand out, reaching toward the whale as it passed. Still watching, Paul leaned the other way in the kayak just enough to steady it in the water as Yashi reached out the other side. Then, suddenly, Yashi sat straight up, and Paul had to slap the paddle on the water to keep from tipping.

When Yashi turned around, his eyes were as wide as an owl's, and he had a huge grin across his face.

"Weren't you scared?" Paul asked.

"A little bit," said Yashi, still smiling.

Back at Hanson Island, Yashi told George and Linda about his encounter with the whale. "He was *that* close," he said, holding his hands up in front of his face.

As George was fixing supper, Yashi asked Paul, "Would you show me how to make kindling with my knife?" Paul showed Yashi how to shave off little pieces of wood, which Yashi stacked in the firebox as he had seen the adults do many times. "Is that enough?" he asked, and Paul leaned over to look inside.

"Well, there's only one way to find out," said Paul. "Light it."

Yashi got a match from George, and Paul helped him light it. Yashi held it to the fire, and the shavings blazed.

"You have to keep putting pieces on," Paul coached, and Yashi slowly fed the fire until it was blazing. Paul and Linda smiled at each other. Yashi lay down by the stove and stared at the fire while George set out the supper.

The following morning, Linda and Paul were wakened by Yashi coming up to their bedroom from below. He climbed into bed between them and announced that the fire was going and the house would be warm soon.

"You started a fire by yourself?" Linda asked.

"Sure," Yashi replied.

"In the stove?" said Linda, concerned but smiling.

"Of course," Yashi replied, and then added, as if to soothe his mother's anxiety, "Don't worry, I closed the damper down."

The heat was soon rising through the house, and Yashi got up from the bed and went back downstairs. Paul and Linda could hear him go outside.

"Well," said Paul, "it seems as if Yashi's encounter with the whale has given him a certain confidence."

"I like it," said Linda, smiling broadly, curling back under the covers. "Ask him when breakfast is on."

Before the summer was over, Michael Bigg and Graeme Ellis had photographed and identified most of the whales in the orca pods around Blackfish Sound. Michael Bigg had hypothesized that the whales in the southern inside passage were a separate group from those in the north around Hanson Island and that the two groups rarely intermingled. In August, Sealand captured six more whales in Pedder Bay. Bruce Bott and Erich Hoyt sailed the *Four Winds* to Pedder Bay, where Hoyt recorded the orcas' vocalizations. He wrote to Paul, "What amazed me is that they have a totally different dialect from the whales up north." This fascinated Paul, and he began to listen even more carefully to the various orca sounds, trying to pick up possible group accents.

Bruce Bott also succeeded in his quest for underwater footage of orcas. While diving in Robson Bight, he managed to shoot seven seconds of film as a mother and calf swam within ten feet of his camera. The mother's pectoral fin reached out and almost touched the lens, as if gauging her distance. The calf, perhaps less than a year old, was tucked in beside her. It was the first footage ever taken of free orcas underwater. When he saw the unedited footage, Paul immediately wanted to add it to his collection of slides and films, which he had organized into a presentation he called "The Whale Show."

"If people could just see that," he exclaimed, "I know they wouldn't want to capture these whales and put them in aquariums." Paul had a copy of *We Call Them Killers*, but that film showed captive whales. He urged Bruce and editor Jim O'Donnell to get their film completed in time for the first Whale Show presentation that Paul was planning for the winter. The Whale Show would be his method of educating people about cetaceans in the wild, about their intelligence and their benign and majestic power, a way for people to learn about whales without the whales themselves having to be captured.

Bob Hunter sat across the small galley table, his notebook open, scribbling as Paul talked. Bob's 1930s gill-netter, the *Zoe Too*, which he had converted from a fishing boat to a liveaboard, rocked in the choppy waters of English Bay. Bob and Paul had motored out into the bay from Vancouver on a gray autumn afternoon. No other pleasure boats were in the area as a light rain fell. They had cut the engine, drifting in the wind, and sat inside the cabin drinking beer and talking.

Bob Hunter was something of an offbeat success in the Canadian media world. His thrice-weekly column in the Vancouver *Sun* provided him with a platform from which he could introduce radical ideas into the Vancouver, British Columbian, and Canadian body politic. His interviews with therapist Fritz Perls, radical psychologist R. D. Laing, the Karmapa of Tibet, and the famed "Chicken Lady" of Vancouver had positioned him as the premier pop-intelligentsia reporter in the city and as the champion of the downtrodden and different.

Bob kept up a constant "Yep . . . Yep . . . Yep, uh-huh," as Paul unfolded his stories of Skana, Tung Jen, Haida, Nicola, and the orcas of Blackfish Sound. Hunter had promised to give Paul's story a two-part treatment in his popular column, but Paul was looking for more than just another newspaper story. Bob Hunter was a superb journalist in the classical sense, but he was also something of a media double agent, providing the newspaper with an air of hipness and providing certain counterculture movements with public legitimacy. When he was not reporting the news, he was making the news, and sometimes doing both.

In 1971, Hunter had sailed with a protest boat into the U.S. nuclear test zone around Amchitka Island. Feeding stories to the press throughout the voyage, Hunter created a major media event, which was credited, at least in part, with forcing the United States to cease testing nuclear weapons on Amchitka.

Following that voyage, Hunter and a few other local environmentalists had founded the Greenpeace Foundation, a small band of protesters dedicated to stopping nuclear testing around the world. As Paul and Bob spoke in October 1973, a second Greenpeace boat was in the hands of the French Navy after having sailed into the French test zone around Mururoa Atoll in the South Pacific. France had just announced that it was stopping French aboveground testing, and Greenpeace, though its boat had been confiscated, was celebrating its second victory. Paul was hoping that Bob could help him with his whale campaign.

Paul had phoned Bob at his *Sun* office and arranged the interview, ostensibly to tell his whale story, but also to pick Hunter's brain for ideas about how to run an environmental media campaign. Bob had agreed, and offered to take Paul out in the *Zoe Too* for a conference in the middle of the harbor. After finishing the interview, Paul and Bob continued to drink beer and talk as the boat drifted.

Bob had read the works of John Lilly, Gregory Bateson, and Farley Mowat, and he was able to discuss whales with Paul on a more sophisticated level than other reporters Paul had met. "Sounds like you've told that story so many times," Bob laughed, "it's just like turning on a tape recorder. Makes me wonder what else you're thinking."

"It's true," said Paul. "I've told this story to a lot of reporters. They've conditioned me to tell it for the general public, I guess."

"That's a bunch of hogwash," said Bob. "The general public is a lot smarter than most reporters think."

"Well, Bob, the heart of it is, I honestly believe that the whales have a very highly evolved social structure and that they have evolved their large brains by using them for extremely complex social communication. They may not speak in words, but they may create sound pictures. In any event, their huge brains are perhaps the most sophisticated biological computers on the planet in certain ways. Humans don't even come close to whales in the ability to process auditory information. I was a classic behavioral scientist, content with manipulating behavior in animals, until I realized that the animal I was working with was as intelligent as and in some ways quite possibly *more* intelligent than I was. My work now is concerned with trying to reveal—or even just glimpse—a new *kind* of intelligence, something that humans aren't even aware of."

"Well, maybe some humans are aware of it, Paul. In case you haven't noticed, the mechanistic nineteenth-century ways of thinking are crumbling. The industrial nations, blind to the laws of ecology, are coming up against their karmic debts, having ripped off the resources to the point that the machines are starting to grind to a halt. Industrial economies are in trouble, and a more ecological coevolutionary paradigm is emerging. If what you say about whales is true—and I believe it is—then the whales are way ahead of us. They seem to have already learned how to live harmoniously within their surroundings, to control their populations, to live ecologically within their environment, and to manage their societies without aggression and violence. It sounds like the whales have a more *gestalten* language, not really a language at all as we know it, but a way of communicating about relationship. They intuitively understand systems theory. This puts them way ahead of human intellect."

"The problem is, Bob," said Paul, his voice betraying a certain desperation, "humans are wiping them out."

"But didn't you say there was a growing awareness? Isn't the United States pushing for a moratorium?"

"It's too slow, Bob. These celebrations and demonstrations aren't going to convince the Japanese and the Russians to stop whaling, and they're not going to convince the aquariums to stop capturing orcas in British Columbia. At the most, we're like little fleas to them, bothersome maybe, but they can just flick us off."

"Well, I have a theory about that," said Bob matter-of-factly, sipping his beer.

"I was hoping you would," said Paul, a shivery thrill running through him as he leaned across the table to listen.

"You have to jump systems on 'em, Paul. Not even Russia and Japan are impervious to global opinion. These deals they cut behind closed doors are just a bunch of commercial trade-offs. If it really did become unpopular to kill whales, on a worldwide basis, then Russia and Japan would back down. No one wants to be the international bad guy; it's bad for business. They like to stay invisible, to sleaze their deals where no one sees them. You've got to flush 'em out into the open, and I'm sorry to say you're right, protest signs aren't going to do it."

"So what is going to do it?"

"It's a battle for people's minds, Paul. This is where the media come in. I see the global media networks as being sort of like delivery systems, all in place and ready to be used. Only they aren't delivery systems for bombs, they're delivery systems for ideas. I call 'em 'mind bombs.' If you want people, on a worldwide level, to care about whales, then you have to deliver the idea to them with force and with clarity. When we sailed into those test zones, it wasn't because we were naive enough to think that one boat was going to stop the United States or France from testing nuclear weapons; it was because we wanted to send the world a picture of how much we cared. The media networks were glad to deliver our message, but we had to do something dramatic enough to warrant the attention."

Paul sat thoughtfully for quite a while, sipping his beer and looking out the window of the boat. "Okay," he said, sitting up straight. "What if we took a boat out and blockaded the whalers. Sailed right between them and the whalers and didn't let them shoot their harpoons! Do you think the media networks would cover that?"

"They'd probably go for that, but where are you going to find a skipper willing to park his boat in front of an exploding harpoon?"

"I know a guy who makes kayaks. His name is George Dyson. We'll put kayaks on board and put ourselves in front of the whalers. We'll protect the whales with our bodies. If they fire, they have to kill us first."

"You'll never keep up with a whale boat in a kayak. But you might do it with one of those Zodiacs; you know, those inflatables. We have pictures of the French Navy using them when they busted our boat in Mururoa."

"Yeah, the Fisheries Department scientists had one this summer, and we've got an old Avon on Hanson Island. Well!" Paul was excited, standing up in the small cabin, pacing. He paused for a moment, then sat down and looked at Bob. "Would Greenpeace help?"

"I don't know, Paul. Greenpeace is a pretty ragtag bunch. They're already in debt, so I don't know where we would get the money. It's also an antinuclear group, Paul. You're going to have a hard time convincing them that it's worth spending money, which we don't have, to save whales."

"But, Bob," Paul protested, "if we can't save the whales,

what good does it do to save humans? It's going to be a sad planet when there's nothing left but humans. I'm talking about a bigger picture. People have put their lives on the line to protect or help other people, but imagine what a powerful statement it would be if people would put their lives on the line to help other beings! And not just for the whales, Bob, but for the whole planet, and for the future. I'm talking about a shift from the sanctity of human life to the sanctity of all life on the planet. Besides, I don't just want to *save* whales, I want to *know* them."

"Believe me, Paul, I understand. You should come and give one of those speeches at the Greenpeace meeting. I'm with you, but I'm hardly going to be your toughest critic."

"So you'll help?"

"Why not," said Bob.

Paul and Bob performed with considerable political savvy through the winter of 1973–74.

First they confronted the other Greenpeace members with the idea of taking a boat out to intercept the whaling fleets. Of the seven board members, only Rod Marining openly supported the idea, and Rod's presence in their camp did not exactly improve their image of belonging to the lunatic fringe. Rod, a street-theater veteran of virtually every social or political movement imaginable, was a tireless whale devotee, and the three of them formed a whale committee. Physician Dr. Lyle Thurston and Greenpeace lawyer Hamish Bruce also supported the idea, and Paul made a deal with Greenpeace.

Paul agreed to raise the money for the voyage himself. He would produce a whale show at a 2,800-seat theater in town, use the proceeds to take the Whale Show to Japan in an effort to convince Japan to stop whaling, and if that didn't work he and Hunter would launch a boat to find the whalers in the summer of 1975. Greenpeace allowed him to use the organization's name in his fund raising, and the "First Annual Greenpeace Christmas Whale Show" was to be held on December 28, 1973. Greenpeace made Paul sign a notarized letter stating that he would personally be liable for all losses.

Paul and Bob agreed to resolve all their personal differences of opinion with the *I Ching,* which served them well as a political and philosophical arbitrator. "Check it out," Bob would say if they couldn't come to agreement on an issue, and Paul would throw the *I Ching* coins. Bob won as many arguments as he lost that way, so he figured that the ancient oracle was credible; even, at times, uncanny.

At four in the afternoon on the day of the show, Paul and Bob walked into the unlit, cavernous main hall of Vancouver's Queen Elizabeth Theatre and stared at the rows of empty seats. It was anybody's guess how many people would be filling those seats in three hours' time, but Paul had a good feeling.

Bruce Bott had arrived that morning with the completed copy of his underwater orca film. For two weeks Paul and Linda had been scrambling to sell tickets, handing them out to their friends and others on their mailing list to distribute. The promotion budget was small, but the human energy had been almost overwhelming. Bob Hunter's daily column in the Vancouver *Sun* had carried announcements of the show three times.

"Um," said Paul, "nice place, eh?"

Bob surveyed the hall. "What's your gut-level feeling about this one, Paul?"

Paul smiled and held out his arms to the hall. "No problem, mate."

While Paul, Bob, Rod Marining, and other Greenpeacers were backstage setting up for the show, a secretary from the theater staff arrived. "Paul Spong?" Paul looked up. "Phone," he said, and smiled. "There's a phone on the wall there."

Paul walked over to the house phone and picked it up. "Hello?"

"Hi, Paul, this is Gordon Lightfoot. Harry Kemball told me about what you were doing. I tracked you down through Bob Hunter's office."

"Oh . . . hi, Gordon. What's goin' on?"

Paul had not met the Canadian singer before, but the two men chatted for about ten minutes, Paul telling him about the whale campaign and the planned trip to Japan. Japan was the key, Paul told him, to the whaling issue. "We have to turn them

around. I'm going to use the money from the show tonight to go
over there."

"Well, I'm sorry I can't be there," Lightfoot answered, "but
I'm gonna go five for you."

"Five?" Paul didn't quite understand.

"Five thousand. I'm going to write you a check for five thousand dollars, just to bolster your spirits. So you can rest easy
tonight. Have a good time. I wish you luck." Paul and the musician said good-bye, and Paul let out a tremendous whoop as he
hung up the phone.

"You're not going to believe this," he called to the others.
"Now it doesn't matter if no one shows up tonight!"

The hall was packed that evening for the show. Hunter introduced Paul with a natural and witty flair that stirred the full
house to applause. Paul showed the best slides from Hanson
Island and Blackfish Sound, and premiered Bruce Bott's film of
the mother and baby orca underwater. He played selections
from his library of tapes, narrating the whole show himself. At
the end of the show, Paul told the audience about the plan to
save the whales. "It is one of the great ironies of our time that,
just as we are beginning to glimpse the incredible nature of
whales, we are on the verge of exterminating them forever."

By the end of the night, the show had made a three-thou-
sand-dollar profit from ticket sales and donations. With the
addition of Gordon Lightfoot's check for five thousand dollars,
the whale committee's bank account was looking flush compared to the general Greenpeace account. Paul's idea began to
look credible, not only to Greenpeace but to the news media.

Reporter James Wilde from *Time* magazine arrived in town
to interview Paul. Paul asked him to phone the aquarium to
arrange to hold a press conference there that would announce
the forthcoming trip to Japan and the intent to launch a boat to
interfere with the whalers if diplomacy failed. With all of the
local papers, the national press, and *Time* covering the event,
Murray Newman consented, with the proviso that Paul not use
the forum to advocate Skana's release. Paul promised, and the
deal was made. Paul told Bob that he would introduce him to
Skana during the event.

When Paul climbed down onto the training platform on February 26, 1974, both Skana and Tung Jen rushed up to him, impressing the media corps with their animated demonstration of affection for Paul. It had been over four years since they'd seen each other, but it seemed as if it had only been yesterday. Paul knelt down and nuzzled and petted the whales, who were falling all over him. Then Skana and Tung Jen sat motionless in the water before him, looking straight at him, as Paul stood in his long wool overcoat and cap, playing his flute. When he finished playing, Skana opened her mouth, and Paul bent down and put his hand inside, rubbing her gums. "Hi, girl," he said in a soft voice, and then howled, loud enough for the microphones to hear, "Awoooooooooooooo!"

Paul reached back and pulled Bob, who had been waiting by the pool's edge, onto the platform. Bob's hand was shaking. "You all right, Bob?" Paul said, barely above a whisper. Bob nodded, but Paul could see that he was trembling. Cameras were clicking and the aquarium staff was buzzing around—no one quite sure what Paul and Bob were up to. Paul held Bob's arm and moved him toward the front of the platform. "Skana," he said, "this is Bob. Bob"—he looked at this friend, who was staring directly at the whale's gaping mouth—"this is Skana."

Bob knelt down and stroked Skana's jaw and then leaned his head over and rubbed it against hers. If he was feeling frightened, Paul thought, he was holding together pretty well. Skana opened her huge jaws and began massaging Bob's head with her teeth. Paul stiffened as she closed her teeth around Bob, until she looked like a child with a sagging lollipop in her mouth. Then Bob's head reappeared and he began to back away. Skana had a piece of Bob's hair in her mouth, and Bob still had his head bowed, looking something like a choirboy saying his prayers. Paul reached down and lifted him up, and Bob slowly looked up into Paul's eyes. Bob did not say a word as Paul helped him back up onto the pool ledge, where he walked off with a dazed shuffle.

Paul turned quickly to Skana. "I think you got him, girl. He's a quick learner, faster than me." Paul stroked Skana's head and gave a soft howl. He realized how much he had missed seeing Skana and wondered if she understood that he hadn't forgotten her. "Maybe we'll get you out of here yet, Skana. 'Bye," Paul said.

Looking around, he saw that the press assembly had broken up and people were milling about or leaving. Rod Marining was busily passing out a printed news release about the trip to Japan and the planned whale-saving voyages. Bob was nowhere to be seen.

"She had me at her complete mercy," Bob told Paul and Linda later that evening. "I've never been in that situation before. One moment I felt more fear than I ever have before in my life, then the next moment I felt a shower of complete trust. You were right, Paul. I certainly felt tested."

Paul, Bob, Linda, Rod, and a growing army of whale lovers began working on the two-pronged attack on the whalers. Paul, Linda, and Yashi traveled by bus from Vancouver to Seattle, where they were to get a Thai Air flight to Tokyo. Bob and Rod stayed in Vancouver, looking for a boat that would take them out to confront the whaling fleets on the high seas.

At his last press conference before leaving for Japan, Paul had told the gathering, "There is a deeper question here that has not really been asked yet, and it's this: Can we learn anything from these whales? And I think the tentative answer to that question is this: The whales we have been watching and studying do not kill one another; they exist in communities that have long-term stability, and these communities comprise families that have long-term stability. Whale families, so far as we know, stay together for life. And not only that, they very effectively mobilize group energy to satisfy individual needs. Everyone in the whale family, the whale community, the whale society, has all his or her needs provided for life, because they work together. It seems to me that this is a key lesson we have to learn if we are to survive on this planet. If this generation allows the whales to be wiped out like the dinosaurs, future generations will never have the opportunity to make the discoveries that are possible. It will be too late. So we have to do something now. That's all there is to it."

Paul, Linda, and Yashi arrived in Tokyo in mid-March with interpreters Maya Koizumi and Michiko Sakata. A CBC news crew followed them, sending film clips back to Canada. *Time* had just published a two-page story about Paul, featuring color photographs of him and Skana and a glowing review of his Whale Show that applauded his research and his campaign to save the whales. Paul, however, received a mixed welcome in Japan. Whereas schoolchildren and conservationists were thrilled with the Whale Show, there was a hard-hitting opposition to his invasion.

At the first show, the audience—split between conservationists and whaling-industry employees—got into a heated debate. The whalers claimed that they were providing protein and jobs. A conservationist shouted out in Japanese, which Maya translated for Paul, "If the country is short of protein, you should plant soybeans on the golf courses, not kill whales!" Paul realized right away that his tour through Japan was going to require considerable diplomacy.

The *Suisan Neizai,* a fisheries newspaper, claimed that Paul's campaign was a "conspiracy of the United States." They called the campaign a "lunatic and unnatural movement supported by abundant funds, making use of children and politicians." The article went on to accuse Paul of using "brainwashing, lies, and distortion." But other Japanese newspapers gave the story a more balanced treatment, running charts that displayed the decline of whale populations and photographs of Paul with Skana. Some people were confused at first when Paul told them that he was in Japan for the *kujira,* the whale. One man thought Paul was a gourmet chef who was learning how to cook the *kujira* with "green peas."

"No," explained Paul. "Greenpeace. We want to *save* the whale."

The Japan Wildlife Club invited Paul to attend its weekly meetings, and Linda and Yashi became the first woman and child to be invited to the all-male gatherings. Paul and Linda invited two friendly wildlife photographers to visit them on Hanson Island. The wildlife group, which had just put whales

on their environmental agenda, took up the whale campaign
with enthusiasm inside Japan.

Paul and Linda were at times overwhelmed by the hospital-
ity of their Japanese hosts. Michiko's father, a bank president,
put a car and driver at their disposal and treated them to a
three-day holiday at a seaside resort. Japanese conservationists, business people, and press reporters took care of them as
they traveled from city to city. When the wildlife club found
out it was Yashi's birthday, they put on a gala party for him; a
Japanese artist, Shuji Kimura, gave Yashi a book that he had
written and illustrated especially for the occasion, a story of a
young boy and a whale called *Yasha and Orca*.

At the Far Seas Laboratory in Tokyo, Professor Omura, the
leading Japanese whale scientist, acknowledged to Paul that
the sperm whale possessed an advanced brain capable of complex thought. Baleen whales, however, were regarded by
Omura as "ocean cows." Nevertheless, Paul was encouraged
that someday Japanese scientists might share his own beliefs.

Paul realized that he had penetrated the mass mind of Japan
when he found himself the subject of a cartoon in one of the
largest circulation newspapers. The caricature even looked like
him. However, when Japan's oldest whaling town refused to
allow him to present the Whale Show at the local museum, he
knew he had a long way to go.

Paul and Linda presented nineteen Whale Shows during
their Japan tour, their audiences ranging from science groups
and whaling-company officials to schoolchildren and the general public. After a presentation to the Taiyo Fisheries, the
largest Japanese whaling company, a public-relations officer
told Paul, "I know the ten-year moratorium is inevitable; it is
only a matter of time." In Osaka, Paul addressed fourteen million viewers through a television talk show.

Most of all, Paul loved the school shows. Children thronged
around him to see more pictures of the whales, and they gave
him drawings that they had made, some of them with "Save the
Whales" written in Japanese. Paul's final press conference in
Tokyo was attended by over fifty journalists, cameras whirring
and tape recorders humming.

Paul left a raging debate in his wake as he boarded the plane back to Canada, but he realized that the Japanese whaling industry had no intention of stopping whaling on the say-so of a few environmentalists. "I hope Bob and Rod find us a boat," he told Linda as they looked down over the Bering Sea and the Aleutian Islands. "But Bob is right about one thing," Paul added. "It's a big ocean."

Paul knew that finding the whaling fleets in the vast ocean would not be easy. The next step, he thought, was to find out where the whalers go, and when. He gazed down through the scattered clouds at the blue North Pacific and heaved a great sigh of anticipation and concern.

6

Pirates and Ambassadors

In one of the back dressing rooms of Vancouver's Queen Elizabeth Theatre, Paul sat silently in a swirl of excited talk. Twenty-five hundred people had just left the theater after the Second Annual Christmas Whale Show, a roaring success covered by city, national, and international media. The campaign to hunt down the Japanese and Russian whalers on the high seas was in full, unstoppable, even uncontrollable swing. The campaign seemed to be charmed, with a special magic that always brought the right person at the right time whenever needed.

Sitting next to Paul, Bob Hunter talked with Captain John Cormack, the skipper of the first Greenpeace voyage, who had agreed to take the whale crusaders out on his eighty-foot seiner, the *Phyllis Cormack*, to find the whalers. Captain Cormack, known more affectionately as Captain John, was an ex-wrestler who had become one of the most respected fishboat skippers on the West Coast. He was gruff and practical on the surface, but his eyes constantly betrayed a mischievous sense of humor and wonder. John teased the whale lovers about being "hippies" and, worse, "farmers," but he loved the hullabaloo as much as anybody. Since he was the one person in the group who could challenge Hunter's verbal wit and

Paul's manic drive, he became a stabilizing force. "Put that hocus-pocus *Ching-Ching* thing away and listen to reason," he would bellow at Bob and Paul.

In the crowded dressing room, Linda was talking to Mel, a Vancouver street musician whom she and Paul had met at Harry Krishna's Last Chance Saloon, a Fourth Avenue coffee house where Fireweed often played—the band that had played for the whales from *D'Sonoqua*. Mel had agreed to come on the trip to "conduct interspecies communication experiments." If Captain Cormack was a rock-hard rationalist, Mel filled out the other end of the spectrum as a flaming mystic. He had talked to whales before he had ever seen one. His long, graying beard and beady eyes gave him the look of an ancient mariner, though he had not yet stood on the deck of a seagoing vessel. Mel had complete faith in his mystical intuitions. He seemed to be forever interpreting the signs, and could almost produce rainbows at will; he was also a good musician, and kept the meetings and gatherings light and festive. His full name was Melville Gregory, and since Herman Melville had written *Moby Dick* and Gregory Peck had played Ahab in the movie, everyone agreed that this was another example of whale magic, the spooky synchronicity that seemed to creep into everything.

Rod Marining brought a case of cold beer into the room and passed the bottles around. The night crew was cleaning the hall, moving stage props around with occasional booming thuds. Bob Hunter's girlfriend, Bobbie Innes, sat talking with Paul Watson, a young radical who had made a career out of political street theater. Watson had agreed to pilot the small inflatable boats between the whales and the harpoons of the whalers. Paul Watson was the type of young man who never flinched. Macho wasn't the word: He didn't seem to overcome fear with a dash of bravery, but rather seemed, in fact, fearless. He was a self-styled eco-guerrilla; the *idea* of risking one's life to save whales appealed to many, but Paul Watson was the first to come forward and say he would *do* it.

They had a boat and a crew, but the Great Whale Conspiracy had some problems that magic had not solved. First, they had almost no money left, and the campaign was going to cost sixty or seventy thousand dollars. Second, even if they raised the money and even if they got out to sea, they would still have to find a moving whaling fleet in the vast Pacific Ocean. At sea, a ship only a few miles away can be invisible, and radar only reaches so far. Paul sat brooding over these issues as the party raged on.

"Paul," said Bobbie, "we have to come up with some fund-raising plans."

"Yeah," Paul replied with an exhausted sigh. He was already feeling burned out by the pace of international politics, and he was faced with more problems than he could handle by himself. His faith in magic was slipping.

Bobbie proposed that they hold a raffle, but Paul pointed out that they would need something to raffle off. As they talked, a Merlinesque old man with long, flowing white hair moved over beside Paul. He carried an eagle feather, and his clothes were studded with pins, patches, beads, and other ornaments. He would have looked like a shaman, except that his stubbly white beard gave him a street rather than a forest look. Paul was getting used to strangers, but this one caught his attention more than most.

"The great whales must be saved!" he said emphatically, waving the tip of his eagle feather in Paul's face. "Every creeping, crawling thing, every flowering bush, every winged being, every finned creature is sacred."

The whole room stopped talking, trying to hear what the mystery man was saying. Captain Cormack screwed his lips at Bob, and Bob shrugged his shoulders. Mel was transfixed by the old man, measuring his every move. Paul looked straight at the man and asked plainly, "What's your name?"

"My name is Henry Payne. I heard you talking about a raffle. Well, I have some land. You can have it. I'll give it to you, free. I don't care about the land; you can have it. Raffle it off."

Paul sat up. "Where is this land?"

"Not far from here; it doesn't matter. We can work it all out later."

Henry Payne agreed to come to the next Greenpeace meeting

to settle the details of the land transfer. Before he left, he stood up and blessed the circle with his feather; at the door he turned and said, "I am the I of eternal I-am."

Was Henry Payne a madman, or was this more whale magic, the right person spontaneously showing up at the right time? Cormack doubted the story, but Mel insisted that the offer would turn out to be real. The night crew at the hall eventually kicked the party out of the dressing room, and it dwindled until only Paul, Linda, Bob Hunter, and Bobbie Innes were sitting around a table at the Cecil.

"The IWC meeting is in June," Paul told them, "with a ten-day Scientific Committee meeting beforehand. We have to have the confrontation with the whalers during the meeting for maximum effect." The four of them split the tasks. Bob and Bobbie would stay in Vancouver. Bob would get the boat out to sea, and Bobbie would raise the money, starting by checking out Henry Payne's land offer. Paul and Linda would take the Whale Show across Canada, raising consciousness and new members. Then they would go on what amounted to a spy mission to seek out the information that could lead them to the whaling ships.

"Where are you going to get the information?" Bobbie asked.

"Oh, I don't know," said Paul vaguely. "Something will happen."

"It's going to look pretty dumb," Bob said, "if we make this big announcement that we're going out into the middle of the ocean to confront the whalers and we can't even find them. Everyone I talk to who knows says it will be a miracle. Cormack just laughs. 'I don't know how you're going to pull this one out of the bag,' he told me. It's too big an ocean to expect to run into them; we need the coordinates of the whaling fleets. We need to know exactly where they are. Then we might have a prayer."

"Oh," Paul laughed, "we've always got a prayer. Listen, just trust me, okay? Bobbie, I trust you to get the money trip together; Bob, I trust you to get the boat off the dock and deal with the crew; you guys have to trust Linda and me. Somehow we'll find the coordinates. There has to be at least one person in the world who knows and who will tell us."

The four agreed on the plan. Paul would use the Whale Show tour as a cover for his espionage assignment. He would take the show around the world if necessary. The boat would leave Vancouver in late April 1975, and they would have to find the whalers by June. Paul had five months to find the coordinates of the Russian and Japanese whaling fleets.

Paul and Linda, with Yashi in tow, were on a pay-as-you-go, whistlestop tour that led across Canada. In each city they would put on a Whale Show and collect enough money to make it to the next city. In Ottawa, Paul and Linda talked to the Icelandic honorary consul general, a friendly woman who had a painting in her house of the waterways near Hanson Island. They chatted about the beautiful British Columbia coast, and she told them about the state Marine Institute in Reykjavík, where Paul might get the information he wanted. Paul, in the role of a whale scientist who wanted to do a study of sperm whales, the species currently hunted by the large factory ships, wanted to know if the Icelandic Marine Institute might have the coordinates of the whaling fleets.

Paul, Linda, and Yashi flew to Iceland in March, but no one at the Marine Institute knew, or would reveal, the whalers' hunting patterns. However, the scientists at the institute gave them the name of Dr. A. Jonsgard, the leading whale scientist in Norway. Dr. Jonsgard, they were told, might know where the information was, and they immediately made plans to go to Norway. Before leaving Iceland, Paul called Bob, told him that the espionage was progressing, and learned that Henry Payne's land offer was legitimate and that the raffle was going well. The confrontation crew was assembled and included Japanese and Russian translators. Before leaving Reykjavík, Paul and Linda had gathered a list of over fifty volunteers who formed a local Greenpeace group.

In Oslo, Paul's lead at the Ministry of Fisheries proved futile. "No, sir, we can't do that," he was told when he asked for the records of whaling routes. However, at the University of Oslo,

Dr. Jonsgard was very receptive. Paul had been referred by scientists in Iceland, and Dr. Jonsgard was pleased to trade scientific information with Dr. Spong, the whale researcher from Canada. Dr. Jonsgard even invited Paul to give a lecture at the university on the natural behavior of *Orcinus orca*. Paul told the friendly, paternal professor that he needed to find out where he could observe wild sperm whales and asked if the Norwegian whaling industry would not have that information from the whaling ships themselves.

Dr. Jonsgard suggested that Paul contact Mr. E. Vangstein, the director of the Bureau of International Whaling Statistics in Sandefjord, a hundred kilometers south of Oslo. Dr. Jonsgard even phoned ahead to arrange the meeting. Paul sensed that he was close to his goal as he stood under a towering arch of blue-whale jawbones at the entrance to a grassy waterfront park in which stood the modern office building that housed the most comprehensive collection of whaling statistics in the world. Near the building, a sculpture depicted the back of a surfacing whale and a small boat of men with hand-held harpoons about to strike it. Paul felt a rush of anticipation as he walked into Mr. Vangstein's tidy office, lined with rows of file cabinets and overlooking Sandefjord Harbor, once one of the world's greatest whaling ports.

In the late nineteenth and early twentieth centuries, when the oceans were alive with millions of whales, the Norwegians had been dauntless and skillful whalers. By 1930, however, the ocean populations had dropped from some five million whales to approximately one and a half million. In 1931, the whalers killed over thirty thousand blue whales in the Antarctic. The kill declined each year as the blue whale was driven to near extinction. By 1965, the population of blue whales in the oceans had dropped from two hundred thousand to two thousand; 1 percent were left. The Norwegians knew that the whales were disappearing, and they were shrewd business entrepreneurs as well as good whalers. They sold most of their whaling fleet (except for a large number of small vessels that continued a relentless pursuit of minke whales in the North Atlantic) and invested their capital in crude-oil supertankers and North Sea

oil exploration. Almost nothing was left of the once great Norwegian whaling industry but a few rusting whaling ships and
Mr. Vangstein's room full of files.

Paul, Linda, and Yashi sat in Mr. Vangstein's inner office,
decorated with whalebones, old photographs, and other whaling memorabilia. The elderly gentleman seemed a bit lonely,
stuck as he was in this modern office standing guard over the
records of a dying industry, a far cry from the heroes depicted
in the sculpture below on the lawn. Yet Mr. Vangstein was
openly enthusiastic talking to Paul about whales, and he show-
ered Linda and Yashi with paternal affection. When Paul
asked, gingerly, for the recent routes of the whaling fleets, however, Mr. Vangstein became hesitant. "Well, Dr. Spong," he
said, shaking his head, "those are company secrets. I really
couldn't let you have them without a written request from the
Scientific Committee of the IWC."

Paul's heart jumped. "He's got them," he thought. Paul knew
that he would never again be so close to his goal. He launched
into what he knew would be his one and only chance to secure
the documents. He explained that he wanted to observe sperm
whales in the wild, that science would be furthered, and that
the political bickering at the IWC would most certainly preclude his getting a request from the Scientific Committee.

Paul, Linda, and Yashi all sat across the desk holding their
breath while Mr. Vangstein scribbled with his pencil in silence.
It was most certainly the kindly old gentleman's compassion
for the young scientist and his family so far away from home,
rather than Paul's reasoning, that softened his heart.

"Well," he said, looking up and pausing, then smiling, "I
guess this is innocent enough."

Paul's chest was pounding as Mr. Vangstein led him out to
the main office and into a back room filled with file cabinets
and shelves crowded with records. Over the course of the afternoon, while Linda, Yashi, and Mr. Vangstein entertained
each other in the inner office, Paul combed the files. He gulped
and looked over his shoulder when he found what he was looking for; then his eyes fell back onto the files. *Nisshin Maru,
Tonan Maru, Kyukuyo Maru,* the Japanese factory ships. Paul

copied down the coordinates of their most recent routes. Then he found the Soviet ships, the *Dalniy Vostok* and the *Vladivostok,* and he copied those logs out into his own notebook, filling thirteen pages with handwritten figures.

Mr. Vangstein was genuinely enjoying his play with Yashi when Paul, having finished, returned to the inner office. Paul felt a bit embarrassed that he had misled the kindly gentleman about the purpose of his visit, but he knew that his guilt was the price he had to pay for being a spy, even if the cause was justifiable. "Thank you," he said to Mr. Vangstein. He wanted to walk over and hug the man, but he just smiled warmly.

Back out in the park, Linda and Paul were bursting with excitement.

"Can you believe what just happened?" Paul said. "That guy just opened the vault and handed us the crown jewels!"

On their way home, they picked up some food and a bottle of champagne, and in their hotel room they cooked a feast on a little camp cookstove.

As they celebrated, they phoned Bob in Vancouver. According to the records from the previous years, the Japanese fleets would be far away from the western coast of North America, in the North Pacific west of Hawaii, for most of the summer. One Soviet fleet, however—the factory ship *Dalniy Vostok* and her escort of fourteen harpoon boats—would be just off the coast of California in June, just in time for the IWC meeting. Bob told Paul that the fund raising was going well and that the crew was ready. The *Phyllis Cormack,* renamed the *Greenpeace V,* was scheduled to depart from Vancouver Harbor on April 27.

"Well, you'll just have to kill some time, Bob," Paul said over the phone. "Try to find some whales. Linda and I are going to see if we can get campaigns going in Norway and Denmark before we head for London. When do you think the best time to confront the whalers would be?"

"At the opening of the meeting. Those guys already have their agenda set, and probably their votes. I'm not sure what we can hope to affect this year, but if there is any chance of swinging votes, we should hit the whalers right as the meeting opens, or maybe the day after."

"Okay, on the twenty-third of June the Russians will be—"
Paul stopped.

"What is it, Paul?"

"Uh, Bob?" Paul drawled out his question.

"Yes?"

"Do you think we should be careful about what we say over
the phone?"

"Well, it's not as if we're trying to keep anything secret, and
if we were, we've already blown it. It's already in all the papers around here that we're planning to blockade the whalers
this summer. You wouldn't believe what is going on here.
We've got the City Council, the premier of the province, Trudeau himself, and a million grandmothers all giving us blessings as if we were the Crusaders. *No* one is coming out in favor
of killing whales. The Canadian delegation is completely isolated, and quiet. There's going to be ten thousand people at
Jericho Park for the send-off, money is flowing in—and out,
faster—and the phone rings in my dreams! Man, this is no secret."

"Okay. The Russians will be off the coast of California in
June. We'll be in London in the middle of June in time for the
Scientific Committee meetings. I'm asking to be given observer
status at the Scientific Committee. I'll send you copies of the
Russian fleet coordinates. Your assignment, Captain Kirk, is to
stop the Russians from killing any whales during the IWC
meeting. The meeting opens on the twenty-third."

"Roger, Roger. Have you been in telepathic communication
with Commander Skana?" said Bob.

"Well, yes, she had planted a comrade in the records office."

"Over and out. How's Linda and Yash?"

"Great. Give our love to Rod and Bobbie and John and everyone. Are you sure this story will make it to London?"

"I promise you a front-page, six-column banner headline, if
not in the *Times,* well, at least in one of those sleazy tabloids."

As they were talking, Paul considered the danger into which
Bob and the others were about to place themselves. The sea is
dangerous anytime, and his friends were going to be placing
themselves between frantic whales and exploding whalers'

14. *Captain John Cormack and Robert Hunter on the first Greenpeace boat, the* Phyllis Cormack, *searching for Russian whalers in 1975 [Photo by the author]*

15. *The two Greenpeace boats in 1976: the* James Bay *and the* Phyllis Cormack *[Photo by the author]*

16. (Above) Musician
and interspecies communicator
Melville Gregory
[Photo by the author]

17. (Left) Musicians
Melville Gregory and
Paul Winter, on board
the Greenpeace boat,
playing
to the whales
[Photo by the author]

18. *The Russian factory ship* Dalniy Vostok *and the Greenpeace protest boat, the* James Bay *[Photo by the author]*

19. *Russian harpoon boat (left) and factory ship, hauling whale carcasses [Photo by the author]*

20. (Left) Greenpeace protesters
Paul Watson and Marilyn Kaga
in front of
Russian harpoon boat
[Photo by the author]

21. (Below) Russian whalers
on the Dalniy Vostok
[Photo by the author]

22. *Paul Spong and Greenpeace volunteer loading bananas onto protest boat during stop in Hawaii [Photo courtesy of Paul Spong]*

23. Russian sailors on deck of factory ship [Photo by Paul Spong]

24. Sperm whales on deck of pirate whaling vessel Sierra operating illegally out of Panama with Norwegian and Japanese owners [Photo courtesy of Paul Spong]

25. *Japanese factory ship* Nisshin Maru No. 3 *[Photo by Kazumi Tanaka]*

26. *Greenpeace members meet with the Japan Whaling Association in November 1976. Chairman, Mr. Inagaki (center, with hand on table), told the ecologists that "Japan will continue whaling—forever!" [Photo by Kazumi Tanaka]*

27. *Protesters sit in at International Whaling Commission meeting in London, 1977 [Photo courtesy of Greenpeace]*

28. *Protesters hold signs indicting Whaling Commissioners for "crimes against nature" [Photo courtesy of Greenpeace]*

harpoons. The reason this thing was going to work was because it *was* dangerous. It would certainly be news if people put their life on the line—not just for their own kind or own country—but for other, nonhuman beings. The thought occurred to Paul that this might be the last time he ever talked to Bob.

"Okay, Paul," said Bob. "Hang in there. Not to worry."

"Okay, Bob, 'bye."

As Paul was hanging up the phone, he suddenly pulled it back. "Bob!" Paul called into the phone, but the line was dead, and he felt tears well up in his eyes as he clicked the phone back onto the hook.

On their way to London, Paul and Linda helped set up Greenpeace groups in Norway and Denmark to put pressure on those countries' IWC delegations. In Copenhagen, Paul performed the Whale Show nightly at an English-language club called The Purple Door. Financial and organizational help poured in, and the Danish Prime Minister, Anker Jorgensen, and the Danish commissioner to the IWC, Mr. Hertoft, received hundreds of letters and petitions.

The Spongs arrived in London on May 29, 1975, two weeks before the Scientific Committee meetings opened, and Paul began the delicate process of negotiating for observer status. Before leaving Vancouver, he had been promised help in his campaign by British Columbia Premier Dave Barrett. British Columbia's representative in London, Admiral Sterling, put himself at Paul's service as Paul arranged to host a reception for IWC delegates and diplomats during the week of the meetings. Paul let it be known among the throngs of protesters and the media that Greenpeace would be attempting to stop the whalers by "nonviolent intervention."

The *Phyllis Cormack*, alias *Greenpeace V*, bobbed in the gray mist off the west coast of Vancouver Island. Bob Hunter had six weeks to kill before he could hope to get close to the Russians off the coast of California. He had not told anybody, not even Captain Cormack, that he had the coordinates for the whaling fleets stuffed at the bottom of his duffel bag. The story in the news media was that Greenpeace was "hunting" for the whalers. Bob was wringing every drop of creative savvy from his exhausted head in an attempt to keep the story alive. He filed stories of "Battles of the Titans of the Sea," hypothesizing a meeting under the full moon between a sperm whale and a giant squid. It was artistry lost on some. The press was becoming skeptical, and so was the crew.

The current story was that they were "conducting interspecies communication experiments" with the local gray whales and the human musicians on board. Mel Gregory, synthesizer player Will Jackson from San Francisco, and jazz composer Paul Winter were, in fact, having some success in getting the gray whales of Wickaninnish Bay to swim around the boat and listen to their music. The sessions served two purposes: The crew loved hanging out with the whales, which distracted them from asking Bob when they were going to find the whalers, and the photographs kept the press interested in the lonely Greenpeace boat.

For three days the crew played music to the whales and even swam in the water with them. One day they saw two orcas mating in the waters of Queen Charlotte Sound along the B.C. coast. The two whales, belly to belly, rotated in the water so that each could breathe in turn. Bob managed to turn the event into a front-page story. They visited an abandoned West Coast whaling station on the Queen Charlotte Islands and made a heroic run through a fierce storm for the Cobb seamounts—underwater peaks where sperm whales sometimes fed and where "the whalers might be found." On the way down the coast in early June, the boat, with a crew of twelve and Captain Cormack at the helm, stopped into Portland, Oregon, for a press conference, vowing to find the whalers "soon."

On June 12, they were back out to sea, this time to make one last desperate lunge at the phantom whalers. The crew members fell into one of two very distinct camps: the mechanics and the mystics. The mechanics kept everybody alive and the mystics read the signs, predicted rainbows, played flutes to the dolphins at the bow, sped Zodiacs alongside the *Phyllis Cormack* as she cut through the sunny Pacific seas, and threw *I*

Ching coins on the galley table at 3 A.M. Bob hammered out press releases, which he read over the marine radio to newspapers and radio stations.

Mel, the undeclared guru of the mystics, hung high on the rigging, the ocean breeze in his face, keeping "whale watch." Whenever whales or dolphins were sighted, the entire crew, even the hard-core mechanics, would rush to the decks to see them. Mel kept a "dream book" in the galley, in which anyone's dreams could be recorded, just in case some dreams might bear important information.

After John Cormack, electrician Al Hewitt was the leader of the mechanics. He kept the boat's entire electrical and mechanical systems humming, and he built a makeshift radio directional finder, which—if the Greenpeace boat ever got close enough—could pick up the radio transmissions of the Soviets and tell the crew which direction to go to make contact with them. While Mel was up in the rigging, Al Hewitt was down in the bowels of the engine room greasing the chugging Atlas diesel engine, or locked in the radio room fiddling with dials, scanning the marine bands for transmissions.

The Russian interpreter was a bruising, blond Czechoslovakian named George Korotva. Carlie Trueman, a deep-sea diver and law student, was the only woman on board, and that only after convincing John Cormack that it would be socially acceptable. Ecologist Dr. Patrick Moore and oceanographer Gary Zimmerman from San Francisco gave the crew its scientific credentials, but even they were often lured into the camp of the mystics. The big question was, How were they going to find the whalers? The *I Ching* or the radio directional finder?

Even Bob was not sure. He had the previous three years' coordinates for the fleet, but what if they didn't take the same route this year? What would happen if they picked up the Greenpeace radio transmissions and simply stayed far away? Bob would lie awake in his bunk at night dreading the possible task of having to explain a big failure. The entire crew began to go through a sort of collective manic-depressive cycle, where one day everybody would be singing, "We are whales, swimming in the sea . . ." to Mel's thundering guitar, and by the next day they would all be arguing over where they should be going. They ran out of booze and tobacco after about two weeks, and the addicts became even edgier. One of the diesel fuel tanks leaked over the food stores, and half the food was ruined.

When the IWC meeting opened on June 23, the *Phyllis Cormack* was forty miles off the coast of northern California, chugging under a full moon, too far from shore to make radio contact, low on food, low on fuel, with film crews and photographers pacing nervously, and without a clue as to how to find the Soviet whalers, supposedly somewhere within a two-hundred-mile radius. The twenty-four-hour radio watch heard not a single Russian transmission, and Al Hewitt was only guessing which bands to monitor. Half the crew was seasick and couldn't eat, and the other half was overworked and starving. Walrus, the cook, kept up a furious pace, trying to make edible food from diesel-soaked staples. Walrus and Mel propped up spirits with music and wild mystical tales.

Bob had revealed the secret coordinates to the crew, and Al Hewitt and Patrick Moore had pored over them, plotting a course on the wheelhouse chart. They were proceeding at about eight knots in the general direction of the Mendocino Ridge, one of the underwater seamounts that attracted deep-sea whales and therefore whalers. A lone albatross followed mythically behind the tiny fishboat as it traveled day and night, south-southeast into warmer breezes. There were cloudless days when the sea was a vast blue plate under the burning sun, and then, without warning, a squall would rock the boat violently. Captain Cormack bulled around the vessel with constantly watchful eyes, one minute grunting terse instructions to his amateur crew and the next minute playing practical jokes on them. His antics kept all on their toes, watchful. His way of encouraging crew members to take their tasks seriously was to remind them that there was "nothing but a one-inch plank between you and the devil." Captain Cormack was the lifeline holding the environmentalists together, and his authority was absolute.

Hewitt had hooked speakers into the galley so that he could

listen for the Soviets during mealtime or late at night over coffee. On this particular night, Hewitt, Pat Moore, Bob, Walrus, Carlie, Will Jackson, and Mel were sitting up late in the galley, singing, plotting, debating, throwing *I Ching* coins, and wishing they had cigarettes. Hewitt had revealed his secret stash of homemade moonshine, so spirits were high. Suddenly, through the crackle and distortion of the Pacific airwaves, came an unmistakably Russian voice. All heads snapped in the direction of the speaker, and a leaden hush fell over the galley. After about thirty seconds, they heard what sounded like "Vawshtok, Vawshtok," and then more untranslatable Russian chatter. Bob ran to the wheelhouse to fetch George Korotva, but by the time he got there, George was already sitting with his ear up to the radio speaker and hushed Bob into silence.

There was no doubt about it. The *Phyllis Cormack* was within fifty miles of the Soviet whalers, and Hewitt trained his radio directional finder on the incoming transmission, determining that the whalers were almost due south, perhaps a bit south-southwest, right on the Mendocino Ridge, where Spong's information said they would be. But they were moving. Hewitt fashioned a new antenna from bits of wire and pipe that extended the range of the radio directional finder. They monitored the radio night and day, chasing the phantom ships through the ocean swells, waiting for a transmission, changing direction, waiting again, changing direction again, maintaining a twenty-four-hour watch in the hope of seeing lights of the Soviet ships at night. They saw nothing.

In Vancouver, Rod Marining and Bobbie Innes were going crazy. The last radio contact with the *Phyllis Cormack* had been a broken, crackling call from Bob that said they were "amidst the Russian fleet." What did that mean? Since then there had been no contact. The media called every day, friends and family called, politicians called. The question was always the same: "What is happening?" And the answer was always the same: "We don't know. They are with the Russian fleet."

In London, Paul was tense. The environmental protesters, lobbyists, and scientists were all wondering if his story about a "nonviolent confrontation at sea" was a lunatic fantasy. Paul had no answer for them; maybe it was. Whale magic, obviously, was not the most prevalent force at work in London. Paul was completely stonewalled in his effort to get observer status at the Scientific Committee meetings. He lobbied with any international delegate who would talk to him, in hotel bars, on streets, and in cafés. Many of the scientists would have nothing to do with him, as their perspective was one of "proving" that the whale "stocks" were not endangered. The Atlantic gray whale was long extinct. There were possibly only a thousand or so blue whales left in all the oceans. There were perhaps just a few hundred of the once mighty bowhead—or "right" whale, so named because it was the most lucrative to the early whalers—left in the Arctic, and approximately two thousand humpbacks. In total only one tenth the number of whales that had been in the ocean at the advent of modern whaling remained in existence. The "proof," needless to say, was somewhat convoluted. The whaling companies' so-called scientists didn't really want to look Paul in the eye.

Without credentials, Paul would be barred from the commission meetings. In the days before the opening he schemed constantly, trying to find a way in. He surveyed the site, Riverside House, a squat, gray government office tower on the bank of the Thames, with a well-secured single entrance. The door would be guarded and credentials checked. On the first morning of the commission meetings, Paul's hopes were low, although he held on to the remote possibility that a delegate might lend him credentials so he could slip in. Gloomily he watched as taxis and limousines deposited the exalted few who would decide the fate of the whales.

During the lunch break, Paul joined a noisy throng of delegates, observers, and environmentalists in a pub near Riverside House. Greenpeace cameraman Michael Chechik had obtained press credentials and had penetrated the meeting, filming the opening proceedings. "You wouldn't have believed it," Michael told Paul. "Ten minutes into the meeting and one of the delegates is already sound asleep." As Michael told Paul about the meeting, Paul was preoccupied, half listening while glancing around among the delegates and wondering whom he might ask to help him get inside. Each delegate or official observer had a red or blue lapel badge. As the lunch ended, the crowd filed out of the pub to return to the meeting, and Paul sat alone feeling dejected. As he pushed his chair back to get another beer, his eye caught a flash of red. There, under the table, was a red delegate's badge! Without hesitation he bent over, picked it up, and pinned it to his jacket. He swung his bag over his shoulder and hurried to catch the crowd going into the meeting. Paul mingled in the line passing security, smiled cheerily, and walked casually in. When the Canadian commissioner, Robert Martin, noticed Paul, he edged toward him and asked, "Who let you in?"

"God," said Paul, smiling.

Later, when a secretary from the commission staff tried to get Paul's attention as he sat in the meeting, he ignored her. "What shall I do?" Paul asked Joanna Gordon Clark, observer for Friends of the Earth, explaining his dilemma to her.

"Tell them you're the alternate for FOE," Joanna whispered back. The story worked, and Paul stayed to witness the proceedings. On the second day, the commission did vote in favor of a ban on the killing of fin whales, as they had previously done for other rare species. There were approximately fifty thousand fin whales in the oceans, 5 percent of their original population. The fin whale ban was expected as a sort of sop to the environmentalists. The papers ate it up, quoting company scientists who insisted that they were "responsibly monitoring the whale stocks."

But the fin whales had already been reduced to numbers that made hunting them uneconomical; the whalers were more interested in the sperm whales, of which there were still some two hundred thousand. A sperm whale was a more difficult catch in the days of the *Pequod* and Moby Dick. They were too far out at sea and too wily a creature to be easily hunted; but in the days of sonar, factory ships, and exploding harpoons, picking off sperm whales was just another profitable, high-tech resource-gathering operation and would likely remain profitable for another decade, until the sperm whales, too, had been reduced to a few thousand in number. Furthermore, it was com-

mon knowledge that no one could really monitor either the
quotas or the kinds of whales that the whalers took. The factory ships processed the carcasses at sea and had nothing but
huge drums of whale oil in the hold when they got back to
shore. A Russian scientist would monitor the operation on *one*
of the Japanese ships, and a Japanese scientist would monitor
the operation on a Soviet ship. "The wolves are guarding the
sheep," Paul complained to the press.

On June 24, Paul's reception at the Landsdowne Club was
attended by many IWC delegates—including Japanese and
Russians—the Spanish ambassador, several British Members
of Parliament, and many of the environmentalists. Paul showed
his films of orcas and gave a light pro-whale speech. The event
was a success, but one nagging question remained: What about
the boat? The confrontation? The media representatives were
beginning to doubt his story.

By June 25, two days before the commission meetings ended,
Paul still had no idea where the Greenpeace boat was, or what
it was doing. Had he known, he would have been even more
distraught. The *Phyllis Cormack* was in fact bouncing around
forty miles off the California coast, having been on a wild-
goose chase with a Russian and Polish deep-sea dragging fleet.
On another escapade, Mel, taking the night shift at the wheel,
had followed the moon—which, of course, moves across the
sky—rather than the compass bearing, and by morning he was
heading sixty degrees off course. He naturally maintained that
following the silver path of the moon was as wise and fruitful a
course as anything the chart-room analysts had come up with,
but Cormack, Moore, Hewitt, and almost everybody but the
hard-core mystics were upset with him.

Bob was beyond upset, he was a basket case—the crew used
the term "bow case" because it seemed as if anyone who went
crazy would end up standing on the bow for hours on end
watching the gray void. Bob could not make contact with Vancouver and therefore could not reach Paul in London. The
Whaling Commission meetings were two days from being over,
and the whole expedition was a big, embarrassing flop. Nevertheless, they *did* continue to hear Russian voices on the radio,

stronger day by day, and there was still hope. Mel was going around the boat saying, "We'll find 'em, don't worry, it's gonna happen."

Mel was on the wheel at noon, June 27, the last day of the commission meetings. He had strict orders from Captain Cormack to bear 190 degrees south-south-southwest. A morning rain had passed, and the sun broke through. Most of the crew were either in their bunks or sitting around the galley table. Cameramen Fred Easton and Ron Precious were the only crew members on deck, and Cormack had gone into his quarters for one of his daily fifteen-minute catnaps. Off to his left, Mel saw a rainbow. Gently he guided the *Phyllis Cormack* 35 degrees off course and began heading south-southeast, straight for the rainbow, which he "just knew" had to be the right direction. It was a sign.

When Captain Cormack woke up after fifteen minutes, he walked out into the wheelhouse and glanced casually at the compass. Mel was sent flying out the wheelhouse door, and Cormack took the wheel. Five minutes later Patrick Moore, who had come up to the wheelhouse to soothe the captain after hearing Mel's story, peered into the distance, squinting. "John!" he said. "What's that?" Seven black dots sat on the horizon like ants on a faraway window ledge. Ron Precious screamed, "It's them!" The *Dalniy Vostok,* a six-hundred-foot factory ship, and the Soviet fleet of harpoon boats was dead ahead.

To add to the miracle, Bob was suddenly able to contact Vancouver by the ship's radio; whether it was just the clear weather or the final stroke of whale magic, he couldn't be sure. Paul Watson, Pat Moore, George Korotva, Bob, and the film crews leaped into Zodiacs as the Greenpeace boat approached the whalers. Carlie Trueman hoisted the UN flag up the mast; the Kwakiutl flag went up, the Tibetan prayer flags, whale banners, and rainbow streamers all went up. Everyone scurried around the deck, Mel and Will Jackson making music that blared out over the ocean. Russian sailors lined the decks of the *Vostok* to watch the strange, small fish boat putter alongside. It was like a circus that had traveled in trailers through a desolate, rainy night and that suddenly unfolded its tents and

flags in an explosion of color and sound. The Soviet whalers
had never seen such a sight at sea and were more amused and
befuddled than hostile.

Mel did his best to play "Russian-type" music, making his
guitar sound like a balalaika and throwing in lots of *Oh! Ah!'s*
for foot stamping. On board the factory ship, Russian sailors,
men and women, clapped and waved. The factory ship was the
largest ship most of the ecologists had ever seen, its huge steel
hull rising from the water like a canyon wall. At the stern of the
ship, whales were being hauled from the water to the deck, and
blood was pouring from a drain back into the ocean. Smaller
killer boats swarmed around the factory ship, and among them
the *Phyllis Cormack* looked like a tiny, colorful toy.

As Mel played music to the Russian sailors, Bob and Paul
Watson sped away in a Zodiac, bouncing over the choppy blue
waves in pursuit of the killer boats as they left the factory ship
to resume their hunt. In the water all around, there were carcasses of sperm whales, massive gray islands in the sea, blood
pouring out in twisting red currents, and blue sharks cutting
here and there. Bob had heaved more than one gulp as the
reality of this crazy stunt descended upon him, and he held on
for dear life as Paul Watson, full-throttle, raced a 150-foot killer
boat, which in turn was chasing down a pod of frantic, spout-
ing whales.

Killer boats have sonar equipment that allows them to track
the great sperm whales underwater, so that when the whales
emerge to breathe, the boats are there waiting, and they are
fast enough to keep pace with the fleeing whales. Soon the
whales become exhausted by this chase, and the whalers are
able to train their harpoon gun on them. The harpoon has an
exploding head that blows up and expands inside the whale's
body. From his sea-level view, gripping the sides of the Zodiac,
Bob looked up to catch his first view of the harpoon projecting
over the bow of the steel-hulled ship. Protruding from the barrel of a cannon, it looked like a bulky, rusty arrow with en-
folded mechanical barbs. Behind the harpoon gun stood a
bulky Russian in a blue sea cap, appearing and disappearing

behind the slicing metal bow of the boat as it slammed through the waves.

Ahead, the sperm whales spouted and keened in the air. As Paul Watson moved the Zodiac closer to the whales, Bob could feel the splash and spray of their frenzy on his back as he stared up at the harpooner, a Russian worker in tattered dungarees. He twisted his head around to get a quick glimpse of the whales' arching gray bodies. Then the whales dove, and Watson kept the Zodiac positioned in front of the harpoon, as the whalers tracked the whales on their sonar. Suddenly Bob was jerked forward as the engine sputtered and stopped. The fuel tank had bounced into the air and had landed on the rubber fuel line, cutting off the flow, and the engine had died. Paul stood at the stern of the Zodiac hauling the tank from the line, then yanking madly at the starter cord as the harpoon ship bore down on them. Over Paul's head, Bob could see the monstrous hull rising above them, and he screamed at Paul to jump. Just at that instant, however, the bow wave from the Russian ship lifted them like a feather in the wind and deposited them gently to the side, where they bobbed dumbfounded in the waves.

Bob's head was still spinning when George Korotva roared up in another Zodiac and grabbed for his hand. Bob stumbled into George's rubber boat, and they sped again after the whalers. Paul managed to restart his boat, and he and Patrick Moore followed with the film crews. Within minutes, Bob was again staring up at the rusty hulk of metal that moved back and forth like a surveying insect. Bob watched as the gunner left the bow, walked along a catwalk to the ship's wheelhouse, and then returned. A messenger continued to run between the bow and the wheelhouse, and Bob imagined that someone, somewhere—either the captain on the bridge, or the commander of the fleet on the *Vostok,* or some admiral on the other end of a radio in Moscow—was collecting the information and giving the orders. Bob had always assumed that the Russians would never shoot an innocent whale saver, but he now found himself searching the void between his thoughts for this faceless man who was deciding his fate. Under his breath he muttered, shaking his head, "You wouldn't do it!"

Then the messenger came down the catwalk with a bit more spunk, stomping his boots on the narrow metal walkway. He whispered something into the gunner's ear and spun back around for the wheelhouse. Bob had the nauseating feeling that whatever the order was, it had just been given. He tried to look into the gunner's eyes, but the man seemed to look right through him. George saw Bob's jaw drop wide open as Bob watched the man on the bow take aim at the whales that were gasping just over his shoulder.

The explosion of the gun cracked in Bob's ears, and he instinctively fell facedown to the floorboards of the Zodiac, covering his head. George ducked, clutching the engine controls behind him and peering over the bow in front. The strong Czechoslovakian swerved to the side as the harpoon cable slashed down beside him, and a fountain of blood sprayed into the air with the explosion of the harpoon tip inside one of the whales. George then wheeled around, out of the way, as the cable sprang tight and the whale thrashed its powerful flukes.

Bob and George watched helplessly from the side as a massive sperm whale, perhaps the mate of the one thrashing on the end of the whalers' line, turned and charged the killer boat, lunging up at the bow. The gunner quickly loaded another harpoon and shot the second whale. The film crews had captured the entire incident, and Fred Easton moved in closer to film the bleeding, dying whales. George Korotva screamed, ordering the Zodiacs to back out of the way. Nothing would be gained now by a needless accident. The Greenpeace Zodiac crews huddled in silence, breathing heavily, watching the red trails of blood flow from the carcasses as they were lashed to the sides of the harpoon ship. Perhaps fearing that the Greenpeace protesters would spoil their day's catch, the Russian whalers stopped hunting and picked up the whale carcasses that they had already left scattered on the surface of the water.

Back on board the *Phyllis Cormack,* Bob and the crew were emotionally drained. On the one hand, they had succeeded; they had found the whalers and interfered with the hunt. On the other hand, what they had seen, the carnage, the continuous flow of blood from the side of the *Vostok,* had dampened their celebration. Bob filed press stories to Vancouver and San Francisco via the boat's radio. The Greenpeace crew followed the Russians for two days, but—perhaps under orders—the Russian fleet turned south and outran the slower *Phyllis Cormack.* The protesters then turned toward San Francisco to bring back their photographs and films.

The news came to London just as the IWC meeting was closing on the last day. All the wire services were carrying the story: A band of Canadian and American conservationists calling themselves Greenpeace had confronted Russian whalers at sea. They had maneuvered their inflatable boats between the whalers' exploding harpoons and fleeing sperm whales. The Russians had fired a harpoon over the heads of the protesters, narrowly missing George Korotva, a thirty-four-year-old Czechoslovakian, and Robert Hunter, a thirty-three-year-old Canadian, the leader of the expedition. The conservation group claimed that the whalers were driving the whales to extinction through unsound management, and they were demanding an end to commercial whaling.

Every newspaper in London carried the story, and Bob even made good on his promise of a six-column, front-page headline. The confrontation could in no way affect the quotas already handed out by the commission to the whalers, but suddenly the entire controversy took an abrupt turn. The media swarmed around the Russian and Japanese delegates, trying to get a comment. The confused delegates dodged and stuttered, calling the Greenpeacers "pirates" and claiming that the Scientific Committee had already ruled on the responsible management of the stocks. Both the Russian and Japanese embassies in London were forced to make a statement, and the Soviet and Japanese delegation leaders had their pictures going around the world on the wire services.

Paul Spong's credibility rose abruptly among the protesters and scientists and reporters in London. The UPI and AP called him for quotes, U.S. television crews interviewed him, and he was *the* man in town for several days. Bob and the Greenpeace boat were heading back into San Francisco, carrying with them not only photographs and film of the confrontation itself but also, reportedly, pictures of illegal, undersized whales killed by the Soviet whalers in violation of IWC regulations.

In Vancouver, Rod and Bobbie were fielding inquiries from every continent on the planet. They had a twenty-four-hour answering service giving the latest developments. Yes, Greenpeace had interfered with the hunt. Yes, they had absolute proof that the whalers were taking undersized whales. Yes, they would go out again. Money poured in. An estate lawyer rang up to say that a dying man had left a "considerably large portion" of his estate to the whale-saving campaign.

In San Francisco, some two hundred people were on the dock when the *Phyllis Cormack* pulled in along the Embarcadero. News reporters and cameramen had to be restrained by immigration officers, and they took interviews by leaning across the gunwale with cameras and microphones. UPI envoys picked up the Greenpeacers in taxicabs and drove them and their film to processing labs. Bob talked on virtually every radio and television station in San Francisco, and Walter Cronkite played the film as the highlight of his "That's the way it is" evening broadcast. A New York film company, Artists Entertainment Complex, flew an executive to San Francisco to try to buy the motion picture, publishing, and television world rights for twenty-five thousand dollars. She offered Bob 10 percent down, twenty-five hundred dollars, and a promise for the rest if a film was actually made. Bob was no entrepreneur, but he knew the offer was, as they say, peanuts. Nevertheless, he wanted to push the campaign forward, and money was not an issue, at least not with Bob. However, with fame and money up for grabs, Greenpeace politics changed rapidly. Bob found that he could no longer make deals without a massive bureaucratic hubbub. "Fear success," he told a friend, quoting his media mentor Ben Metcalf. "I can already feel it beginning to bog down. We didn't plan what to do after this worked."

The campaign to save whales exploded onto the world scene. Aside from some environmental groups who accused the Greenpeacers of "stealing the media," some hard-core revolutionaries who considered the whale issue "soft," and a handful of whalers, the whole world loved the whale savers. The Soviets and the Japanese had been put on center stage with the lights on full blast. Paul was an international celebrity, not just the darling of a few pub crawlers and ecology nuts. By the time he got back to Vancouver, he was a local legend. Everyone *expected* miracles to follow him around. When the *Phyllis Cormack* entered Vancouver Harbor on July 22, Paul, Linda, and Bobbie had organized a massive welcoming, with banners, television crews, bands, and a crowd of over ten thousand people who waded into the surf to greet the returning crew.

As bands played, Bob and Paul sneaked away to a quiet spot behind the stage to figure out what to do next. The whale campaign had amassed a forty-thousand-dollar debt, but, on the other hand, donations were rolling in as never before. Both Bob and Paul admitted that they had no idea how to handle all the money and deals and exposure they were getting, but the question of what to do next took care of itself.

A few weeks after the Greenpeace boat arrived back in Vancouver, on August 16, Bob Wright captured six orcas at Pedder Bay. Paul, who had gone back to Hanson Island, returned to Vancouver vowing to free them. The confrontation with Bob Wright, his onetime guest on Hanson Island, was imminent. Paul began to prepare a brief for the British Columbia government, which would propose an outright ban on the capture of orcas in provincial waters.

Mel led a Greenpeace group to Pedder Bay, where Bob Wright had already established a tight security perimeter to keep out protesters. The Royal Canadian Mounted Police had just arrested someone who was suspected of trying to cut the nets and release the captive whales. By sneaking along the coast at night, Mel was able to record calls from the orcas inside the nets, as well as the calls of family members outside the nets, and he sent these tapes to radio stations, for which Paul did telephone interviews.

Then Paul headed for Victoria with Bob Hunter. Through the

provincial press secretary, John Twigg, an old newspaper buddy of Bob's, they scheduled a meeting with the premier of the province of British Columbia, Dave Barrett. Paul's brief outlined the legal and scientific reasoning behind his suggestion that capturing orcas should be outlawed. He pointed out that over the previous twelve years, 263 orcas had been captured in the waters of Washington State and British Columbia. Twelve orcas had died during capture, and of the forty-eight that had been shipped to aquariums, more than half had died.

The demand was obviously going to grow for more orcas, and the capturing, in addition to the shooting of orcas, was depleting the local populations. Paul made the case that the orcas were a bigger asset to the province alive and free than wasting away in aquariums, sold for a few thousand dollars, or dead.

Behind closed doors, Barrett listened and talked frankly with Bob and Paul. "It's not a simple question," he told them. "Sure, I like whales, too, but to Wright and those guys the whales are just a resource to be harvested. It's kind of hard for the government to tell people that they can't harvest the natural resources and make a living."

In a flash, Paul realized that he wouldn't have much time with the premier, and that the only hope was to appeal to the man's heart. "Listen," Paul began measuredly, "I know this is not an easy thing for you to do, but these whales are a lot more than a 'resource.' I live with them. I know these whales. They have families; their families are outside the nets right now calling to the whales inside. I've been watching these whales for six years, and I can tell you that they are remarkably intelligent creatures with tight social bonds. It is not entirely a question of 'resource management'; it is also a question of how we as humans treat other intelligent beings."

Bob finally broke in. "Mr. Barrett, *everybody* is in favor of saving whales, probably ninety-five percent of the population."

The premier smiled in such a way that Paul could not tell if he was being friendly or evasive. "I'll give all this to Jack Radford," the premier said, referring to the conservation minister.

"By the way," he said in an amiable tone, "how did you guys find those Russians?"

Bob and Paul looked at each other. Paul turned back to the smiling premier, broke into a smile himself, and said, "Spies."

"Thanks, gentlemen." The premier was in a good humor. "I promise you I'll do what I can."

Two weeks later, on September 1, 1975, Conservation Minister Radford announced that the provincial government had declared a moratorium on capturing orcas in the territorial waters of British Columbia. Citing the survival rate of captured whales, the number of whales already captured, and the value of whales as a part of the natural heritage of the province, Radford added in his statement to the press that capturing orcas was "neither morally nor biologically justified," and that Bob Wright, operator of Sealand, was "morally obligated to release the whales."

"Did you hear that!" Paul exclaimed over the phone to Bob when he heard the news. *"Morally* wrong to capture whales. He said Bob Wright has a *moral* obligation to release them. Barrett heard us! He understood!"

Bob Wright let four of the six whales go. One was already at the Sealand aquarium, and the last whale—a three-thousand-pound male already sold to Marineland in Niagara Falls—was held at Pedder Bay pending transportation. The government-operated B.C. Ferries Corporation refused to move the orca to the airport as they had done previously, citing the new provincial regulations. Greenpeace called Air Canada, the scheduled carrier from Vancouver to Ontario, and made the case that if they transported the whale, the adverse publicity would have a negative effect on the airline's corporate image. Air Canada quickly canceled. The provincial government told Bob Wright that if the whale was not delivered by September 16, then it must be released.

Marineland hired a Calgary-based charter firm, International Jet Air, to fly the orca from Victoria to Ontario. From Pedder Bay to Victoria, a truck carried the young male orca, named Kandu IV after three previously captured orcas, all of whom had died in aquariums. Protesters met the truck all along its route into Victoria, waving signs and honking from cars. The whale lovers jammed the Victoria airport as Kandu IV was loaded into the belly of the transport plane and carried away. He would be the last orca legally captured in British Columbia waters.

Paul, on Hanson Island at the time of the move, was upset that none of the protesters had tried to stop it. "Sounds like a bloody party," he'd complained to Linda.

Paul was henceforth persona non grata at Sealand as well as at the Vancouver Public Aquarium. He genuinely did not want to make the aquarium directors, Bob Wright and Murray Newman, his enemies. Yet he was locked into a battle for the whales' sake, and this necessarily estranged him from some people. Orca capturing was big business; Sea World alone, with three aquarium facilities in the United States, had grossed thirty-five million dollars the previous year. Prices for a single orca ranged between seventy-five thousand and two hundred thousand dollars. Bob Wright had been offered a million dollars for Chimo before she died. Historically, it has always been risky for a scientist to mess with the merchants' cash flows.

In practical terms, Paul had also been cut off from all sources of funding. His militant stance on behalf of whales had alienated the very sources of income that might help him continue his studies. After 1972 he had received no more money from the university. He was not interested in government grants, no longer wanting the constraints and strings of government sponsorship. Besides, it was very unlikely that the Federal Fisheries or Wildlife agencies would be supportive anyway. As someone with the whales' interests in mind, Paul was not exactly cooperating with the bureaucratic pecking order, even though Prime Minister Pierre Trudeau himself had publicly wished him well. Furthermore, the well-funded aquariums were not about to support research that was so much in conflict with their plans to capture show orcas for their aquarium pools. And in his work with Greenpeace, he concentrated on raising funds to save the whales, not to support his orca research.

Paul returned briefly to Hanson Island, but the autumn wind and rains held the balance of power there, making it virtually impossible to create a livable, functioning home in the water-soaked camp. Paul was astonished at how fast the wild forest had taken back his little homestead. The house and lab looked as if they had been abandoned ten years ago, and Paul felt a longing for his summer days in Blackfish Sound.

During the winter he traveled to Bloomington, Indiana, for the National Whale Symposium, where he presented his ideas on *Orcinus orca* social structure to the other scientists, artists, philosophers, politicians, and conservationists gathered at Indiana University. He learned there, from Dr. Roger Payne, that the humpback whales have distinct dialects among their several groups. Furthermore, Payne said, they had new and different songs each year, which all the whales seemed to know. "Whales have been swimming in the midst of echoing choruses for millions of years," Dr. Payne told the audience. "Only in the last few years have we considered them to be more than shoe polish and floor wax, and begun to hear the music."

Michael Bigg was also at the symposium, and in presenting an outline of his population research he said there were approximately 210 orcas inhabiting the waters between Namu, B.C., and Olympia, Washington. The B.C. orcas were divided into three groups: the northern group of at least a hundred whales that was centered in the Johnstone Strait area; a southern group that remained in the Strait of Juan de Fuca and the Strait of Georgia; and a third group, which Bigg called the Transient Group, that seemed to move in and out of both areas. Nicola's pod ("A pod" to Bigg) and Hooker's pod ("B pod") were northern residents. The "A5" pod was considered a subgroup of Nicola's. This was the family from which Tung Jen and Corky had been captured in 1968 and 1969. Paul was impressed by the detail that Bigg presented about orca pods, but he cringed when he heard about an experiment in which an orca was marked surgically with two deep notches in its dorsal fin and then released.

Ken Norris, Peter Beamish, and other whale scientists were at the symposium. Dr. Miwa, a Japanese-American scientist, introduced the idea that jojoba beans could be cultivated to replace the oil taken from sperm whales. Paul also got to know

Sidney Holt, a distinguished professor of ocean sciences at the University of Malta. Holt, a British citizen, had worked for the United Nations Food and Agriculture Organization in Rome. He was a small, intense man with gray hair and beard. His expertise was an inspiration to Paul. Sidney Holt was a man of incontestable scientific repute who was absolutely convinced, on purely scientific grounds, that whaling had to stop, and soon, if the whales were to be saved. Dr. Holt, a founding member of the IWC Scientific Committee, was advocating a complete moratorium. Paul developed a natural friendship with him, and Holt was fascinated by Paul's stories, having never even seen a free whale. Paul invited the scientist to Hanson Island.

After Bloomington, Paul went to Washington State, where he was a featured guest at the First Annual Orca Symposium held at Evergreen State College in the spring of 1976. During the symposium, eight orcas were captured in Puget Sound at a place called Budd Inlet, only two miles from the campus. The whales had been corralled by Donald Goldsberry, who worked for Sea World in Seattle and whose airplanes had dropped explosive charges into the water to force the whales into the nets. An assistant to the governor, Ralph Munroe, had been out for a Sunday sail when he found himself literally in the middle of the melee. Outraged, Munroe asked the governor to intervene. Paul and a band of local whale lovers, joined by Mel Gregory from Vancouver, set out to have them released.

Three days later, after a massive uproar, Governor Dan Evans ordered the orcas to be freed. A court case followed in which Sea World subpoenaed whale scientists who testified to the value of captive whales as research animals. Among the witnesses for Sea World was Paul's former mentor, Ken Norris. Paul was the chief witness for the state of Washington, testifying that, in his opinion, the whales were being taken as circus animals, not for serious research. The court ruled that the whales had to be released within sixty days, backing up the governor's orders. University of Washington scientists riveted radio beacons to their dorsal fins before releasing them near the San Juan Islands. Two weeks after the whales were released, their radio signals stopped, and they disappeared, to turn up later, permanently disfigured where the bolts holding the transmitters had torn through the dorsal fins.

Yashi sat on a log looking out to sea. Paul had taught him how to cut the end from the hollow bulb at the end of a long piece of kelp and make it sound like a Tibetan horn by blowing through the other end. Yashi had been playing for hours, hardly noticing the spring rain that blew in a mist about him. Mesmerized by the sound, he blew on the horn until his lips were sore.

When the orcas came by, Paul and Linda joined him on the shore. The orcas blew great fountains of mist in the bay while the three of them blew the kelp horns. "What do you think, Yashi?" said Paul. "They like the kelp horns, eh?" It was the early summer of 1976, and Paul was glad to be back on Hanson Island, weary of politics, scientific meetings, media interviews, and the steamrolling machinations of governments and industries. He and Bob had planned another voyage for the summer, which would attempt to intercept the Japanese whalers, and he had been lobbying the IWC Scientific Committee to allow him observer status at the summer meeting, but he had returned to Hanson Island to spend some time with the whales. He was expecting the two Japanese photographers whom he had met in Tokyo to arrive any day, anxious to photograph free orcas.

Mel Gregory spent part of the summer at OrcaLab, as the Hanson Island research center had come to be called, playing music to the whales through the underwater speakers. Mel's music, picked up by the hydrophones, could be heard by Paul, Linda, and Yashi as they lounged around on pillows in their ever more comfortable house. The living room was a fifteen-by-six-foot platform covered with a carpet and surrounded with windows. There were skylights in the cedar-shake roof, and a wood stove in one corner. Sometimes the whales came by, and sometimes they didn't, but Mel played on, totally dedicated to sending out his song to the orcas. Surely the whales heard the music, he thought, and they recognized it as human-made. Perhaps they even appreciated the artistic offering and were conscious of the fine melodies and spirited rhythms. "Hi, Nicola.

Hi, Wavy. Whooooop! Whoooouuuuup!" Mel sang over the microphone.

One afternoon, explosions of lightning began to crack through the island hills. By nightfall, seen from the house, Parson Island, Compton Island, and Red Point on Harbledown were all silhouetted against the quaking yellow light. Orcas screeched and wailed in Blackfish Sound. Only a few drops of rain fell in the camp, and then the sky cleared.

Everyone sat out on the rocky shore watching the sky and listening to the orcas in Blackfish Sound. They could hear the blows of the whales through the air. Mel beat a drum while Yashi sent out great, booming howls from the kelp horn.

Streamers of the northern lights appeared, shooting out in slow motion across the sky like giant laser fingers of light, changing color and shape, waving like flags in the wind. "Look, an eagle!" Yashi hollered.

"Where? Where?" The others looked around.

"No, in the lights," explained Yashi. Sure enough, the northern lights formed a huge eagle that was flashing on and off as the lights pulsated rhythmically. It was a full show of whale magic, something no one would ever see at Disneyland or an aquarium in Vancouver or Seattle or Dallas. It was a sight that could not be purchased with any amount of funding. Only the wild, uncontrollable universe, brandishing its own unnameable power, could put on such a show.

A few days later, Paul motored into Alert Bay to pick up Tomatsu Aoki and Koichi Koaze, the two photographers from the Japan Wildlife Club. The photographers were wide-eyed and excited when they got back to Hanson Island, and completely stunned by the natural beauty of the place. They wanted to waste no time getting to meet the whales. "You have to sort of go on their schedule," Linda explained, but Aoki and Koaze could hardly be calmed.

When the whales did come by, signaling their arrival with calls over the speakers, the two photographers scurried about, packing film, lenses, and cameras into their bags, and ran down to the beach. Paul got the inflatable ready, motoring up ahead of the whales and waiting for them to pass. Aoki and

Koaze got pictures that day, and were pleased, but eager to try again. As the days passed, they took photographs of families cruising along together, of huge dorsal fins, and even a spyhopping orca; but what they wanted most was a *jumping* orca. They told Paul their wish.

"Well," said Paul quite seriously, "if you want the orcas to jump, you could try asking them." Aoki and Koaze looked at each other quizzically, neither of them sure whether to take Paul seriously and neither wanting to be played for a fool.

Paul took them to Robson Bight in the inflatable, the two photographers in the bow, and himself steering the outboard engine in the stern. Nicola's pod was in the bight, and the youngsters were particularly playful. Wavy rolled on his back while some of the calves splashed in the shallows. Paul cut the engine and drifted in the middle of the bight; Aoki and Koaze clicked several rolls of pictures before they got bored, or tired, and Koaze brought up the subject of a jumping orca. One of the younger whales was swimming near the inflatable boat. "Orca, jump!" cried Koaze, and the two photographers put their cameras up to their eyes. The whales blew and dove in the choppy blue-gray water. "Jump, Orca-san!" Koaze called out. Both photographers watched through their viewfinders. Aoki changed to a wide-angled lens so that he would get a broader view.

Koaze carried on for quite a while, calling, "Jump, jump," but the orcas only swam around, ignoring the humans. Aoki sat with his camera in his lap, and Koaze stood in the bow with his camera hanging at his side.

"Don't give up," said Paul cheerfully.

The sun hung like a huge orange ball on the horizon. Koaze called again, "Jump, Orca, jump," but his heart was not in it, and he stood dejected. Suddenly, as if erupting, the sea burst open thirty meters in front of them, and a young orca bolted perfectly out of the water and hung horizontal for a tiny eternity, its bulk blocking the sun, white belly toward them. Cascades of orange water rained down, and then came the crash of the body slamming onto the surface and sending another shining fountain skyward.

Both photographers nearly knocked themselves out hurling

their equipment into position, but by the time they focused, there was nothing left but a circle of ripples in the water. They called out again, but the orca did not reappear. Minutes later, as the sun disappeared from sight, the orcas were suddenly gone, and the trio headed home.

"If you don't really believe," Linda explained at the house, "then it doesn't work. You have to believe."

Aoki and Koaze nodded. Yes, they believed; they wanted to try again the next day.

"Wait until the whales come by," Linda suggested. "Then you won't have to go all the way over to Robson Bight."

Aoki and Koaze agreed, and they waited around for a full day, watching the waters of Blackfish Sound from the rocks of Hanson Island.

When Nicola's pod next came by, Paul, Linda, Aoki, and Koaze motored ahead of the whales in the inflatable. At Bold Head, on the northwest tip of Swanson Island, Linda and Koaze got into the kayak, which they had carried on board. Nicola was leading the pod in a leisurely swim along the north shore of Blackfish Sound toward Queen Charlotte Strait. When they turned the corner around Swanson Island, eight kilometers from their home on Hanson Island, the whales slowed down even more and began to linger in the waterways of the White Cliff Islets.

Paul had cut the engine and was paddling the inflatable sitting on the bow. Up ahead of them, Linda paddled the kayak as Koaze clicked his camera and urged her forward. They were close enough to the meandering whales to get vivid shots of the black and white bodies of the orcas cruising along. The air became very still as the afternoon sun hung over Donegal Head to the west. In about an hour it would be setting.

"Not much time," Aoki said to Paul, nodding toward the sun. "Maybe I should ask Orca to jump."

"Okay." Paul nodded and smiled.

Aoki turned back toward the pod of whales. "Jump, Orca, jump," he called out. Soon Koaze joined him from the kayak, calling across the water: "Jump, Orca, jump!" Wavy turned and swam directly toward the kayak. "Jump, Orca, jump!" the pho-

tographers continued to shout while they held their cameras to their eyes. Wavy dove below and disappeared. A long minute passed as Aoki and Koaze continued their chant in a hushed whisper; the words "Jump, Orca, jump" fell like a mist over the water. Then Wavy broke the surface, not fifteen feet from the side of the kayak, with a thundering rush of air and water churning around his body.

From where Paul sat, on the bow of the inflatable, he could not see the kayak, which had disappeared behind Wavy's huge, arcing shape. His heart pounded, and he wondered for a moment if the whale had leaped right on top of the kayak. Aoki screamed out.

Linda watched as Wavy's black and white belly soared high above them, making an arch that ended in an enormous splash. Too excited to be afraid, she instinctively gripped the sides of the kayak, then realized that not a single drop of water had landed on her and that the boat only rocked gently in the wake of the splash. Neither Aoki nor Koaze had managed to snap the shutter, and they both shook their heads, groaning.

Without the slightest warning, Wavy burst out of the water again. Aoki and Koaze scrambled to get the leaping whale into the frame, but it was all over too fast again. "Keep your cameras up!" screamed Paul, and the two photographers—Aoki rocking on trembling legs in the inflatable, and Koaze sitting in the front of the kayak—raised their cameras. Paul and Linda steadied the boats with their paddles.

"Jump, Wavy," Linda started this time. Aoki and Koaze joined in, holding their cameras fast to their eyes, fingers on the shutter release, scanning the blue water as golden light fell on the rocks and tiny islets. "Jump, Orca. Jump, Wavy," everyone called out together.

When Aoki saw the huge whale coming out of the water for a third time, this time right in his viewfinder, he let out an excited squeal. Koaze thought the whale must be traveling in slow motion, as it seemed to rise gently until its whole body was out of the water and seemed to hang in the air. He had time to notice the background, get the horizon level, and frame the islands just right, and then he clicked the shutter. Aoki got two shots, one as Wavy was halfway out of the water and another just before the tip of his head touched the water at the other end of his jump. Aoki and Koaze were ecstatic, screaming and howling as the sun began to set over Malcolm Island. "Thank you, whales. Thank you, Orca. Thank you, Wavy-san," they called out.

The photographs were seen throughout Japan, published in a full-color spread in *Mainichi Graphic* magazine. Aoki and Koaze went home as dedicated ambassadors for the whales and as full-fledged believers in whale magic.

For Paul, being back on Hanson Island and spending time with his family and with the whales was a calming retreat from the worldly affairs he had plunged into.

He hiked up to the bluff by himself on a summer day. Dall's porpoises played in the water below him, and a huge bald eagle with a two-meter wingspan glided silently in front of him in the cool breeze, hovering just above the windswept tops of the pine trees. Soon Paul would be going back to the city and the buzz of international politics, but in the meantime he could enjoy the quiet blessings of Blackfish Sound.

He and Bob had planned a second Greenpeace voyage to seek out the Japanese fleet near Hawaii. Perhaps by the time the whales were free in all the oceans, he would have his floating laboratory.

Counting the two years at the Vancouver Aquarium, Paul had been studying orcas for eight years. For six of those years he had been watching Nicola and her family. He had drafted a ten-year plan, and a budget. He had plans for ongoing research and observation that could take all his time. Yet he thought there was still time to convince the whole world that humans should stop killing whales. He had taken on a lot of responsibility, but for a few warm, summery days, he felt completely at ease with it all.

His only regret was that he had been spending less and less time with the whales, and with his family, on Hanson Island. But he could be proud of what he had actually accomplished in the previous year. A growing network of Greenpeace offices dedicated to saving whales now flourished across Canada, in

Iceland, Norway, Denmark, England, and the United States. The decisions and actions of the International Whaling Commission were under the scrutiny of the world media. Whales' rights to life and liberty had become an international issue. Directly, the Greenpeace boat had saved eight sperm whales from the Soviet harpoons. Premier David Barrett and Governor Dan Evans had been convinced that the orcas of British Columbia and Washington State should be free, untroubled by capture expeditions. Nicola, Wavy, Hooker, Saddle, A5, and all the other orcas, young and old, in British Columbia and Washington State waters were safe.

Paul Spong's work might have been snubbed by some of the scientific elite, but as an act of compassion it took on historical proportions. With his love for these nonhuman creatures Paul had crossed some ineffable threshold that seemed to separate humans from the wonder of other living beings. In so doing he had touched a primal nerve in hundreds of thousands of people who intuitively had reached out to help make amends for the ravages of human civilization—not just against the whales, but against all the winged, four-legged, or finned citizens of the earth.

7
Nicola

It was the first spring salmon run of 1977. Paul sat listening to the familiar orca vocalizations, guessing it was Nicola's pod that he was hearing. When they passed, Paul could indeed see Nicola through the binoculars as she traveled close to the far shoreline. A light spring rain fell outside. He wrote "Nicola's Pod," with the date and time, on the tape box and in his notebook.

After leaving Hanson Island the summer before, Paul had sailed with Bob Hunter and a crew of sixteen on the second Greenpeace campaign to interrupt the whale hunt. In an effort to reach farther into the North Pacific and to keep up with the whaling fleets once they had found them, they had refitted a retired Canadian navy minesweeper, the 150-foot *James Bay*, into a Greenpeace boat. Artist Kurt Musgrove had completed the transformation of the old gray warship, painting whales on the hull and rainbows on the bow. Their espionage efforts produced even better results than in the previous year. Through the Washington office of sympathetic U.S. Congressman Leo Ryan, they received daily reports on the exact positions of the Soviet whalers. Greenpeace intercepted the Soviets eleven hundred miles northeast of Hawaii, where Paul—with Bob Hunter and Bobbie Innes aboard the inflatable—was able to dart in front of a hulking whaling ship as it chased a fleeing pod of sperm whales. As Paul raced his small boat past the whalers, he raised his arm in a gesture of determination, trying to catch the eye of the harpooner, but the man was intent on his target. Once Paul, Bob, and Bobbie were in front of the Soviet ship, Paul could see a messenger hurry down the catwalk and speak to the harpooner, who immediately clicked the harpoon down and walked away. The whaling ship stopped dead still in the water, and a crewman covered the harpoon with canvas. Perhaps, thought Paul, the whalers had orders from the Kremlin not to kill whales while Greenpeace was around. In any event, the hunt was stopped.

Later that day, as the Greenpeace boat shadowed the Russian factory ship, a pod of sperm whales surfaced alongside, frolicking and playing while the excited crew watched and played flutes from the rail of the *James Bay*. It was rare that sperm whales would approach so close, play around a boat, and remain for so long. The crew was ecstatic, sure that this must be the pod they had saved earlier in the day. Perhaps the whales knew that the colorful boat was friendly. The rainbows on the hull were matched by rainbows that appeared in the spray of the whales' spouts, an auspicious sign that fortunes were turning in favor of the whales. In the end, the protest was so disruptive to the Soviet whalers that they abandoned their hunt in the Pacific between Hawaii and California.

Paul had not been able, however, to obtain the coordinates for the Japanese fleet from Congressman Ryan, who claimed that he himself could not get them. Somewhere along the line, someone thought it was okay for the Greenpeacers to confront Russian whalers, but the Japanese were being protected. Several sympathetic Coast Guard crewmen visited the Greenpeace boat in Hawaii, and one of them gave the Greenpeacers photographs, taken only the day before, of Japanese whalers operating near the French Frigate Shoals off Hawaii. The photographs showed baby sperm whales being flensed on the decks of the Japanese boats, probably in violation of IWC size regulations. Paul sensed that the chance had come at last, and he wanted to go out after the Japanese right away, but fuel was short, and others wanted to confirm the position of the whalers. In the end, the Japanese eluded Greenpeace, much to Paul's disappointment.

Determined to confront the Japanese this summer, Paul would leave for Hawaii soon to outfit a ship there that could strike out after the Japanese fleets operating in the northwestern Pacific. In the meantime, Paul would work on Hanson Island alone, as Linda and Yashi had stayed in Vancouver, where Yashi was going to school.

The early outlines that Paul had drawn of the orcas' social structure were being detailed by the added census data from researchers Michael Bigg and Graeme Ellis. There seemed to be nine family groups that frequented the waters of Johnstone Strait and Blackfish Sound. Bigg, in his exhaustive study, had labeled the pods A, B, C, D, G, H, I, R, and W. A-pod was Nicola's group of thirty-two whales. Hooker was one of the eight whales in B-pod. Three bulls, four females, two juveniles, and a calf made up the ten whales of the C-pod. In all, there were about 140 orcas in the nine family groups that summered in Blackfish Sound and Johnstone Strait.

The southern population, made up of three distinct pods, seemed to center in the area between Vancouver Island and the San Juan Islands of Washington State. This southern population totaled seventy-nine whales.

In addition to the northern and southern "resident" pods, there were also 47 "transient" orcas that traveled in small groups and sometimes alone. Altogether, an estimated 267 orcas lived at least part of the year in the inside waters of British Columbia.

The northern and southern populations were, according to Bigg's research, completely segregated. Only twice had whales from the north been seen in the south. One of these occasions was in 1969, when A5's group was captured in Pender Harbor. At Marineland in Los Angeles, one of these whales, Corky, had just recently delivered the first orca calf conceived and born in captivity. Orky, the father, helped the baby to the surface for its first breath of air. The baby battered itself on the pool walls, had difficulty suckling, and died on March 16, 1977, after less than three weeks of life in the concrete pool. Paul wondered if it would ever be possible to get Corky released back to her pod in Johnstone Strait.

There was still some confusion over the exact structure of Nicola's pod. By 1977, there was a growing awareness that A-pod was, in fact, three separate pods that sometimes traveled alone, together, or indeed with other distinct pods. Nicola and her immediate family formed one group, the A1 pod; A5 and his family of twelve whales made up another, the A5 pod; and a smaller group with a large bull, A4, and three adult females with one juvenile formed the final group, the A4 pod. In general, these groups were present during the summer in the Johnstone Strait area more often than any other pod. For this reason they were considered the resident pod/pods of the area. Other pods, such as B-pod, were viewed more as visitors, though they, too, were part of the Northern Resident Community. Later, when John Ford, a doctoral candidate from the University of British Columbia, conducted his acoustic research, he found that indeed the A-pods shared many similar calls, indicating their ancestral relatedness. Possibly, long-ago associations had drifted with succeeding generations, leaving an affiliation but also a preference for their closer and more immediate families.

The orca vocalizations that Paul recorded were of two distinct kinds: the repertoire of calls and the echolocation clicks. The echolocation clicks could be heard at various rates. Sometimes, when the whales came into Blackney Passage, Paul would hear a single train of clicks, as if one whale was sending out an echolocation signal that gave a reading of the area for all the whales in the pod. A staccato burst of high-frequency clicks could also be heard. By using a higher-toned click and more clicks per second, whales are able to get a more detailed readout of objects, their shape, and their precise location.

Paul knew from the work of Dr. Roger Payne that humpback whales would sing long, intricate songs that would be repeated, note for note, by the same whale or other whales. Dr. Payne had even noticed that certain songs would be sung in one season, only to be modified or replaced by new songs the following year—a sort of cetacean hit parade. Such creative vocal behavior is obviously the work of a mindful creature, but human science was only just beginning to penetrate that vast mystery. Paul hypothesized that the orca language was of the analogue type rather than digital; that is, the orcas were most likely communicating whole sound pictures, or sound environments, that carried meaning or image synergistically. An example in human language is that the statement "Open the door" is digital information, whereas a sigh is analogue information. The whales may have perfected analogue communication beyond anything that humans could imagine or comprehend.

The orcas, if Paul was correct, used a system of communication that defies any direct translation, because the sounds are not words as such. The calls may include information about the immediate environment, about who is calling, where the callers are, where they are coming from, where they are going, how they feel, to whom the message is directed, or even perhaps information concerning every member of the pod. All of this was, of course, pure speculation. Paul still had no idea what the orcas were saying to each other, but there was no doubt that they were saying something and that their communications were meaningful.

Moreover, orcas, it seemed, worked out their social roles peacefully. The most powerful predators in the seas, they rarely—if ever—turned their aggression toward one another. Paul marveled at this absence of physical force, of the aggressive instinct that was so prevalent among land mammals, including the supposed paragon of animals, the human. In comparison, the orcas were exquisitely self-controlled.

Paul was walking in the forest; the bright afternoon sun sent shafts of light through the misty air between the boughs of the spruce, fir, and cedar trees. On his return, as he approached the house, he heard the blows of orcas. He walked along the rock cliff until he could see orca fins through the trees. Nicola's pod came by, close to the rocks, moving very slowly. Nicola herself, swimming alone, drifted at the surface outside the bay, directly in front of the camp.

"Hi, Nicola." Paul startled himself. Living alone, he had not heard the sound of his own voice for several days. Nicola milled about, drifting. Paul guessed Nicola to be perhaps fifty or sixty years old, a creature of considerable experience to go along with her natural intelligence.

"Niiicolaaaaa!" Paul called her name. The orcas assembled into a tighter group, but still were silent. "Niiicolaaa," he called again. No sounds came through the speaker. The group was Nicola's closest family, the ones who were usually with her. Wavy swam nearby, with a female that was accompanied by a calf and two youngsters.

"Reeeeeeeeeow!" A single cry came through the speakers. Paul answered with a high-pitched, wavering howl that echoed in Blackfish Sound as the whales began to move off along the shoreline.

A few days later, Paul was motoring into Alert Bay in the inflatable when he saw Nicola's pod again, swimming in a heavy chop whipped by wind and current. He turned off the engine and drifted. When he saw Nicola surface, he screamed her name, "Niiicolaaaa!" through the wind. Immediately Nicola slapped the surface of the water with her flukes, then she raised and thrashed them down again, and again, and again. "Niiicolaaaaaa!" Paul called out once more.

"She knows her name," Paul thought. Maybe it was only his wishful projection—and it was not something he could prove in a scientific sense—but Paul felt that Nicola knew him. For his own part he knew that he sensed the presence of some*one,* as he had felt when Skana first caught his attention.

Paul had felt accepted by the orcas ever since he had first paddled among them. Now, as he sat in the bouncing boat, Paul once again felt warmed by the presence of his friends. The whales dove together and came up at a distance. He watched as the whales moved away; then he started his engine and continued into town.

"Even if they *do* know me," Paul told his friends Michael Berry and Jim Bates in Alert Bay, "I wouldn't say I'm very important in their life. They have more pressing things to do than hang out and play with me." Paul was torn between his scientific skepticism and his sense of wonder.

Paul left Hanson Island for Hawaii, where he met George Korotva, the Czechoslovakian seaman who had sailed on the *Phyllis Cormack* in 1975 and had skippered the *James Bay* during the second Greenpeace confrontation with whalers in 1976. George, Paul, and a virtual army of volunteers in Honolulu refitted a 176-foot World War II sub chaser to serve as a Greenpeace boat. In Vancouver, Bob Hunter and Patrick Moore launched the *James Bay*. For the third year of protests, the whale savers would have two ships in the Pacific chasing whalers.

With George at the helm of the sub chaser, renamed *Ohana Kai*, "Family of the Sea," Paul and a crew of thirty-five headed into the Pacific. They carried on board a complete ABC television camera crew with a helicopter lashed to a landing pad on the stern deck. As they traveled north, Paul was painfully aware that the waters around the Hawaiian Islands had once teemed with whales. Native Hawaiians told him that even fifty years ago, whales could be seen on any given day. Old ship logbooks documented sperm whales, blue whales, humpbacks, fins, the smaller whales like the sei and minke, and a host of dolphin and porpoise species.

Nevertheless, for days the *Ohana Kai* plowed through a lifeless sea. The camera crew would fly off in their helicopter, covering a hundred-mile sweep across the path of the Greenpeace boat, but they came back day after day reporting no sightings of whalers or whales. Paul knew what the graph of declining whale populations looked like, he knew the percentages and the numbers that were left, but day after day each crashing gray wave punctuated his scientific knowledge with the actual experience of the vast emptiness, the tragedy.

When the *Ohana Kai*, chosen for its sub-chaser speed as well as its cheap price, finally did come upon the Soviet whalers fifteen hundred kilometers north-northeast of Hawaii, the *Dalniy Vostok* and its fleet of harpoon boats, these, too, had been cruising over an empty sea. Not even the whalers could

find whales. The *Dalniy Vostok,* a floating factory, rose six
stories above the waterline, just to the deck. Above deck, the
wheelhouse rose another fifty feet and was topped with an
array of electronic equipment that made it look more like a
space station than a whaling boat. The hull towered straight
out of the water, a sheer iron wall with little pinpoint openings
where men and women stood, looking out at the rainbow-
painted *Ohana Kai.* On his first encounter with the Soviet fleet,
Paul had seen blood pouring continually from the deck drains
in the side of the hull; but the decks were now dry, though the
brownish red stains still painted the iron wall, a grim vestige of
once-living whales converted by modern man and machine
into dog food, lubricating oil, and cosmetics.

A week passed and the *Dalniy Vostok* continued to cruise,
fourteen harpoon boats fanning out and returning like puppies
to their mother. The ABC camera crew followed the harpoon
boats by helicopter, but they saw no hunting going on. The
Greenpeace crew learned that the landing of a helicopter on
the deck of a narrow ship bobbing in the choppy sea was a
highly technical and dangerous operation, but the veteran pilot
managed without a mishap. Day and night the harpoon boats,
sleek, fast cutters with 150-pound exploding harpoons mounted
on the high bows, came and went, but no whales were hauled
onto the deck of the factory ship. With no whales to kill, there
would be no confrontation. Paul decided that he would take his
message directly to the captain and crew of the Soviet vessel.

The Greenpeacers organized a boarding party consisting of
Paul, Nancy Jack from the Honolulu Greenpeace office, and
Kazumi Tanaka, a Japanese photographer. Kazumi would take
photographs and speak with the Japanese observer who was
supposedly monitoring the Soviet operation. The three set off
from the *Ohana Kai* in one of the inflatable Zodiacs, which
Paul maneuvered to the stern of the factory ship; there a huge
slipway plunged from the deck into the churning ocean. A
winch on the deck was used to haul whale carcasses from the
harpoon boats to the deck of the factory ship, where the
whales were flensed and rendered into vats of oil.

Paul ran the little inflatable, like a gnat biting at a giant beast, right up against the stern slip of the factory ship and quickly lashed the bowline to a rail on the side. Paul, Kazumi, and Nancy walked up the slip and presented themselves politely. The Soviet crew, obviously not feeling threatened by these high-seas, whale-loving pirates, shook their hands and tried to speak in broken English. The Greenpeacers had learned a few words of Russian, so polite introductions and nods went all around. Paul handed out Russian broadsheets like an old union organizer. He could have been on New York's East River docks urging the workers to rise up against their bosses, but he was petitioning the workers themselves on behalf of the whales. "The whales are your comrades." Paul smiled, hoping someone would understand. The Soviet sailors were reading the handout and talking among themselves, nodding, shaking their heads. Some seemed to agree with Paul's analysis; others didn't.

Then a man came on deck who Paul ascertained to be some sort of political commissar, casually dressed in a striped sports shirt and definitely not a working seaman. The short, stocky man took quiet but firm control of the scene on the deck, escorting Paul, Nancy, Kazumi, and the ABC film crew—who had just arrived on the Soviet ship—to an officers' lounge upstairs. Paul asked to speak to the captain, a messenger was sent, and the captain arrived in the lounge. He was a tall, clean-shaven man, wearing a fresh white shirt with a braided collar and white slacks.

"You found us again. Very good," the captain said in English that was quite understandable. He nodded his head as though impressed with the Greenpeacers' tenacity and their skilled, albeit unorthodox, seamanship.

Sensing that his time was short, Paul spoke quickly to the captain. "Excuse us, sir, for this unexpected intrusion, but we have a serious concern to bring to your attention. Even you can see there are very few whales left, no whales to catch. People from all over the world are asking you to stop killing the whales, to let the remaining whales be free to live in the oceans."

Paul waited for a moment, and the captain nodded again. He

seemed to be an attentive man, giving the intruders a fair hearing, and he struck Paul as being an experienced seaman, unruffled by this unprecedented disruption in his routine. The commissar, on the other hand, seemed agitated and hurried, wanting to end the exchange quickly.

"You've met us before," Paul ended quickly, "and you know we are determined, that we'll keep coming back. Please stop. That is what we are asking you. Just please stop now."

Kazumi asked, "Why have you found no whales?"

The captain only shrugged, perhaps having strict orders or at least the good sense not to say anything quotable about whales. He was just a sea captain; policy concerning resource management was made far away, among bigger bosses, with far more to win or lose. Paul could see the Japanese scientist and other dignified-looking Soviet officers standing in the back of the crowd. When Kazumi called for the Japanese scientist, however, he and the men with him simply disappeared. The commissar signaled that the exchange was over, directing Paul toward the door. The captain shook Paul's hand as the commissar ushered the Greenpeace crew and the film crew back down to the deck.

As they passed among the deckhands, Paul and Nancy handed out whale buttons to anyone who would take one, and many of the crew unabashedly wore them with pride, giving little thumbs-up signs and flashing smiles. As a friendship tour, they were doing fine. Paul stopped and pinned a whale button on the shirt of the commissar, who did not object. Then the Greenpeacers were shown courteously, though swiftly, to their boat. The visit had come to an end.

For several more days, they followed the *Dalniy Vostok* on its lonely hunt. Paul knew that the whaling captain and the crew of the *Dalniy Vostok* were not the ones who could change the tide of history, though he was glad that he had been able to deliver his message firsthand. When the Greenpeacers were down to just enough fuel to make it home, they left the hapless whalers, and the *Ohana Kai* turned back to Hawaii.

In Honolulu, the local volunteers wanted to go back out after the whalers, but Paul had seen enough. Due to the overwhelming scientific evidence, the IWC, meeting in Canberra, Australia, had cut the whaling quotas by 36 percent. However, a special meeting of the International Whaling Commission had been called for December to be held in Tokyo, and the Scientific Committee was reconvening in Cronulla, Australia. The news on the grapevine was that Japan had some "new" data. Paul boarded a jet for Australia, feeling that his efforts would be better spent there, where decisions were actually being made.

Paul was able to obtain observer status to the Scientific Committee meeting in Cronulla, and there he met Jean-Paul Fortom-Gouin, a fiery French businessman turned whale saver, Jean-Paul was the quintessential jet-setter, tanned from life in the Caribbean, flying around the world cutting business and political deals, and puffing constantly on French Gauloises while peering out from behind his designer sunglasses.

But Jean-Paul was also a very serious whale crusader who had donated heavily to the *Ohana Kai* expedition and had been financing an Australian campaign. He had organized a demonstration at Cheynes Beach Whaling Station, Australia's last whaling operation, bankrolling the grassroots Australian Whale and Dolphin Coalition. Jean-Paul had flown Bob Hunter in to help with the confrontation. He had also managed to get himself appointed as an adviser with the Panamanian IWC delegation.

Among Jean-Paul's many international businesses, he owned a dolphin research facility and show aquarium in the Florida Keys. He had become fascinated with the dolphins and came to regard them as extraordinarily intelligent. He had made friends with the dolphins and had come to the same conclusions as Paul Spong. As a result, he had leaped—with all his entrepreneurial gusto—into the battle to save the whales. Naturally, Jean-Paul and Paul Spong formed an immediate camaraderie in Cronulla, recognizing in each other the same deeply felt understanding about whales and unbending devotion to saving them.

As foretold, Japan had "new" data in Cronulla, which they claimed showed that sperm whale numbers in the North Pacific were increasing rather than decreasing. Sidney Holt, one of the most influential and genuine scientists on the committee, was not present, and his levelheaded knowledge would be missed. The whaling-nation scientists presented their new scientific data with bold self-confidence. The Japanese scientist, Dr. Ohsumi, maintained that new evidence showed that the pregnancy rate among sperm whales increased under the pressure of harvesting by whalers, and that future birth-rate projections should be adjusted upward. "New" data regarding sex ratios of whales taken showed that the female sperm whales were not endangered. Moreover, it was argued that new technologies, such as the sonar-ranging ASDIC systems that the whalers used to find the whales, were not very effective. By changing a few percentage figures, the scientists were able to feed the new data into their computerized population model, and—not surprisingly—come up with a new recommendation, raising the catch quota for sperm whales in the North Pacific from 763 to 6,444.

Paul and Jean-Paul lobbied furiously, but to no avail. The recommendation would be sent to the upcoming special meeting of the IWC in Tokyo. After the meeting, Paul continued his campaign around the country, presenting the Whale Show in many cities, speaking to the people through the media, and pressuring the Australian government to change its position on whaling. Australia was a key. In the past, it had voted solidly with the whalers, but the government was under a great deal of public pressure, ripe for a change. Prime Minister Malcolm Fraser's daughter, Phoebe, was a member of Project Jonah, the group that had brought Paul to Australia, and reports came back to Paul that the politician was getting heavy pressure from his family at home. By the end of October, when Paul left Australia, Fraser had appointed Sir Sydney Frost to head an independent Australian Inquiry into Whales and Whaling. A great wheel had begun to turn in the international politics of whale killing and whale saving.

Paul then flew to New Zealand, where he petitioned the government to appoint him—a New Zealand citizen, after all—as its representative to the Scientific Committee of the IWC. J. V.

Scott, the New Zealand Secretary of Foreign Affairs, arranged
a meeting between Paul and J. B. Bolger, Minister of Fisheries,
but the wheels of the bureaucracy turned too slowly, and the
appointment was not forthcoming. Paul then flew to Tonga,
where he teamed up with Sidney Holt in an effort to persuade
the Tongan government to stop killing humpback whales and to
join the IWC as a pro-whale nation.

In November, Paul received a forwarded letter from the Congress of the United States. He opened it, noticing that it was
from Leo Ryan, Democratic representative from California and
chairman of the House Environment, Energy and Natural Resources Subcommittee of the United States Congress. The letter read:

> Dear Dr. Spong:
>
> The Environment, Energy and Natural Resources Subcommittee
> is very concerned over the plight of our great whales. Several of
> these species are rapidly approaching extinction. Specifically, the
> subcommittee is concerned that the U.S. policy position and re-
> cent actions taken at the International Whaling Commission
> (IWC) may not be effective in protecting whales.
>
> In 1973, the U.S. advocated a ten-year moratorium on the taking
> of whales. But recent U.S. conduct at the IWC suggests a shift
> away from a moratorium stance. The result has been confusion as
> to what specific policy the U.S. is pursuing. We wish to pinpoint
> these inconsistencies and unresolved questions which have
> caused confusion as to our current posture on whale protection.
> This is especially important in light of the upcoming December
> meeting of the IWC in Tokyo.
>
> I extend this invitation for you to appear before the subcommit-
> tee on Tuesday, November 28, to give us the benefit of your views
> on the issues mentioned above.
>
> In particular, I would ask you to focus your testimony before
> the subcommittee on the intrinsic value of a whale, as well as the
> significance of extinction of a species. The subcommittee would
> also like to hear of your personal efforts as a member of Green-
> peace to prevent the killing of whales.

The letter was signed, with "best regards," by Leo J. Ryan,
one of the most outspoken environmental watchdogs of the

U.S. Congress. Ryan had played a major role in saving thousands of acres of giant redwood trees in California and in passing the Marine Mammal Protection Act. Through his connections in Washington, he had helped Greenpeace monitor the movements of whalers. What struck Paul most profoundly, however, was that Congressman Ryan was able to seriously address the notion that whales had "intrinsic value." Such a man, Paul thought, was no ordinary politician groveling for the "environmental vote," but was someone with deep insight into what Paul felt was a completely new approach to the other life forms on the planet. Such a man, in such a powerful position, would no doubt prove immeasurably helpful in Paul's campaign.

Paul's hopes in this regard, however, were cut tragically short. The Environment, Energy and Natural Resources Subcommittee would never hear Paul's testimony, because the scheduled meeting was not fated to occur. Congressman Ryan was brutally gunned down at Jonestown in the jungle of Guyana just before the meeting was to take place. Paul mourned not only the man who had done so much to help usher in a dawning of deep ecological awareness, but also the tragic setback to the whales.

In December, saddened by the untimely and tragic death of Leo Ryan, Paul flew to Japan for what he suspected would be a gargantuan battle of words and data. In Tokyo, Jean-Paul and Paul concluded that in order to get the moratorium passed at the IWC, it would be necessary to convince countries who were not yet members to join and to vote with the pro-whale faction against the whaling nations.

"It's absurd for a few nations to claim that all the whales in all the oceans belong to them alone," said Jean-Paul. "Rightfully, every nation with an interest in the ocean should be a member of the IWC. And that doesn't just mean the oceangoing nations, either. Every *person* on the planet has an interest in the whales, and they should have the *right* to have their interest represented."

Jean-Paul had already succeeded in convincing Panama to put *him* on their delegation. In that capacity he had placed the moratorium on the agenda for the next summer's meeting. He also placed the issue of ethics on the summer agenda. The Japanese, however, were not to be so easily outmaneuvered. They would play the political chess game with their own brand of steely international political savvy.

In Tokyo, the Scientific Committee's new recommendations were passed by the full Whaling Commission in forty-two minutes and with almost no discussion. Japan had obviously done some effective back-room lobbying. Environmentalists and many delegates at the meeting were stunned and incensed. Dr. Holt told reporters that the "so-called scientists" were not using the data to arrive at a population estimate, but that they made up a population estimate and worked backward to arrive at the data they needed to "prove" their opinions. He called the exercise a "travesty of science."

During a discussion in a restaurant, Paul heard the real story of the vote. IWC Chairman A. G. Bollen, from Australia, said casually, "It was simple. The Americans wanted the bowheads; it all comes down to politics." The American delegation had been under pressure to get a quota for endangered bowhead whales for the Inuit in Alaska. It was a tricky issue for the Americans, pitting native claims against environmental concerns. In the end, the United States apparently made a deal with Japan. "The Americans sold out the sperm whales for a few bowheads!" Paul exclaimed to his friend Jean-Paul.

Jean-Paul, however, was full of hope. "So we lose this round. We'll get them in London. The Australian inquiry is the secret, Paul. If Australia turns around, that could make all the difference." Sidney Holt, Jean-Paul, Paul, and the other pro-whale advocates gathered their forces for the next summer's IWC meetings to be held in London.

While the whalers were slaughtering virtually every whale they could find—the quotas being higher than the previous year's catch—a major showdown was brewing for the scheduled meeting in London. The flamboyant Jean-Paul, in his role as the Panamanian delegate, was leading the assault against the whaling nations by placing the moratorium and ethics debates on the agenda and by bankrolling several whale-savers' budgets. Although Jean-Paul infused the often ragtag anti-whaling movement with his jet-setting corporate efficiency, he was to find that the Japanese were not so easily outfoxed in the realm of multinational wheeling and dealing.

During the first week of June 1978, Mr. Kuniaka Asomura, director of the Fisheries Division of the Economics Bureau of Japan's Ministry of Foreign Affairs, traveled to Panama for a meeting with the Panamanian Minister of Industry, Mr. Julio Sosa. Ostensibly Mr. Asomura was in Panama to conclude negotiations on several trade deals, including a Japanese purchase of fifty thousand tons of sugar. Such a meeting, under normal circumstances of commerce, would have nothing to do with whale quotas, but in this instance it did.

Jean-Paul Fortom-Gouin was in London for the IWC meeting when he received word from the Panamanian ambassador to Britain that he had been fired from his post as IWC commissioner, and that the new commissioner was instructed to withdraw the moratorium item from the IWC agenda. Through his friends in Panama, Jean-Paul discovered that Kuniaka Asomura had alluded to the IWC and the whaling moratorium during his meetings with Julio Sosa. Asomura called the moratorium proposal "an unfriendly action" and—according to Jean-Paul's sources—threatened to "quit the IWC" if the moratorium passed, and hinted that the sugar deal hung in the balance. Whether or not such a threat actually was leveled, Sosa *did* cable the Panamanian ambassador in London, ordering Jean-Paul's removal and the deletion of Panama's moratorium item from the agenda.

By the time the meetings opened, an all-out war was being waged in the media, in back rooms of London hotels, and in Cambridge, where the Scientific Committee met. Since the IWC meeting in Japan, Paul had flown back to Vancouver, visited Hanson Island, and then returned to Japan, where he worked toward establishing a Greenpeace Japan Environmental Center. In April 1978, his father, Richard, died suddenly, and he flew from Japan to New Zealand to attend the funeral and spend a few days with his mother. In May, he flew back to

Vancouver from Tokyo and then went to Seattle for a special
IWC Scientific Committee meeting on minke whales, then flew
to London. Paul arrived in Cambridge a few days before the
Scientific Committee meetings began, having been on the road
—or in the air—for over a year.

Paul met Sidney and Jean-Paul in Cambridge. During the ethics debate in the Scientific Committee meeting, Jean-Paul sat
with a model of a sperm whale brain in front of him. In Canberra, at the commission meeting the year before, Jean-Paul
had paraded before the delegates with the model sperm-whale
brain above his head, shouting, *"Cachalot!"* in reference to the
sperm whale. *"Cachalot! Cachalot!"* Jean-Paul had harangued
the meeting, pointing out the size of the sperm-whale brain,
bigger than a full human head, and condemning the politicians
and scientists for crimes against nature.

Now he sat poised, agitated by his political frustrations. He
tapped menacingly on the whale brain and stared around at
the scientists in the room. During breaks in the meetings he
held his own personal demonstrations with the sperm-whale
brain, accusing the scientists of destroying the "greatest brain
on the planet." Such carnival-style histrionics were not simply
the mad ravings of an outfoxed Jean-Paul, but were calculated
guerrilla theater, playing to the divided mood of the scientists,
and—more directly—to the story-hungry press. After being
fired, with nothing to lose, Jean-Paul erupted in the full blossoming of his impassioned sense of stewardship on behalf of
the whales. Paul, in the shadow of Jean-Paul's unrestrained,
uncompromising advocacy, was able to maintain a lower, more
congenial profile, appealing to the scientists in earnest.

He even managed to strike up an amiable relationship with
Dr. Ivashin, the diminutive Soviet scientist, perhaps helped
along by the fact that the two of them were about the same size
and build. Dr. Ivashin was gentlemanly and serious, and
seemed to welcome Paul's gracious, diplomatic overtures. His
hair was gray and neatly combed back, not a single strand out
of place. In contrast to the other Soviets, notably the silent
KGB who lolled about in obvious boredom, Dr. Ivashin seemed
almost elegant, and certainly cultured.

Paul's convivial diplomacy produced some of the few light, warmhearted, and even comical exchanges of the otherwise titanic battle. During the meetings, Paul took photographs, discreetly at first, and then more openly. Wanting to stay on friendly terms, he took care to photograph the delegates in flattering expressions, and then showed them the pictures. The photos were a success, and many of the scientists ordered reprints. Dr. Ivashin gave Paul an order for the Soviets. Paul dutifully obtained the reprints and—in his own conciliatory efforts to win the hearts and minds of the delegates—brought them back and distributed them during the commission meeting. When Paul delivered the Soviet order to Dr. Ivashin, the scientist indicated that Paul should see the aide—one of the KGB—for his payment.

The KGB agent, a pale, square-jowled, reticent Soviet official, neither overtly friendly nor hostile, caught Paul's eye and gestured for him to come to the back of the room where he stood away from the crowd. Quickly surveying the assembled delegates with classic B-movie paranoia, the agent motioned Paul behind a curtain, where he took the pictures gingerly in his hand, glanced quickly at them, and plunged them into his pocket. Paul chuckled to himself as the man pulled out a handful of pound notes and counted them into Paul's hand, stopping halfway through to start over. During this exercise in international trade, Paul noticed that they had caught the attention of a house security guard. Immediately seeing the scene from the onlooker's perspective, Paul smiled while the Soviet agent counted out the change. When the paranoid KGB man looked up, noticing that he was being observed, he quickly stuffed the remaining pound notes into his pocket and walked away muttering. The joke was too good to spoil, so Paul didn't bother explaining the circumstances to the security guard, preferring to savor another brief moment on the stage of international espionage and intrigue. Jean-Paul laughed uproariously when he heard the story, and the KGB agent stayed away from Paul for the remainder of the meetings.

Jean-Paul had arranged for two distinguished scientists, Dr. Georgio Pilleri from Switzerland and Dr. Peter Morgane from the United States, to address the Scientific Committee on the subject of cetacean intelligence. For the first time in the history of the International Whaling Commission, the subject of ethics, whales' rights, and whales' intelligence surfaced among the delegates. Dr. Pilleri was a distinguished neurophysiologist, internationally renowned and unassailably objective as a scientist. His neatly trimmed, snow-white hair and beard and his piercing, intelligent gaze gave him a formidable presence.

Discussing the hypothesis of whale intelligence, Dr. Pilleri summarized the known neurophysiology of cetaceans, pointing out that the cetacean brain attains a degree of centralization far exceeding that of the human brain. As centralization is one of the several indexes of brain development, Dr. Pilleri suggested that the scientific community "keep an open mind" to the possibilities inherent in the further study of cetacean intelligence. As Dr. Pilleri spoke, some of the scientists huffed in obvious disinterest, and Paul could detect a frustration growing in the scientist. Closing his presentation, Dr. Pilleri brought out a photograph in which a sperm-whale brain dramatically dwarfed the human brain beside it. Standing at the front of the room, Dr. Pilleri, with pointer in hand, tapped at the cerebral cortex of the whale brain.

"Science is missing a great aspect of the whale," he said. "Please stop and think; these are highly developed mammals."

Continuing to tap at the whale brain, more than twice the size of the human brain, Dr. Pilleri noted that scientists could not help but be impressed and curious about the nature of cetacean intelligence. Moving his stick to the relatively diminutive human brain, Dr. Pilleri pursed his lips, surveyed the scientists who had sat up, taking notice. Tapping the pointer at the human brain, he smiled. *"Nada,"* he said emphatically, using the quasi-international negative. *"Nada!"* Compared to the brain of the sperm whale, the human brain is nothing. Jean-Paul beamed.

Dr. Morgane was a neurophysiologist and neuroatomist who —with Drs. Eugene Nagle, Will McFarland, and Paul Yakovlev of Harvard University Medical School—had completed a definitive survey of the dolphin's central nervous system and published *A Dolphin Brain Atlas*. Before the Scientific Committee he outlined the map of the cetacean brain, the internal connections of neurons, the convolutions of gray matter, the chemical network, and the electronic circuitry as it was understood in the laboratories at the cutting edge of neurophysiological science. As Morgane pointed out, it was interesting and important to note that cetaceans were well adapted to the aquatic life. The massive, highly centralized neocortex of the whale's brain was especially more impressive because it was so highly specialized and precisely differentiated. "There are no other brains like these on the planet," he explained, and for this "if for no other reason, the cetaceans are deserving of protection and preservation." He was firm and assured in his tone, and he closed by telling the delegate scientists, "Enough is known to lead us to believe we are dealing with special creatures with remarkably developed brains. Major riddles of nature and relations between species may indeed be answered by study of these brains, and these opportunities may die with the whales."

Jean-Paul rose to thank the guest scientists. He took the opportunity to speak in his usual unabashed, uncompromising fashion. Citing the work of scientists like Drs. Spong, Pilleri, Morgane, Lilly, and others, Jean-Paul concluded, "From a moral point of view, the mere possibility that whales may be intelligent beings with whom we might someday communicate and from whom we might learn is enough to make it grossly unethical to kill them. If whales are intelligent, then whales are people, people from the oceans. If whales are people, then whaling is not the harvesting of a resource, it is murder. And if whales are people"—the speaker was now in full, chanting stride, sounding like a cross between Jean-Paul Belmondo and Martin Luthur King—"then destroying the whales is genocide. If whales are people, it is morally criminal to kill them, and it should become legally criminal as soon as possible!"

With the Scientific Committee meetings completed, quota recommendations set in Cambridge, the scientists, delegates, their entourages, the press, protesters, KGB agents, and onlookers all moved to London, where the IWC plenary would be held over five days. Jean-Paul sped along the road from Cambridge to London, with Paul at his side in the passenger seat. "They think they have us, eh?" he laughed. "Well, *mon ami,* they are wrong."

Paul laughed with his friend, but his mind was busy wondering what to do next.

"Heh, Paul." Jean-Paul nudged him. "It's okay. I have a bomb."

Paul turned to stare at him, and Jean-Paul laughed again.

"You want to see it?" The Frenchman, driving with one hand, reached into his black bag and pulled out a small package wrapped in brown paper. "It's a *mind* bomb," he said, using Bob Hunter's term. He handed the package to Paul, who carefully unwrapped it and leaned his head back smiling. Jean-Paul smiled, too, as Paul held the bundle of cash. "We still have some tricks for them." The Frenchman laughed, and Paul could not help laughing along as the car sped toward London.

With Jean-Paul deposed as the Panamanian delegate, only Professor C. Roux of France and I. Villaseñor of Mexico were advocating the preservation of the whales. Their voices, however, were drowned in the tide of business-as-usual; the political momentum seemed to have swung against whales during the hot, humid days of June.

Because the Inuit of Alaska had lobbied the U.S. government to preserve for them a quota on the rare, nearly extinct bowhead whale, the United States had backed off completely from its conservationist stance, agreeing to support the pelagic whaling nations in return for the Japanese and Soviet votes in favor of allowing bowheads to be hunted in Alaska. Argentina, Australia, Denmark, South Africa, Norway, Iceland, and Canada were also voting in a solid block with Japan and the Soviet Union.

Paul spent his days in London lobbying for every bit of support he could and trying to keep the story alive in the international media. The London *Sunday Times* published a letter from a Soviet scientist to a British scientist, claiming that the Soviet whalers had exceeded their quotas by some two thousand whales during the previous summer and that undersized whales, infants, and lactating females were illegally taken by the whalers. Behind closed doors the IWC Infractions Committee met, listened to the official Soviet denial, and announced to the media that there was no evidence to substantiate the accusation. Nevertheless, the whalers were getting rough treatment in the media. They were portrayed as sinister, cold, calculating manipulators of truth in their search for short-term profits. When it was revealed that the Japanese were supporting pirate whaling efforts, buying whales from outlaw whaling operations completely outside the jurisdiction of the IWC, their image reached an all-time low.

The principal ray of hope in the otherwise dismal atmosphere of London was the presence at the meetings of Sir Sydney Frost, the Australian judge who was conducting an inquiry into whales and whaling. Sir Sydney, as the demonstrators affectionately called him, was responding to the Australian Prime Minister's order to determine whether or not the Australian whaling industry should be closed, a response in turn to the burgeoning pro-whale movement within Australia. The judge was tight-lipped on the issue, maintaining impeccable judicial detachment; but the travesty of scientific method and the overt political nature of the decision-making process at the IWC meeting could not have escaped his astute eyes. Furthermore, he showed an open-minded objectivity that left Paul feeling very hopeful about the outcome of the inquiry. And if whaling could be stopped in Australia, perhaps that might be the first falling domino in a larger political victory.

On the last day of the IWC meeting, held at the posh Mount Royal Hotel in London, the demonstrators, locked outside during the entire proceedings, conspired to make a final statement of protest. A growing radicalism among the protesters was fueled by their frustration and anger over what seemed a coldhearted, mocking disregard by the IWC delegates, not only for compassion but for rational science. With the help of a sympathetic hotel watchman, twenty-one conservationists entered the building through a back-door fire exit, climbed the staircase to the third floor where the final plenary session was about to begin, and hid in an empty room.

When the closing session began, with the media corps attending in full, the demonstrators stole silently into the room. They stopped before the French and Mexican delegates, presenting them with bouquets of roses and praise for their courageous stance in favor of the whales in defiance of the overall tide of opinion that surrounded them. To the other delegates, the gentlemen from the Soviet Union, Japan, Canada, the United States, and other countries who voted consistently with the whaling nations, the demonstrators presented large scrolls indicting them individually, in huge letters that television viewers around the world could read, for CRIMES AGAINST NATURE. The group then sat quietly in the center of the room, peacefully prolonging the disruption while the cameras whirled and reporters scribbled notes.

Among the protesters was Richard Jones, a lean, frizzy-haired, wild-eyed young Australian environmentalist whom Paul had met the previous summer in Australia. Richard had his own private, theatrical plot circling in his head. He held in his hands a small, unnoticeable vial closed tightly with a cork and containing a few ounces of blood. Richard surveyed the room, noting the exact location of the Soviet and Japanese delegates and of the hotel security guards. As the demonstrators concluded their sit-in, they began slowly, quietly to file out of the room, passing behind the seated delegates. As he passed the Japanese delegation, headed by a Mr. Yonisawa, who sat beside Dr. Ohsumi, Richard Jones uncorked his vial of blood and poured it across the papers and over the expensive suits of the Japanese men. A horrifying squeal erupted, and Richard was instantly overpowered by two hulking Japanese bodyguards, whose massive bodies bulged inside their tailored suits and who flung themselves at Richard with all the flair and precision of crack antiterrorist security specialists. With both arms bent up behind his back, Richard was dragged out of sight, Mr. Yonisawa still shrieking.

Nevertheless, the deals were made, and the whalers got their quotas. For all their efforts, the environmentalists had to admit that they had been outhustled by the experienced politicians whose job it was to look after the interests of an outdated but still gasping industry. The scientists had tolerated the discussion of ethics and intelligence, and the plenary delegates played to the press with the belated protection of the seriously depleted sei whales in the Antarctic, but for the most part the IWC dealt out generous quotas, to the whalers' smug satisfaction.

"Humans are barbaric!" Paul told Jean-Paul. "I think I'd rather hang out with whales. Maybe I should just go home."

Resignation was not an option in Jean-Paul Fortom-Gouin's game plan, and he unleashed his charismatic penchant for emotional speeches in an effort to rally Paul. *"Absurdité!"* he bellowed. "Paul, we aren't finished yet. I'll go to every country in the world, get them *all* to join this commission and vote for the whales. You think I'm going to let these bandits get away with a few cheap tricks? Paul, you might be frustrated because you can't speak out in these meetings, you have to listen to all this scientific—how you say? *Bave. Bêtises*—chatter—"

"Bullshit."

"Yes, bullshit. But, Paul, you are the conscience in those meetings. You sit there taking those notes of yours, and sometimes I see the others looking at you. They admire you. They know they are mercenary hypocrites, and they know that you are a man with love and feelings and truth. They know the whales are disappearing as well as you or I know it, and every day that they have to look at you in those meetings they have to face the mirror, they have to see their own dark, greedy souls! These whales we are trying to save, Paul, these are Nicola's cousins, Skana's cousins. You have to fight. That's it. You don't have a choice. It isn't over, Paul, I swear!"

Jean-Paul laughed. "Don't forget my *bomb,* eh! I made some money because I was a clever businessman, just as clever as these cowards. Now I want to do something worthwhile. Anything the whale movement needs, you ask me. We'll have campaigns in every ocean of the world. These—how you say? turkeys?—these turkeys aren't going to win so easy."

Paul was touched, not so much by Jean-Paul's generosity, and not by his competitive vitality, but by his unyielding dedication, his absolute belief in the importance of the cause they were fighting. Only a handful of people had really ever demonstrated such unbending allegiance to the whales.

Paul smiled. "You're a true believer, mate—how you say? *mon ami?* Okay, Jean-Paul, you're right. I think I'm just homesick. I'm glad you said what you did in the Scientific Committee. It *is* murder, what they are doing. Don't worry, I'm with you all the way, mate. Still, I need to get back to Hanson Island."

"Next year, Paul, things will be different. You'll see, my friend." Jean-Paul exuded a dauntless confidence.

Jean-Paul drove Paul to the airport, and on the way they discussed plans for the future. Jean-Paul was planning a whirlwind tour of the Caribbean to see if he could convince independent countries to join the IWC. At the airport, they sat at the bar drinking a final beer together. As they talked, they overheard a table of travelers discussing whether or not whales were intelligent and whether or not they should be protected.

"See?" Jean-Paul said. "It's everywhere. We're winning, Paul. It might not look like it sometimes, but we're winning. No doubt about it."

Paul took a direct flight from London to Vancouver. He spent a few days in town gathering supplies, visiting with Bob Hunter and other friends and spending some time with Linda and with Yashi, who was now ten and soon to start fifth grade at a local elementary school. Paul also visited Skana one day, buying a ticket at the front gate. The visit further dampened Paul's spirits, however, as Skana looked weak and lethargic. Her dorsal fin flopped over in a pathetic arch, something seldom seen among orcas in the wild. Skana was still just a young whale, yet her fin was sagging over completely and looked lifeless. She was in an obvious state of mental and physical decay. When Paul left, he felt a wave of despondency and frustration wash over him.

Sitting by himself on a park bench, Paul felt a sadness, not just for Skana in her degenerating condition but also for his own life, which seemed fragmented and pointless. He had spent so much time away from Linda and Yashi that he had felt estranged during his visit, certainly not the husband and father that he wanted to be. They were making their life in Vancouver, and Paul was torn in his desire to return to Hanson Island. The Great Whale Conspiracy seemed to be a fizzling dud in spite of thousands of whale-savers all over the planet and Jean-Paul's singular, indomitable enthusiasm. Bob Hunter had quit as president of Greenpeace, and Paul was discouraged by the petty infighting and political jockeying that had followed the organization in the wake of media fame and financial success. Paul's laboratory on Hanson Island sat vacant and incomplete, probably crumbling under the onslaught of wind and rain. Perhaps he had taken on too much, too many commitments and goals. His energy and his attention were scattered and ineffectual, he thought as he sat bleary-eyed, watching the park strollers.

He heard the trainer's whistle blow at the aquarium pool and heard the insipid voice of the announcer introduce Skana's first trick. Paul picked up his shoulder bag and walked away, far enough away through the trees so as not to hear the haunting charade that was being played out at the pool, echoing somehow his own internal despondency and sense of floundering collapse.

Paul sat by the warm wood stove on a late-summer evening, listening to the sporadic orca vocalizations transmitted by the speaker system. His few days on Hanson Island had already begun to lift him from his depression. Only two days before, he had paddled out into Blackfish Sound as B-pod passed by in the direction of the Plumper Islands. He had followed for a while, but the eight whales, moving swiftly, soon outdistanced him. The brief encounter had, however, bolstered his spirits.

More importantly, Yashi had come with him this time, and the two had shared many precious moments exploring Hanson Island together, and watching whales from the rocks. For supper this night, Paul had cooked rice and stir-fried vegetables with some cod that he had caught that day. After eating, Paul said, "You did well, Yashi."

"What do you mean?" Yashi asked.

"Your vegetables, you ate a lot of vegetables."

"Well," said Yashi, "I'm ten now, and I've decided I'm old enough to eat vegetables."

Paul had laughed, and now he laughed again, recalling the incident. He sat by the stove, by the light of a kerosene lamp, and wrote in his notebook, scribbling ideas and remembrances of the previous days and making drawings of his visionary floating OrcaLab. Wondering where his life was taking him, he took out his *I Ching* coins. By throwing the coins six times, he obtained five yin lines with a single yang line in the third place, signifying the fifteenth hexagram, "Modesty." Paul knew the text fairly well, but he opened the book to read it word for word. The first verse read:

> Modesty creates success.
> The superior man carries things through.

The commentary explained:

> The superior man can carry out his work to the end without boasting of what he has achieved.

Paul's throw of the coins had left him with one changing line, the top line, which changed from a yin line to a yang line in this ancient Chinese binary code. Paul read the verse for the changing line:

> Modesty that comes to expression.
> It is favorable to set armies marching,
> To chastise one's own city and one's country.

Again, Paul perused the commentary for a deeper explanation of the meaning. He read:

> A person who is really sincere in his modesty must make it show in reality. Genuine modesty sets one to creating order and inspires one to begin by disciplining one's own ego and one's immediate circle. Only through having the courage to marshal one's armies against oneself, will something forceful really be achieved.

The changing line, when changed from a yin line to a yang line, changed the hexagram and indicated a direction in which the situation would tend to evolve. As Paul thumbed through the book, he heard a distant "Reeeeeeooooooo" from the orcas

that seemed to be lingering in the dark waters of Blackfish
Sound. Finding the new hexagram, number fifty-two, "Keeping
Still," he read:

> Keeping his back still
> So that he no longer feels his body.
> He goes into his courtyard
> and does not see his people.
> No blame.

The commentary added:

> When a man has become calm, he may turn to the outside world.
> He no longer sees in it the struggle and tumult of individual be-
> ings, and therefore he has that true peace of mind which is
> needed for understanding the great laws of the universe and for
> acting in harmony with them. Whoever acts from these deep
> levels makes no mistakes.

The orcas called out again, and Paul read the last verse:

> Mountains standing close together:
> The image of KEEPING STILL.
> Thus the superior man
> Does not permit his thoughts
> To go beyond his situation.

Paul closed his eyes and relaxed. He felt the cold floor, the
warm fire, the darkness, and he heard the haunting, compelling
calls coming from Blackfish Sound. He thought that he must be
listening to Nicola, Wavy, and others of A-pod. As he sat with
his eyes closed, only the hard floor reminded him that he
wasn't himself swimming below the choppy surface of Blackfish Sound, with the throbbing tide and currents massaging his
body. He noticed how sore his neck had become, aching from
tension and pent-up concern. The orcas, as they had done so
many times before, reminded him to carry his woes more
lightly. Paul curled up in a blanket and slept.

When he awoke, the fire was out, the air in the house was
cool, and the red light from the rising sun was just emblazing
the tops of the fir trees outside. Later, at noon, the sun had long
since disappeared back into the thin overcast of effervescent

white clouds that diffused the light, making even the deep reaches of the forest glow with a pulsating softness. This was real rain-coast light—no blinding glare and harsh shadows, but each leaf reflecting the same delicate, misty glow, as if the light were not in the sky but in the earth somewhere, and all the salal bushes and fir trees were lamps.

Paul chopped wood, carrying it in armloads into the kitchen. Between the sharp thwacks of the hatchet on wood, Paul heard the breathy exhalations of orcas wafting in the air among the trees. He walked out to the rock ledge to watch. The whales were far off, just entering the sound from Blackney Passage, on the far side near Parson Island. Straining, Paul thought that he could see Wavy and the rest of his group. There were other large bulls, A5 among them, so it looked like Nicola's entire extended family. Nicola, however, was not at the head of the pod, and Paul could not see her in the several groups that moved together, silently, swimming in the unison that so typified their meanderings.

Paddling out in the kayak, Paul and Yashi could still hear the velvety blow of their breaths carried on the southeast breeze as the whales came through Blackney Passage. That same wind, however, carried the sounds of the whales in front of them far away, up Blackfish Sound toward Queen Charlotte Strait. The whales themselves would soon be leaving through those same waters, before the blustery equinox turned to dank winter and the salmon left the inland seaways for their mysterious exploits along unchartable ocean depths.

In the silvery light, A5 was swimming by himself, off to the side, and Saddle, or A14, swam with a young calf. Saddle's other calf of earlier years had grown into a healthy teenager, its dorsal fin still too immature to distinguish it as a male or female. This young whale's fin had a distinctive shape, broad at the base and pointed at the tip, making it look something like a shark's fin. He, or she, was named Sharky.

The year-old calf nuzzled close to its mother, swimming at her pectoral fin. The young calf was maybe ten feet long and probably weighed four or five hundred pounds. It splashed and darted about with the same sort of youthful exuberance one would expect from a young kitten, puppy, bear cub, or human child. Other mature females swam nearby.

The calf, Paul knew, could still be nursing; it was probably gaining approximately twenty pounds a day on its mother's milk, on which it would feed for perhaps two years. When fully matured, in fifteen or twenty years, the young orca might weigh as much as eight or nine thousand pounds and would have grown into the most powerful predator in the ocean.

Paul and Yashi drifted, watching the orcas loll about in the middle of Blackfish Sound, diving and surfacing in little circles, no longer moving in one direction. "Nicola!" Paul exclaimed out loud when he saw her for the first time. Apparently having traveled near the end of the caravan, Nicola was swimming alone, closing the ranks as the family milled about, probably feeding on salmon. Nicola stayed aloof from the others and swam in a large circle to the Hanson Island side of the sound, so that Paul and Yashi were between her and the other orcas.

Not wanting to disturb the scene in any way, Paul just leaned back in the kayak and watched. Nicola would dive below the surface, then reappear either closer or farther away, to the right or to the left, in a seemingly random or at least undefinable pattern. The loud "Whoooosh! Uhhh" of the exhalations and inhalations sounded all around.

Looking about, Paul realized that Nicola had been out of sight for some time; he could not spot her anywhere as he surveyed the gray water. Then he caught a glimpse of movement just below the kayak, and he knew immediately that it was Nicola. The black and white body of the whale passed under the kayak on its side, with one eye staring straight up. The sleek body slowly disappeared from sight, then surfaced about ten meters from the kayak. The identity was certain: it was Nicola, come by for a close inspection.

Several times Nicola passed directly under the kayak, and Paul leaned over to get a better view. He felt no fear. Nicola certainly possessed the physical power to come up from below, smash his little kayak in two, and swallow him whole if she decided to, but Paul trusted her completely. Nicola, he sensed, was not an animal ruled by primal instincts of hunger and self-

protection—as, say, a great white shark might be. Nicola had a
mind that could preempt or control her actions; she was conscious of her environment and her relationships. Again, as
often before, Paul was impressed by the peacefulness of her
complete mastery over her awesome power.

The orcas were having a leisurely day, in no great hurry to
get anywhere, content to gobble salmon and splash in the water near Double Bay at the northwest end of Hanson Island.
Nicola mingled with the groups and was joined by several
young whales, perhaps giving their mothers a much-needed
break. Nicola, in her social role of family grandmother, moved
slowly into Weynton Passage to the west of the Plumper Islands, with three youngsters splashing beside her. One by one,
the other family groups followed, until all the whales were
moving nimbly around the outcroppings of rocks and through
the passage back to Johnstone Strait.

Paul and Yashi stayed near Nicola and the youngsters who
dove in unison alongside the kayak. Paul felt comfortable in his
growing knowledge of the whales. He was content to observe.
With each excursion the puzzle of their way of being revealed
itself by subtle increments. He felt there was a lot of teaching
going on with the young orcas. Mike Bigg had found that the
birth rate among the orcas was low, perhaps 4 or 5 percent per
year. The natural death rate seemed about the same, so the
overall population was virtually stable; certainly any population increases over the past few decades had been offset by
captures and rifle shots. The long gestation and weaning peri-
ods bespoke a delicately evolved creature. The orcas took
great care with each individual, keeping it healthy and teaching it the ways of the family and the style and traditions of its
social legacy.

Paul had long been fascinated by the nature of this social
continuity. He knew that Roger Payne's recordings of humpback whales revealed songs up to thirty minutes in length that
were taught to and repeated by other whales. The orcas of
Blackfish Sound, as well, seemed to share, at the very least,
common inflections or accents in their vocalizations. To call
these "songs" was perhaps something of a human projection,

but Dr. Payne's work and Paul's own experience led him to believe that a great deal of information was passed on to young whales, probably through both vocalizations and behavior modeling, by elders such as Nicola.

Floating with the tide in Johnstone Strait, Paul and Yashi saw the sun reappear at last below the clouds to the west, once again throwing its red light across the waters. Arriving at Blackney Passage, they turned north and paddled home, leaving Nicola and her clan to carry on toward Robson Bight.

On his next trip to Alert Bay, Paul phoned Bob Hunter, who told him that Australia had closed the Cheynes Beach Whaling Company and banned whaling in their territorial waters. The Australian inquiry, led by Sir Sydney Frost, had cited as a reason the "high intelligence potential" of whales. Australia was vital, and its attitude toward whales was turning favorable. If Australia changed its position at the IWC, the whole house of cards could come down and a new order might just coalesce around live whales rather than dead ones.

At the post office, Paul picked up his mail. Shuffling through the letters, he found a postcard from the Seychelles, from Sidney Holt. Paul stood in the street in front of the Alert Bay post office, read the card, and smiled broadly. "Ah," he thought, "maybe the great pendulum is swinging back."

8
Passages

Paul sat looking out the window of a Pan American Boeing jet airliner as it cruised at thirty thousand feet over the coastal range, having just lifted off from Seattle International Airport on its way to Washington, D.C., where Paul would attend a meeting with the world's leading cetacean experts, scientists, and researchers who had begun to fashion a new approach to studying whales. Sidney Holt, John Lilly, Roger Payne, and other cetologists would be gathering at the Smithsonian Institution for a special session of the International Whaling Commission's Scientific Committee, on "Ethics and Intelligence." Paul sipped a beer as he casually sat back for the ride; he had grown accustomed to these airplane jaunts and quite enjoyed the peaceful moments aloft. It occurred to him as he sat and pondered—watching Mount Baker, Mount Rainier, and Mount St. Helens pass below like pyramid ships in a white cloud sea —that he was not really anything more than an electrical blip himself, a single tiny piece of an idea passing through the neurons of the global brain. Or at least so it seemed as he sipped his beer and watched the scene below.

Paul had realized long ago, somewhere along the journey from meeting Skana to finding Hanson Island, becoming an international agent of espionage to meeting Nicola's family to struggling through the hard-knock lessons of global diplomacy, that he was not the only one who felt the way he did or had experienced the realizations that had come to him through his meetings with the whales. And the idea was bigger even than whales. Although Paul's interest in saving whales from human folly was inspired by compassion for the whales, he saw that the whales had, in fact, come to symbolize a new way of thinking, a new way for human beings to feel connected to their planet.

It wasn't just the "ecology movement," either, although that was part of it as well. But the elusive idea around which Paul turned his thoughts had something to do with the end of human loneliness, the human passage through some great barrier of thought that had kept the human family isolated from the full richness of the life blossoming all around. The late Congressman Ryan had asked specifically that Paul speak on the "intrinsic value of a whale." That phrase had often since echoed in his thoughts and was a large part of the puzzle with which Paul played as he passed over the Rocky Mountains.

If the amorphous philosophical questions were still defying precise articulation, the political questions were becoming ever more crystallized. While Paul had retreated to the sanctuary of Hanson Island, the "Whale War," as the newspapers were calling it, raged on. During the previous summer, former Greenpeace member Paul Watson, who had struck out on his own with more heavy-handed tactics than Greenpeace employed, had put the pirate whaling ship *Sierra* out of business by ramming it on the high seas with a concrete-reinforced, steel-hulled sub chaser called the *Sea Shepherd*. The impact was crippling to the illicit whalers, staving in the *Sierra*'s rusting hull and exposing its tonnage of clandestine whale meat to the world media. Although Paul Watson's less-than-peaceful tactics received mixed reviews within the "nonviolent" whale movement, they had completely and permanently stilled the outlaw whaling vessel and painfully embarrassed Japan, South Africa, and the Norwegian Forretningsbanken, who were silent partners in the operation. Watson's bravado had spread a sense of urgency through both the pro-whale movement and the whaling industry.

Gazing out the window, Paul fingered the postcard he had stuffed in his jacket pocket shortly before leaving. He pulled the card out and read it again; it was from Sidney Holt. Dr. Holt was as close as anyone could come to being the human encyclopedia of cetology. The overtly political, embarrassingly unscientific charade taking place in the Scientific Committee had at times driven him to despair over the possible uselessness of the IWC, though he had, as they say, hung in. Dr. Holt, however, had seen the light long enough to realize that there had to be a political, rather than simply a scientific, solution. He had encouraged Jean-Paul Fortom-Gouin in petitioning various governments to join the commission, selling them on the idea that self-interested commercialism was perpetrating an ecological holocaust and threatening their common heritage, the sea. During the previous year, Paul had attended a meeting with Dr. Holt in Mexico, sponsored by the International Union for the Conservation of Nature, to discuss the development of cetacean sanctuaries. The gathering had produced funding for a santuary in the gray-whale breeding grounds of Baja, Mexico, and Holt had introduced a plan to make the entire Indian Ocean a whale sanctuary. Paul had proposed that an orca sanctuary be established in Washington, British Columbia, and Alaska.

The postcard that Paul held had arrived from Victoria, in the island nation of the Seychelles. Victoria was on the island of Mahé, largest of the five tiny peaks of the Seychelles-Mauritius undersea ridge piercing through the surface of the Indian Ocean nine hundred miles off the east coast of Africa, between Madagascar and the Arabian Sea. The card read:

> The Seychelles have joined IWC & will put on agenda (a) Sanctuary in whole Indian Ocean (b) Moratorium on Sperm whaling. Supporting other conservation positions. You will be one of two scientific advisers (I am other). This is serious—O.K.? Your fare to

U.K. & expenses will be paid. You'll hear from Lyall Watson. This
is a *great* day.

Love to you,
Sidney

At the next IWC meeting, Paul would have official government status to offer his opinion at the Scientific Committee
meetings, and he would be able, through the Seychelles delegate, to participate in the plenary sessions. More important, the
whales would have another vote in their favor. Several more
votes, actually. The nations of St. Lucia and Jamaica, as well as
Oman and India, had also joined the commission. The pendulum, indeed, was swinging back. Even a Soviet scientist, Dr.
A. A. Gerzin, had been quoted in the press as having said, "The
sperm whale brain structure is such that this can be said to be
a thinking animal capable of displaying high intellectual abilities." Jean-Paul was ever more hopeful that the coming summer
would mark the end of modern whaling.

Whether it was wishful thinking or an accurate reading of
the political winds, Paul, too, felt they just might be on the
verge of a great victory—and not merely a political victory, but
a victory over the outdated human chauvinism that, at the root
of the problem, allowed human governments to treat all of nature as a bottomless pit of resources to be plundered at will. If
the whales could be saved, then Paul could turn his full attention to his lab and the orcas of Blackfish Sound.

Through the magnanimous generosity of an enthusiastic
whale-lover, Paul had at last been able to make some far-
reaching improvements on Hanson Island. He had commissioned some carpenter friends to rebuild the physical struc-
tures. The new lab was built on the rocks overlooking Blackney
Passage, and a new house was built on the old, original site. He
had begun to experiment with remote monitoring of whales,
placing hydrophones at various underwater locations around
the area, transmitting by radio and microwave to the lab.
Paul's library of orca recordings grew, and the photographs he
had collected from Michael Bigg identified almost every whale
in the local pods.

John Ford had already begun his study of orca vocalizations, and in the first two years had amassed some interesting data on the existence of dialects among the various orca pods in both the southern and northern orca communities. Through analysis of the sound waves, Ford had determined that dialects did, in fact, exist. He noted that pods had unique calls, unique vocalization formats, and unique intonations or accents. Paul was encouraged that so much attention and comprehensive work was being centered on the free orca. In the last frantic political years, he had not been able to accomplish all the research goals he had once set for himself. He had little choice; his life was hurtling forward as if slung from a catapult. His fate was not so much sealed as soaring to meet him.

Flying east, Paul watched the sun disappear quickly behind him as if in a time-lapse movie, then watched the stars twinkle on until the entire sky was alight. The waxing moon rose, capping the celestial light show. The thoughts that occupied Paul's mind, as he flew through the darkness toward Washington, D.C., turned from politics and science to his personal life.

During the last few years, Paul and Linda had drifted into two disparate lives, primarily because of Paul's hectic pace. Fortunately for both of them, each had found new love. Linda still managed the Pacific Killer Whale *(Orcinus orca)* Foundation, and was working with Paul to gather the best orca recordings into a long-playing record album to be called *Songs and Sounds of Orcinus Orca.* Yashi—a quick-witted, quick-tongued twelve-year-old with the demeanor of a glib college professor and a debating tenacity to match anyone's—spent his school year in Vancouver with Linda and most of the summers on Hanson Island. Linda had fallen in love with Bill Gannon, an accountant who had played a major role in extricating Greenpeace from its early financial debt.

Paul, for his part, had become involved in several new relationships. He now had a new daughter, Milora, born to Norma Rejall at the end of the previous year. A second daughter, Anna, was soon to be born. Anna's mother, Helena Symonds, had moved to Hanson Island with Paul. Paul and Helena had worked together organizing the vast files of information and data. Tapes, books, papers, IWC reports, scientific journals, slides, films, and photographs were retrieved from boxes and filed in a new wing of the house on Hanson Island. The Hanson Island outpost was being transformed from a summer observation camp into a year-round laboratory, office, and home.

Through all his affairs of the heart, Paul had not emerged unscathed. But as the great Boeing jet screeched on the tarmac across the river from Washington, D.C., he was feeling almost blissful. He had had some time to deepen his relationship with Yashi, and he and Linda had an amiable working friendship, based on mutual respect and compassion. Nicola and the other whales kept returning year after year, the Hanson Island outpost was in its best condition ever, great forces were rolling like a tidal wave against the whaling industry, and Paul was in love.

The only blot on this pleasant mental tableau was the stabbing memory of his last visit with Skana. Her condition troubled and saddened him, and his helplessness was frustrating. For years he had been hatching a plot in his mind to free her. Now it seemed almost real. The plot had a glistening simplicity about it. Through a friend in the movie industry, Paul had arranged to get a feature-film script written that involved the fictional freeing of a whale by means of a helicopter, with a sling to lift the whale from its pool. The plan was to convince the Vancouver Aquarium to allow them to film the scene of the whale's release at the aquarium pool, using Skana as the whale. Then, during the filming, rather than return Skana to the pool, they would take her to a holding facility in Georgia Strait, eventually releasing her back to her family. The screenplay had already been written, and the producer was raising money for the shooting to begin. As farfetched, impossible, and illegal as the plot was, it was Paul's only hope for Skana.

And as the plane rumbled to a stop at the gate, the thought went through Paul's mind, "Well, Skana, this could be it. I don't think you'll last much longer." He was soon lost in the shuffle of humanity inside National Airport.

Paul sat down at his designated spot at the oak meeting table in the Smithsonian Institution and quietly set his notebook before him, writing the date: 4-28-80. Paul always took detailed notes, and for this meeting he had been asked by Sidney Holt to be one of the official rapporteurs. He looked up and around the room. He smiled at his comrade, Jean-Paul, whose round face was beaming with its bronze glow as he jotted notes, looking elegant as usual in his fine cotton suit and silk tie. Sidney Holt, with his sagelike white beard, his flowing white hair, and deep-set eyes that betrayed a busy mind, sat at the head of the table talking with John Lilly and Lyall Watson. The other scientist-delegates included IWC secretary Raymond Gambell, Puget Sound orca researcher Kenneth Balcomb, dolphin researcher Karen Pryor, Masaharu Nishiwaki from Japan, Roger Payne, and others whom Paul had never before seen. They all shared an interest in the biological sciences, particularly cetology—the neurophysiology, the sociology, the encephalology of whales—and with at least a passing interest in whether or not whales were intelligent beings. Whether or not any one of the scientists present could define intelligence was a question that perched in several, if not all, of their minds.

First to broach the subject was Professor Harry J. Jerison, who presented an evolutionary history of the brain, beginning four hundred million years ago with early vertebrate species. Sharks, which ironically now have the reputation of being dumb, were the earliest vertebrates to evolve what science now calls a "big brain," a brain that had developed some "silent" or "associational" areas that did more than register input and issue a reaction—a brain that, to some degree, mixed information together and analyzed it. As fish and then mammal brains evolved, the associational area grew ever larger: Intelligence had survival value. In cetaceans and primates the associational area of the brain, the cerebral cortex, has reached its most complex stage.

The human brain, Dr. Jerison explained, has grown in size from 450 cc five million years ago to 700 cc a million years ago, to just over 1,500 cc today, the biggest growth spurt taking place over the last two hundred thousand years. River dolphins had a 700-cc brain thirty million years ago, long before humans existed, and the largest sperm-whale brains today measure 9,000 cc, six times the size of a human brain. Although size of brain and what can be called intelligent behavior are unquestionably linked, brain size alone, Dr. Jerison pointed out, was certainly no absolute measure of intelligence.

The whales, however, were the only animals with a brain physiology comparable to that of humans. Dr. Jerison pointed out that there are ten billion neurons in the human cerebral cortex, and thirty billion in the larger whales'. "We can assume," he told his colleagues, "that unusual mental processes occur in whales. The volume of the brain reflects the amount of information it can handle, the information-processing capacity. Many species of whales, in this regard, can match humans. What they are doing with it, with this capacity, we don't know, but to propose that they're doing nothing with it is a stupid conjecture."

Roger Payne likened whaling to slavery, once acceptable in many so-called civilized countries. "The moral justification for slavery and other forms of human oppression has often been that the slave was 'not equal,' a being of 'lower' status," Payne went on. "That same mistake is being made with whales today. Modern whaling may be the lowest point to which our species has ever sunk. Like the conquistadores, who completely destroyed incredible civilizations, so modern whaling, having found the magnificent whales to be easily killed and sold, has destroyed the culture of the whales." In defense of his use of the word "culture" with respect to whales, Dr. Payne presented some of his data regarding humpback whale vocalizations: the length of the songs being often over thirty minutes, several whales singing exactly the same song, the introduction of new songs each year, the whales breathing at the same point in the song like well-trained choir singers, remembering entire complex strings of sounds from one year to the next, and the transference of songs between groups on either side of the Atlantic Ocean.

Dr. Payne had broken the songs down into six parts for detailed analysis: the original song, themes, phrases, subphrases, units, and subunits. Through spectral analysis, he had been able to glimpse the wonderful precision with which the humpbacks performed their arias of the ocean. These songs were far more complex, varied, and mindfully performed than the songs of any other animal, comparable if not superior to anything humans could achieve. "The songs alone," Dr. Payne concluded, "suggest advanced mental treatment of the material."

In an abrupt change of pace, Mr. Ryu Kiyomiya from Japan warned against the "dangers in excessive animal-protection activities. It is beyond my comprehension," he went on, "why an ethic of this kind has to be discussed. Every race has its own habits, creeds, religions that are the basis for their culture. Our concepts of ethics and justice differ, and it is impossible to establish a standard throughout the world."

Paul shuddered to hear this. Even at this ostensibly lofty scientific inquiry, the Japanese had sent someone whose job it was, apparently, to uphold the rights of whalers to the bitter end. Sidney Holt answered Mr. Kiyomiya as if taking the thoughts right out of Paul's mind. "Our first task is that we have some bridge-building to do," he said, speaking measuredly and softly, yet with authority. "We have a problem of prejudice. The so-called objectivity of scientists is a myth. We try to pretend that ethical views, moral principles, don't play a part in our interpretation of data, but this is not so. We have perhaps some power to overcome our biases, but it is by no means infallible. I believe, rather, that we should clearly state our biases, our philosophies, declare our views. The purpose of this body is precisely to search for a global ethic; that is why we are here. I will be glad to state my own view: I accept self-awareness of some animals, and certainly among cetaceans. This is another bridge to build, a bridge between species, or more likely a window into the consciousness of other species. We cannot say for certain that a given species of whale is 'rational,' but we cannot say with our current knowledge that it is irrational, either.

"Continued commercial whaling," Dr. Holt went on, "under the present management system of the IWC is unethical on two grounds. Firstly, the scientific advice given to the IWC is formulated through a process that is itself corrupt. Results of the scientific process have only been reported in an incomplete and misleading way. I have noticed that we always get, from the scientists of whaling nations, a higher population estimate than from anyone else. I can't help but notice this bias. And the IWC has been unable to devise an observer scheme to objectively monitor whaling practices. No one can dispute that whale stocks have steadily gone down; there is no substainable yield-management system in place to assure future generations the same abundance that we enjoy today. As a result, purely from the point of view of managing the stocks responsibly, modern whaling is unethical.

"Secondly, if the whales possess the intelligence and mental properties that we assume, then whales have a culture. By continuing with current whaling practices, we are denying the future possibility to discover and understand the culture of the whales. I consider it a great evil to destroy something that we don't understand."

The battle lines, of course, were no different than they had ever been, but Paul was pleased that the discussion among whale scientists had matured beyond calculating population dynamics and guessing how many whales could be killed without driving them to extinction.

The debate carried on for several days. British author and scientific anecdotist Lyall Watson chaired the meeting, adroitly keeping the adversaries from each other's necks. "The root of the marine problem," he said with a grin, "is the unchecked fertility of the human species."

Paul watched all this with a certain detachment and wistfulness. He could see the dividing lines as clearly as if each delegate had worn a team uniform. There were those who unabashedly regarded the whale as a harvestable resource for the taking. There were those to whom the whale was an abstruse object of curiosity that science could probe with its investigatory finger. And there were those who could intellectually and emotionally entertain the notion that whales, and perhaps other animals, perhaps all living creatures, were more complicated, more intelligent, more self-aware than human science had yet supposed. These scientists could, in short, accept the presence of a nonhuman intelligence sharing the planet with them. Scientific knowledge by no means precluded the existence of this intellect, and all the emerging data about cetaceans was leading many scientists to that conclusion. The hypothesis—that our relationship with cetaceans might, therefore, be social, interspecies, interactive, and mutual—was being advanced with all seriousness. Such a hypothesis, if true, did preclude wholesale slaughter of whales, so something had to give.

This would not be the first time that a new idea was bad for business, or that a new truth demanded a radical shift in the popular human belief system. Humans, the paragon, the avatar on earth of God's great knowledge, the Chosen Species, the ones with "higher consciousness," just might not be alone on their lofty plane. Such an idea had a certain charm. And it had a certain inevitable ring to it as well, as when Copernicus announced that the earth was not the center of the universe around which everything turned.

Paul thought back about the people he had known or met in the last few years. Linda somehow knew all along, never doubted, and didn't even think it strange that Skana and Tung Jen were intelligent beings. Bob Hunter, Michael Berry, Mel Gregory, Joan McIntyre, Farley Mowat, Paul Horn—they all knew, they never doubted it. More recently, Jean-Paul, Sidney Holt, Roger Payne, Paul Winter, Helena—they all saw it. There were millions. Just as no one could deny that the hypothesis had been raised, no one could fail to see that a groundswell of popular and professional opinion had already accepted it as an obvious truth.

Paul's own comments to this body, "Reflections from an Orca Eye," amounted to a tracing of the intellectual steps that had led him to his own frame of mind on the question: his work with Skana, her "spontaneous reversal," his recordings of orca vocalizations since 1968, his meetings with Nicola and her clan, and his evolving appreciation of cetacean intelligence based on his observations of the orcas' own social interactions. "Despite the attraction of working with captives," Paul said, "we must study whales in their natural habitat if we wish to fully understand them. To my mind, the key to orca existence is the social group, its stability, interdependence, and efficient utilization of pooled energies over generations of family continuity. A picture emerges of some sort of social organization akin to a tribal system in which several pods harmoniously share an ocean space. The lesson for human civilization is all too obvious."

In the Netherlands, on an earlier trip, Paul had observed a dolphin that had been taught to retrieve rings from its pool while blindfolded, using its echolocation system. The keeper told Paul that when they recorded the dolphin's echolocation, the dolphin let out just *one* echolocation click, and then efficiently retrieved all five rings. Paul had also heard single trains of echolocation clicks used by the Blackfish Sound orcas. A single train of clicks could apparently serve the entire pod, locating for each individual all the objects being scanned. Paul had also observed this "single-source" group readout system with the captured whales at Pender Harbor in 1968. And from his observations of orcas feeding, he had speculated that they also used echolocation bursts to stun fish prey.

As Paul recounted these observations, he pointed out that the ability of cetaceans to share information was not only efficient but "sophisticated, requiring not only considerable acoustic skills, but also self—and group—awareness." Paul elaborated on group salmon fishing and synchronized breathing among orcas, and he ended by emphasizing the paramount feature of their social organization: their ability to coexist peacefully. "The inference is clear," he concluded. "The whales are perfectly capable of managing themselves, and I suggest that the IWC decides to let them do just that."

John Lilly presented a taunting and creative twist to the debate. Lilly had begun research on dolphin brains in 1954, a classical scientific investigation that involved making cross-section viewing slides of the brain tissue of *Tursiops truncatus*, the Atlantic bottlenose dolphin. The *Tursiops* brains that Lilly worked with were just slightly larger than the largest human brain. What had impressed Lilly, however, was not so much the size as the complexity of the cetacean brain, the number of "gyri" and "sulci" on its surface—that is, the "tremendously packed folding of this large brain within its case."

So impressed was Lilly with the neurophysiology of the *Tursiops* brain that he decided to experiment with live dolphins rather than dead tissue. Planting electrodes into "pleasure" regions and "distress" regions of their brains, Lilly was able to apply direct positive or negative electrical reinforcement in an experiment designed to teach the dolphins to make humanoid sounds. The experiment proved successful, and the dolphins Lizzie and Elvar did make sounds in air that mimicked human language. In 1961, Dr. Lilly had predicted that humans and cetaceans would one day communicate intelligible information across the boundary of species. Most observers at that time had laughed at his conjecture, and few scientists took him seriously. But it was neither the ability of the dolphins to mimic human speech nor mere brain physiology in itself that became the primary object of Lilly's scientific attention. What Lilly noticed was more profound than the fact that one species could mimic another, and more startling than the impressive brain.

In the first place, Lilly discovered that dolphins never go to sleep with their whole brain, but rest only half the brain at a time. The reason for this, and the reason he discovered it, is that dolphins, and all cetaceans, have to remain conscious to breathe. A dolphin that goes to sleep fully drowns, as Lilly sadly discovered when he first tried to sedate a dolphin in order to implant electrodes in its brain. He later had to use a respirator in order to perform the operation.

Secondly, Lilly observed that "in spite of negative stimuli, the dolphins would not become angry: They controlled their anger. I realized that this large brain, like man's, could control the built-in instinctive patterns of reaction to pain, which in other animals can lead to aggressive or frightened actions." All this led Dr. Lilly to his first awakening insight about cetaceans. Lilly located the breath-control area of the brain in the thalamus—that is, cetacean breathing is under cerebral control, unlike that of humans and other land mammals, for whom breathing is an instinctual motor function that can operate even in sleep. The cetaceans, with their huge brains, Lilly hypothesized, had learned first to control their breath, and then "the huge cerebral cortex could exert direct inhibitory influences, from higher-level thinking processes, on their expression of emotion."

Lilly told the group of scientists, "The fact that cetacean respiration is controlled at a higher level than in land mammals means that all cetaceans within a community are interdependent twenty-four hours a day, for their whole life. If a dolphin is injured or sinks for any reason, the others have to bring it to the surface to breathe, or it will die." In essence, what Dr. Lilly was saying was that in the world of whales and dolphins, no one can "space out," even for a few moments. All members of the group are constantly aware and conscious of each other lest one of them should need help. Babies must be immediately taught how to breathe, and from that moment on, until the day it dies, each cetacean individual breathes as part of a conscious social group. Long before Marx or Keynes or Fritz Perls, whales were addressing the issues of group and social interaction.

The mental boon that the whales received because of this quirk of evolutionary fate was an acute power of control over their emotions and behavior, a process that began some thirty million years before primates walked. "This impressive control and total interdependence means an awareness of dependence among members of a species," added Lilly. "This leads to social relationships that are hard for humans to appreciate. We'd be nervous wrecks if forced into that sort of situation."

Most of the scientists in the room were at least passingly familiar with Lilly's research, and to them these comments were not so much new as simply placed into a newer, more filled-out context of emerging ideas. The real twist that Lilly offered was what he called his "basic conclusion." Dr. Lilly is an intense man, lithe, almost frail-looking, but with a face drawn taut by decades of personal intellectual struggle, having been shunned by scientists, ignored, ridiculed, attacked, and slandered. Recently, as a wave of data had begun to point in the direction of Lilly's theories, a growing respect was being shown him, but at times he looked like a man too weary or uninterested in respect to acknowledge the admiration with much more than a roguish grin. Lilly spoke slowly, as if thinking of each word for the first time. His smile seemed to betray an absolute confidence.

"When discussing intelligence," Lilly said, "we must be careful not to look on intelligence as an absolute characteristic of the individual in isolation. We must look at intelligence in a new way, as interindividual. When we attempt to measure intelligence that is nonhuman, we should be aware that we are measuring something that is shared, both among the members of the other species—say, dolphins—that we are investigating, and also shared between the dolphin, say, and the human who is doing the measuring. We are measuring an *inter*action."

Lilly's remark struck a resonant chord in Paul's mind. Yes, Paul thought, that was what he had learned from Skana. In the future, the crucial research with cetaceans would not be done with scalpels and dissecting tables, not with probes, electrodes, or the myriad spinning dials of the modern high-tech biological laboratory. In the future, work with cetaceans would become more *interactive*, reflecting evolving relationships between whale and human, participatory observation, an equal meeting of minds. And part of this change in attitude would be a recognition that we are investigating free beings who have a right to life without being captured, brutalized, or harassed.

Paul sat at his dining-room table looking out through the new floor-to-ceiling windows that swung in an arc around the living room, watching the lone great blue heron that lived in the cove in front of his Hanson Island home. It was late summer 1980, and things had changed around Hanson Island. Helena had given birth to Anna, and she and Paul were busy serving the needs of their charming infant.

As Paul stared out of the window, he held Anna in his arms. Helena was napping upstairs in the loft-bedroom that overlooked Blackney Pass. Somewhere outside Paul could hear the guitar and singing of Mel Gregory, the mystic whale-saver who, to that day, still maintained that his following the moon and the rainbows had been the secret weapon through which the Russian whalers had been found, back in 1975. Mel's lack of practicality, not to mention his abhorrence of the work ethic, was offset by his personal charm and delightful music. Among his claims to fame was his unmatched skill for mimicking whale and birdcalls; Mel was something of a walking, breathing synthesizer who could reproduce the calls of ravens, wolves, or orcas with equally adroit fluency. In his jesterlike way, Mel made things happen.

Paul heard the deep hum of an airplane engine and then saw a single-engine Beaver floatplane circle over Blackfish Sound and land outside his bay. Paul knew it would be Jim Nollman, musician and interspecies-communication researcher from California, who was flying up with a camera crew from the American television program, "Those Amazing Animals." Jim had called ahead, wanting to find orcas with whom he could perform his interspecies-communication experiments for the television cameras.

Paul went out to meet the floatplane, picking up Jim and the crew in the inflatable. Back on shore they talked briefly, Jim explaining how he used electronic instruments to improvise sounds with animals. "I've talked with wolves, dolphins, humpback whales, tapirs, even frogs and turkeys."

"Turkeys!" Paul laughed. "Hey, I've been talking to turkeys for years! Come on in."

Inside, Jim explained his project to find free orcas, to set up his sound system—floating drums, chimes, and an electric guitar played through underwater speakers—and to entice the whales into a vocal exchange. Paul outlined the organization of the local pods, and suggested where Jim might find whales, pointing out the spots on a chart.

"Find a quiet place out of the way. Play and wait; they'll come. But you're welcome to stay here until you find your spot."

Mel entered, pointing outside. "Hey, you guys, check this out." He waved them over to the window. "See those ravens? They're trying to trick Victor out of his food." Paul and Jim looked outside, where Victor the dog was being lured away from his food dish by two ravens. While Victor barked at the taunting ravens, who sat on a low branch squawking at the dog, two other ravens swooped down to gobble the food from Victor's dish. "Check *that* out," Mel repeated. "Those ravens have their act together."

"What are they saying, Mel?" Jim asked.

"They're saying, 'Quick, some of you guys go in the back door while all those idiots are looking out the window.' " Mel's laughter echoed from the pole beams of the ceiling. "Cawww! Cawww!" Mel shrieked, the ravens by the dog dish on the porch took off, and Victor, noticing, came running back to guard his plate, too late to save his supper or catch the ravens, who all flew off together in triumph. "See!" said Mel. "Even the ravens communicate. Everything communicates. I'm surprised at Victor, though—he shouldn't let himself get sucked in like that."

The late summer on Hanson Island was busy with a wide variety of projects. Some friends from Oregon built a solar greenhouse at one end of the lab. Paul, as was his custom, assigned visitors chores such as carrying and chopping firewood. Mel hung bells from a gray-whale bone that he had carried all the way from Magdalena Bay in Baja. Jim Nollman found a remote spot for his experiments, returning later with tapes that had captured a midnight session during which a pod of orcas had investigated his ethereal sounds and had responded with vocalizations that led Jim to believe the orcas were curious and interested in the sounds.

Paul continued his remote recording experiments, moving hydrophones around to various spots among the island waterways. He was helped in this by John Gale, an electronics expert who worked in the movie industry in Los Angeles, Mickey Hoolihan, a recording engineer from Colorado, Mike Sofen, a systems designer from Washington State, and by Bill ter Bruge, an amateur radio buff from Alert Bay. The remote systems enabled Paul to monitor the whales without leaving his lab, a technique that kept harassment of the whales to zero. Whenever orca vocalizations were heard, day or night, Paul would record them and note their location, their direction of travel, weather and tide conditions, and anything else that seemed relevant at the time. Paul knew that eventually his massive accumulation of raw data would prove invaluable. Once the analytical problems had been solved and it was possible to identify, for example, which individuals and pods were on the tapes, he would be able to say with some assurance what had been happening with the orcas of Blackfish Sound during all the years he had been observing them. Paul's evolving philosophy increasingly emphasized learning about the whales without interfering with their life. To be consistent, but also in reaction to the growing number of people paddling about in kayaks and zooming around in Zodiacs, Paul largely curtailed his excursions with the whales. It was an approach that demanded patience.

Where all this would lead, Paul did not know. He was primarily interested in observing the orca social structure; he was in for the long haul. He was fascinated by the vocalizations and by the interchanges, but his pace was unhurried. He felt more confidence than ever before. His objective had become one of building the Hanson Island lab into a steady-state base for monitoring the orcas of the area year-round and across generations.

The large male orca that Paul had named Wavy, and who had been the usual companion of Nicola, had not been seen all summer and was presumed dead. In earlier years, Paul had thought that Wavy was Nicola's mate, but Michael Bigg had suggested that Wavy was probably Nicola's son. The males, it seemed, remained in their mother's group throughout their lives. Wavy, in any event, was gone.

As the summer ended, precisely at the equinox, a new calf was born to the A4 pod in shallow water in Johnstone Strait near Blackney Passage. The birth was witnessed by reporters and photographers from the two major daily newspapers in Vancouver. The media had been on a tour arranged by Jim Borrowman, a local whale enthusiast who had launched a campaign to have Robson Bight set aside as a provincial whale sanctuary. It was the first time an orca birth had been observed in the wild, and the photographs made the front pages in Van-

couver the next day. It was a good start to the Robson Bight
Sanctuary campaign, an effort that would eventually succeed.

Paul continued plotting to free Skana, but in September 1980
his worst fears were confirmed. The movie deal was bogged
down in financial negotiations, and Skana—according to
friends in Vancouver—looked pitiful. Skana became somewhat
lethargic during the fall of 1980. On September 18, she was not
able to finish her public show, stopping, atypically, halfway
through the routine of tricks. It was determined that she had
contracted a vaginal infection. Aquarium staff took daily blood
samples and bacterial cultures and treated the infection with
antibiotics and antiseptics. Her food consumption, usually 140
pounds of herring a day, dropped steadily, and she quit eating
altogether on September 28. By the evening of October 4, as the
aquarium staff left for the day, Skana could do little more than
float in catatonic listlessness. A single staff member stayed
with her through the night, but at 8:20 A.M., without a call, without a single sound, Skana sank to the bottom of her pool and
died.

Skana was eighteen when she died, and for thirteen of those
years she had been in human-contrived bondage. She was still
a young whale, not yet middle-aged. Skana was one of the few
who survived more than a few years in captivity, yet she lived
nothing comparable to a full life. Paul was not the only
mourner, to be sure, but he was as sad as if a member of his
own family had passed away. He regretted that he had not
been able to carry through with his plan to release her, and
that he had not been closer to her in her last years, but he was
glad about one thing: Skana was free at last.

In the hope that the summer 1981 IWC meeting would be the
meeting that ended whaling, Bob Hunter joined Paul and the
others in Brighton, England, hiring himself out to the anti-whaling factions as a public-relations consultant and trying to keep
media pressure on the delegates. Paul, though he had not been
appointed to the Seychelles delegation as expected, was none-
theless hopeful for a positive result. The political card game
stacked up like this: There were twenty-seven countries voting

(Jamaica, Oman, St. Lucia, Seychelles, India, and Switzerland had recently joined). It was expected that Japan, the Soviet Union, Norway, Korea, Iceland, and Chile would vote in a solid bloc in favor of the whalers' interests. The moratorium supporters needed all twenty-one of the remaining votes to score the required 75 percent.

Australia, in a complete turnaround from previous years, was proposing a worldwide *ban* on all whaling. Jean-Paul was extremely pleased about this change, hoping that Australia would become the keystone in a new ecological awareness at the IWC. Furthermore, the United States and Britain were back on the whale-saving side, but suggesting a compromise moratorium on selected species. In any case, these three countries, the six new countries, and France, Mexico, the Netherlands, Argentina, Sweden, and Denmark all supported the ban. New Zealand, Brazil, Uruguay, South Africa, and Spain were the mystery votes, the swing votes, and their delegates were served many a cocktail by one and the other side. Paul, Jean-Paul, and Bob were among the lobbyists.

The Japanese delegation threw an unexpected twist into the contest by announcing, a few days before the vote, that Japan acknowleged "no legal or moral obligation to subscribe to a total moratorium should it be carried by vote." Notwithstanding Japan's hint that they would not abide, the day the vote came to the floor was electric with anticipation. All the expected pro and con votes were cast as predicted. Brazil, Uruguay, and South Africa abstained, leaving Spain and New Zealand to settle the question. New Zealand voted for the moratorium, but Spain voted against, so the final tally was sixteen "yes" votes, eight "no" votes, and three abstentions; the proposed moratorium, with 67 percent of the vote, was just short of the three-quarters majority needed.

"Next year" seemed like a whole universe away to Paul's tired mind. He and Bob and Jean-Paul shared a consolatory beer at a quiet pub. After half an hour, Paul was able to laugh at Jean-Paul's childlike indomitability.

"Hey, *amigos,*" the Frenchman said in his best Spaniard caricaturization, "we almost got 'em, eh?"

"Sure, mate." Paul laughed. "They're running scared now, Jean-Paul."

"Shakin' in their silk suits!" chimed in Bob. "Listen, you guys, sometimes I have the feeling that the world isn't going to blow up in a nuclear explosion, it's going to whimper away into a two-thousand-year ecological dark age. In a hundred years they're going to have little bonsai groves in the lobbies of the multinational monoliths to remind them of the forests. We'll be telling our grandchildren, 'No, really, little things used to fly all over the place. They were called birds.' "

"Hey, Hunter." Jean-Paul pounded the table, "You're too burned out. People all over the world are seeing the light."

"Well, you know what they say about politicians," said Bob. "They don't see the light until they feel the heat. I think we should fund Paul Watson to ram 'em all. What are we going to say to our children? 'Oh, sorry, well, you know, uh, we were nonviolent.' Of course then at other times I figure that maybe there is some Almighty hand at work. Who knows, maybe this planet *is* destined for greatness. Maybe the bodhisattvas are going to come down from the Buddha realms and lead us to the incomparable clear light of wisdom."

"Maybe the whales are the bodhisattvas," said Jean-Paul quietly.

"Seriously, mates," said Paul, "I think we've run this one about as far as we can. It's time to change the anti-whaling movement to a pro-whale movement. I think we should start talking about *live* whales, not dead ones. Be realistic. We may never win this political battle. Maybe we've already lost. The whalers are laughing; they have us completely sucked into their game, counting whales, spending two days debating the life span of a bloody sperm whale! It's idiocy. Mortality rates, birth rates, migration patterns, snooping into their breeding habits, liver biopsies: I'm *sick* of it!" Paul's voice had risen steadily, and when he blurted out *"sick* of it!" heads in the pub turned.

"Oh, excuse me, mates," said Paul, looking around, grinning. "Excuse me, I got a little excited. Cheers." Paul held up his glass, and the pub patrons raised their glasses just the tiniest bit in response, and Paul turned back to his friends, nodding, still smiling. "Eh?" Paul whispered, raising his glass. "Here's to humanoid science in the bloody dark ages! Here's to working with beings that are alive and free."

Bob and Jean-Paul raised their glasses, the sorrow-drowning debacle having only just begun.

Back on Hanson Island, Paul was glad to return to the routines of life on the edge of forest and ocean, and with the whales and his family. Yashi came for his usual summer visit, and then Milora arrived, too. Paul was especially happy to have all three of his children with him. He quickly learned how to carry the two girls around together, one in a backpack, the other in a Snugli, and loved to take them on walks through the woods, playing his flute. As the summer days passed, Paul began to feel hopeful again. "It's just a matter of time," he told Helena. "If Japan changes, the world will follow."

In mid-August, two Japanese visitors arrived. One was a photographer, Mitsuaki Iwago, and the other a writer and editor, Ken Takahashi. Paul had met Takahashi in Japan in 1974, when he had been the editor of the wildlife magazine *Anima*. Takahashi was a small, intense man with a quick, perceptive mind. He explained to Paul that he wanted to make a feature film about orcas and had come to Hanson Island because he needed to know if the film could realistically be made. Years earlier, he had written a story about a fox that had altered the attitude of people toward foxes so dramatically that their status had changed from vermin to protected species. Now he believed the same sort of thing could be done for whales. Paul was electrified by the elegant simplicity of the vision and promised to do anything he could to help. "This could be it," he said to Helena, "the key to Japan. If the Japanese take hold of an idea, there's no stopping them. And the beauty of it is, this is a Japanese idea."

In order to write his story and sell the idea, Takahashi needed to know if it was possible to be in a boat in close proximity to a group of orcas that floated quietly at the surface of the water for some time. Paul said he thought it would be possible, if the crew were patient enough.

Late one afternoon, Paul and Helena and the two girls were returning from a trip to Alert Bay in their sixteen-foot fiberglass speedboat. As they entered Blackney Passage from Johnstone Strait, they saw the misty blows and black fins of a group of orcas in the distance directly in front of OrcaLab traveling slowly toward them from Blackfish Sound. They quickly sped into the shore to pick up Yashi and Ken Takahashi, who were watching from the lab deck. Making a wide circuit, they returned to a position in front of the whales, who had paused to play in a kelp bed at the corner of Hanson Island. Paul cut the engine and drifted, setting about putting together his equipment, camera, a hydrophone and video recorder. He had his back to the whales and was explaining to Yashi how the system worked when he heard an urgent "Sshhh!" behind him. He looked, to see Takahashi gesturing for quiet. The boat was drifting toward the whales, more than ten of them, and they were now only fifty meters away. Paul stopped trying to get the equipment working and watched spellbound as a fan-shaped group of five whales swam quietly and continuously at the surface toward them. Takahashi leaned over the side, intent. The whales paused, just a few meters away. The silence rolled on and on. At last, the whales dove together and swam under the boat, their bodies clearly visible below the surface.

Takahashi turned to Paul, smiling, eyes shining. "Thank you," he said, "it's enough." A few days later, he left for Tokyo to spend the next several years working to make the film idea real.

The summer days passed pleasantly. Jim Nollman returned from California and set up his electronic instruments in his usual spot. Paul was intrigued by the fact that the orcas did seem to come around while Jim played music.

Jim came back one day with a story of how a whale had *taught him* a song. "It was under the full moon one night," Jim explained. "The orcas would appear and disappear like dark ghosts. When a single orca issued a modulating, melodic phrase, I tried to copy it on the guitar. Then—and this really made me take notice—the orca responded with an *exact* copy of my imperfect copy. Then I began to feel like a student. The orca broke the phrase down into three component parts, the way one might break down a long word when teaching it to a child. I repeated the three parts as best I could, knowing right away, however, that my rendition was not perfect. The orca was patient, and he or she repeated the three parts, but slowed them down to half speed. I got it and played the phrase perfectly. Then the whale repeated the same phrase quickly, at the original tempo, adding a single upsweep note at the end. I've got the whole thing on tape!"

Linda, meanwhile, working in a Vancouver recording studio, completed her record project. Twelve examples of the orcas' impressively diverse repertoire of clicks, calls, songs, and other interchanges were chosen for the record, *Songs and Sounds of Orcinus Orca*. Most of the selections were recorded around Hanson Island, but Linda also included early recordings of Tung Jen, made during late-night experiments at the aquarium, and a haunting piece titled "Last Words," the cries of a young whale and its family as the calf was being lifted from the water at Pender Harbor in 1969, to be taken away forever into the carnival world of Marineland of the Pacific. The plaintive cries are unmistakably tragic. For the album cover, Linda chose a beautiful picture of a leaping orca, taken by Peter Thomas, a photographer friend who had visited Hanson Island for many years. Later, *Fanfare* magazine would describe the album as the best whale record ever.

A group of Yashi's school friends came to Hanson Island for a summer visit. Paul had not felt so content in a long time. His plan to turn Hanson Island into a year-round research facility was unfolding well. He did venture out in late September, accompanied by Helena and baby Anna, to attend a meeting in Zeist, the Netherlands, which had been convened to discuss cetacean research in the Indian Ocean Sanctuary, recently established by the IWC. Sidney Holt chaired the meeting and Paul served as rapporteur. There were forty participants, gathered from all over the world. The meeting was a big step in the development of a world network of researchers interested in developing whale sanctuaries.

Paul's spirits were high when they returned to Hanson Island. He took ambling walks with Helena and Anna in the forest, collecting chanterelle mushrooms from marshy hollows overgrown with ferns and surrounded by towering fir and cedar trees. Around the porch of the house Helena and Paul had planted a profusely blooming spring garden of tulips, hyacinth, forget-me-nots, and daffodils and other narcissi. Two friends, Joel and Louise, had planted an abundant vegetable garden lush with broccoli, kale, lettuce, and the like. The little island family and their neighbors the orca families seemed to be living in one of earth's rare and blessed sanctuaries, quiet, clean, bountiful, and idyllic. If time had stopped right there, Paul would not have complained.

9

Let the Whale Go

Winters on the British Columbia coast are wet, dripping affairs, not so cold as the winters on the prairies or on the eastern seaboard, not harsh and bitter like Saskatoon or Boise, not charmingly mystical like Quebec or Connecticut. The effect on one's body and psyche can be deep and bleak, and as subtle as the gray mist that seeps into the boards, then the bones, then the brain. Sometimes one cannot really tell if it is still raining or not; one has to listen carefully to know whether it is only the drops falling from the eaves and the evergreen boughs that one is hearing, or whether it is the incessant drizzle itself.

On such a winter night in the waning days of 1981, the redeeming solstice only a few days away, Paul and Helena sat on the sofa where Paul, with Linda and Yashi, had first built a fire in the summer of 1970. There was a carpeted floor, shelves of books, kids' toys, and photographs of whales on the walls. Pole rafters radiated from a central post, and a circle of windows looked out into the garden and across the bay. The house was cozy, warm, dry, and adequate.

Paul was saying to Helena on this wet winter night, "Sometimes I can sit right here and feel this big machine poised, on the ready to destroy this little piece of paradise. It is too beautiful; can such perfection last?" Paul knew—it was common knowledge and much discussed in the press—that MacMillan Bloedel Ltd., a multibillion-dollar corporate logging giant that provided thousands of jobs in British Columbia's leading industry, wanted to log the Tsitika River Valley and drag the logs down to the estuary, where they would build a log-sorting depot in Robson Bight. This logging operation, if it proceeded, would destroy the playground and central gathering point for the 140 orcas, including Nicola's family, who used the area. The dry-land sort itself would require several hundred pounds of dynamite to move rock around, reshaping the land to fit the loggers' needs. The entire Robson Bight shallows and rocks would be awash with log booms and leaky, oily machines.

Paul knew all this and had lent his full support to stopping the plan. A group called the Robson Bight Preservation Committee had sprouted from the local community, led by Jim Borrowman, the whale enthusiast who had witnessed the recent birth to the A4 pod. Borrowman was a carpenter in Port McNeill, a logging town where ecologists are less tolerated than wolves. The town of Port McNeill survives on logging, from the chokermen and fallers themselves to the bar matron and the insurance salesman. To the townspeople, the logging of the Tsitika Valley meant cash flow, a winter's heat, maybe a satellite dish to watch the Movie Channel. To them, the idea that the whales—not to mention the eagles, deer, wolves and owls— had some preemptive claim was absurd. Paul knew all this and knew that British Columbian loggers were no more to blame than the Soviet whalers he had met at sea.

This specific danger, however, had seemed to have passed, as the environmentalists and the logging company had reached something of a compromise. MacMillan Bloedel Ltd. had announced that it would not use the bight for assembling log booms without an "environmental impact assessment," and that it would find another route for the logs. But the Tsitika Valley itself, the last pristine watershed on the entire east coast of Vancouver Island, would still be logged to the ocean. The "compromise" hung there. Many important people, including Dr. Dean Fisher, the distinguished professor of zoology at the University of British Columbia, who had first recorded orca vocalizations in Johnstone Strait in 1964, supported the idea of an orca ecological reserve at Robson Bight. Yet Cracroft Island just across Johnstone Strait from Robson Bight was also slated for clear-cut logging. "Clear-cut" means just that: The land is denuded. First the logging roads cut through the quiet forest with massive D-8 tractors, and then every living thing is scattered, smashed, cut, blown apart, or otherwise dispatched by the logging crews, who haul out the good timber and leave behind a scene reminiscent of Carthage after the Romans' salt and fire or Hiroshima after the bomb.

The replanting process, much touted by the companies, is paid for by the government and employs crews who hire out in the spring to haul sacks of seedlings through the wreckage to plant the "crop" that will be harvested again in fifty to eighty years. The idea of this stalwart band of tree planters even remotely keeping pace with the diesel-fueled, megadollar-driven army of loggers is absurd. Not even the companies pretend it is so, but everyone is "trying."

This forestry drama had been playing over Paul's shoulder since he first set up camp on Hanson Island. Crown Zellerbach, another logging giant, owned the government-issued "tree farm" license on Hanson Island, and Paul had only received his "special-use permit" with their permission. Officially, only the government could revoke Paul's permit, but in British Columbia the government and the logging entrepreneurs are not exactly strangers. The politics of London, Washington, Tokyo, and Moscow were one thing; as Paul was soon to discover, the politics of his own backyard were yet another. Robson Bight might be saved, but what would be next? It was this question, slinking in the unconscious reaches of Paul's mind, that gave birth to the "machine" of his nightmarish premonition, poised to sweep forest and hydrophones to some netherworldly grave.

As the solstice turned and the first furry buds opened up, Paul forgot his fears and turned to his work in the laboratory. His data-gathering and social observations of free orcas continued. He had developed a small network of radio-hydrophones situated at various sites in Johnstone Strait, Blackney Passage, and Blackfish Sound, and he continued experimenting with microwave and VHF transmission of the signals. He could now track much of the daily pattern of movements of the whales from his lab and house.

As year-round residents, Paul and Helena grew ever more aware of the land and water and of the other creatures who, for at least part of the year, made Blackfish Sound and Hanson Island their home. In the summer there were the glaucous-winged, herring, and bonaparte gulls, the black terns with their twangy nasal call, hummingbirds buzzing at the columbines in the garden, and myriad phalaropes. In the autumn came families of harlequin ducks and mergansers, the western grebe, cormorants, the common loon, the kingfisher, the great blue heron. In the winter, many northern and prairie birds—such as the red-necked and arctic loons—came to the Pacific rain-forest coast. And in the spring, the arrival of the robins marked the beginning of a new cycle.

The forest birds fluttered and soared around the house in all seasons: the persistent ravens and crows, chickadees, wrens, and woodpeckers. From deep in the forest, the screech owl called out its high-pitched Ping-Ponging call in the night. And by day the bald eagles kept their majestic place above it all.

The island was home to deer, otter, and mink, and was visited by wandering black bears, and wolves that were known to swim from island to island. Mussels, limpets, and clams inhabited the rocky beaches. The intertidal zone was rich with cryptic caves and jewel-box pools of anemones, sea urchins, crabs, starfish, and other sea life. Communities of acorn barnacles held together, waiting for the next tide to bring them their nourishing wash from the sea.

In the forest, mushroom-picking paths wound along creek beds, up ridges, and into hollows. The stand of three-hundred-year-old spruce trees and the thousand-year-old cedar tree stood as the colossal elders of the forest, the ancient ones, the original occupiers who had witnessed the countless comings and goings of other, more vulnerable and fleeting beings. When the cedar tree had been a seedling, a little sprout in the forest floor, Europe's industrial frenzy had not yet begun to awaken, and cougars, wolves, eagles, ravens, and owls ruled the forest.

The "Big Cedar," as it became known to Paul, had seen many generations of native people come and go, and Paul's eleven years on Hanson Island were but a flash.

Paul was not reminded of his bleak winter vision of disaster until late April, when forest engineer Steve Lackey, in the employ of Crown Zellerbach, showed up and announced that the logging company planned to clear-cut most of Hanson Island. Lackey—his name being the only humorous relief in the drama—was actually a mild, friendly man. He told Paul and Helena that he loved the wilderness as much as anybody, but that it was his job in this case to mark the boundaries of the impending clear-cut. The spruce grove and the ancient cedar were slated to go, the terrible irony being that the cedar giant was too old to make useful lumber but was in the way of the proposed logging road. It would be felled and left to rot.

The plan, as outlined by Lackey, was that the logging roads were to go in later that year, and the clear-cut operation would start soon thereafter. In addition, Dong Chong Bay, around the corner from Paul's house on the north shore of Hanson Island, would be converted into a dry-land log depot. Holes would be drilled into the rock, and dynamite would blast the shoreline to rubble. The forest of Hanson Island would be cut and hauled to Dong Chong Bay, and there the logs would be sorted, boomed, and towed away by tugboat and barge. Paul's "special-use permit" would be entirely honored, Lackey said; that is, the clear-cut operation would stop fifty feet from the back of the bay.

Several days passed before Paul recovered from the shock enough to act. His first call was to the Nimpkish Band in Alert Bay, to whom he proposed that they help preserve Hanson Island, which had been used by native people in the past and was now a living museum of Indian middens. Paul then wrote to Ernest Mitchell, president of Crown Zellerbach International in San Francisco, California. This letter turned out to be useless, because Crown Zellerbach was in the process of selling its Canadian holdings to Fletcher-Challenge, Ltd., a three-billion-dollar resource company located in Paul's native New Zealand. As Paul's fate and Hanson Island's fate fluttered in the corporate breeze, Paul himself wavered between despair and his unrelenting drive to change the course of events.

"We live in a hopeless age," he lamented to Joel one day in the forest, standing before the Big Cedar tree. "We live in a time when the acceptance of the coming end of everything is commonplace. That's one reason why the save-the-whales movement is so important—because it gives us reason to hope that the doomsday course of events on the planet might be reversed. It's the same when people come here to be with the whales. They are moved by the power of this place. I have stood before this cedar tree with people from Tokyo, New York, London, Los Angeles, people from all over the world, and they have all been awestruck. When people stand here, they are put back in touch with the core of their being. And that gives them reason to hope. No price, no profit, no paycheck could ever take the place of the hope that the forest offers in its pristine state.

"Places like this are just as rare and precious as the whales, and destroying them is just as crazy as destroying the whales. But people can identify with whales; after all, they're intelligent and playful. Trees, I don't know. Can people understand the wild intelligence of the forest?"

When Bob Hunter visited Hanson Island, Paul took him walking deep into the forest. Eventually they stood talking on top of a giant cedar tree that had fallen across the forest floor. Bob was recalling the occasion on the first Greenpeace voyage when Pat Moore had coined the line "A flower is your brother."

"Yes," said Paul, "and the forest is your mother."

At that moment, an immense eagle with its wings spread and talons outstretched plunged down through the trees toward them. At shoulder height and only an arm's reach away, it swerved and vanished through the trees.

On July 22, 1982, in London, the International Whaling Commission finally voted a moratorium on all commercial whaling. That is, a moratorium with some provisions, one of them being that it would take effect in 1986 and the other being that the Soviet and Japanese whaling fleets would, in the meantime, be allowed a quota of sperm whales in the North Pacific; aboriginal bowhead whaling would continue. For the most part, the press and the whale movement played it as a victory; after all, it was a major international decision to protect whales.

Paul did not attend the meeting, leaving it to Jean-Paul, Sidney, and the others to usher in the victory. "Of course I'm glad that whaling will stop eventually," Paul told a reporter in Vancouver. "But it is a black victory. How can I be happy about the fact that more than ten thousand whales will still be killed in the coming year? I personally don't want to discuss the numbers of whales that should be killed. *Zero* should be killed, and my position doesn't change. Of course I'm 'glad' the quota is being reduced from fourteen thousand to ten thousand. But I mourn the ten thousand four hundred and sixty incredible beings that are going to be blown up this year, and I don't want to discuss body counts while the atrocity is taking place.

"I cannot say I am 'happy' with the progress. I am *not* happy with the progress. I praise the people who have done this, accomplished the moratorium, worked for so many years, long before me, but I am sorry to say even in this victory we are losing. It's the whalers who are happy. They get to kill whales until they can take the last dollar to be made. In this waiting game, it's the whalers who are winning, not the whales."

After this interview, Paul met Bob Hunter at the Cecil. The old pub had changed over the years: It now boasted a sea of electric lights, strippers, and waiters with muscles bulging from house T-shirts. Ironically, the old, quiet corner where Paul used to drink during his Vancouver Aquarium days was still there. The place, however, was too noisy, so Bob and Paul ended up walking along the waterfront.

"Paul," said Bob, "this woman called me the other day from Abbotsford, or somewhere out there, and told me she raised dogs. She asked if I was the Bob Hunter who wrote about Skana in the newspaper, so I said yes. Then she tells me that she has something for me—she says she bought part of Skana to feed her dogs, and she had been saving this vertebra for me, trying to find me, because she thought I might appreciate it. I'm thinking, 'No, this is impossible,' I thought they said Skana was buried at sea. But this woman takes my address and sends me this bone. It sure looks like an orca vertebra to me, but I'm not exactly an expert."

Sitting by the water, Bob pulled the bone from a bag and handed it to Paul. It was a cylinder the size of a small birthday cake, pasty white, with arcing extensions extruding from each side like breaking waves. An orca vertebra no doubt.

Paul knew it was a tradition in the aquarium business to sell dead orcas for dog food. Moby Doll had ended up that way. But he was surprised. Paul was more disgusted than angry. It just seemed cynical, even slightly sinister, for the aquarium to have made a last dollar from Skana by selling her body for dog food.

"There's no way to prove it's Skana's," said Paul matter-of-factly.

"Well, anyway, Paul"—Bob bowed as he was inclined to do in delicate situations, being at heart a humble man who had been blessed with the dubious boon of a fast mind and fluid tongue—"you take it. Keep it at Hanson Island with you." Paul held the bone in his lap. The two friends sat in silence, something they had rarely done in their wild campaigns together. A few boats chugged in and out of the inner-city marina, and the wind swept over English Bay. Traffic rumbled above them on the bridge.

After several minutes, Paul said, "Whales don't have hands, and they didn't grow up in an environment where they had to manipulate objects in order to survive. Primates are different. Look at them." He held his palms up to the city and continued, "We emerged fighting for a place to live and we won with our minds and with our hands. We became this, modern *Homo sapiens*. But in getting here we killed off all our competitors. Now we're alone. So we combat ourselves. And our destructive genius ensures our end.

"Just look at how many different cetacean species there are. They're not alone, because they followed a different path. They used their big brains to figure out how to live together, to share the abundance of the ocean; peaceful coexistence, that's what the whales figured out.

"We ended up with everything from axes and houses to computers and vaccines and nuclear bombs. We also have Auschwitz and genocide of indigenous peoples all over the world, and slavery and racism, and countless angry and alienated men and women. Sure, we have our pleasures and our graces, but compare us to the whales. We only dream of such a state of grace. We do yoga and we meditate and have therapy and drugs to try in a million ways to relax and look at the world with a calm, kind equanimity. But look at the whales."

Paul was speaking briskly, his mind set freewheeling first by the encounter with the reporter and now by the sight of the whalebone. Bob was nodding, giving his friend free rein to get out his frustration.

"Intelligence *created* this planet," Paul continued. "The whole thing is intelligent. *Gaia* is intelligent. John Lilly says that intelligence is *collective,* mutual, a shared thing. He's absolutely right. Human philosophers have created this special little category for themselves and their species: human beings, the smartest creatures in the known universe, the ones with 'intelligence.'

"Now we've glimpsed the whale." Paul held the whalebone out in front of him. "And we don't need to keep any more whales prisoner in order to find out more about them. We know. We should let them go. We should let every captive cetacean go. They've done enough for us already, and it is time we made some gesture in return. If we want to teach kids about whales, then we should end this masquerade circus trip. Let the kids see films of free orcas in the places where they live, with the mountains and trees and eagles and otters.

"It's time to leave the whales alone, period! Let them go! Let them work out their own destiny. We should leave the planet alone. We should be learning how to live, to survive ourselves without destroying everything in sight. Let's say we have another hundred years' supply of hydrocarbons. But think: It's been two thousand years since Christ and Buddha, two million years since Peking man. What's a hundred years? People had better learn to survive with a gentler hand. Why did we evolve? Why did we rise up out of four billion years of evolution to the point where I can stand up and talk and play with my computer? So it can all be destroyed in a flash? Richness is our problem. We are blinded by our wealth. I'll be impressed with human intelligence when I hear someone talking about a million years of survival, not how to keep things rolling until the next election."

"Can I quote you on that, Dr. Spong?" Bob was still nodding and smiling.

"Yeah." Paul was stone-faced, grave, not quite ready to give up his anger. As he sat looking at the water, the pleasure boats, a few gulls wheeling under the bridge, and the white whalebone, he could feel the anger in his belly. He took a few deep breaths. "We compromise too much. You and I and a host of others know the truth, and we do nothing about it."

Paul spoke more reflectively. "The human brain is a magnificent thing: extraordinary powers of reasoning, logic, creativity, inventiveness. Can the whales match us in these kinds of powers? Maybe. But also think of the ways that we know we cannot match the whale's powers. Their acoustic abilities, both sending and receiving, we can't begin to match in speed or complexity. The physiology of the brain, the size, convolutions, connectivities, the massive associational areas, the sheer bulk of information processing going on! The cerebral control of breath, bodily functions, emotions, we cannot match. They have evolved far beyond humans in the areas of group interdependence and communication. The whales have highly specialized and centralized brains, and yet those individual brains are working in a collective network in ways that humans only dream of. To see fifty whales all hunting together, to see them spread out over ten square miles of ocean and then all turn around at exactly the same time, to see them take a collective readout from a single echolocation train: Such demonstrations of conscious group communication and activity are as impressive as any human achievement. Besides, the whales get along better than the whale-savers! They're playful, humorous, kind, gentle, and nonaggressive with each other, showing enormous patience and compassion for people, even to their captors and tormentors. I stand in total awe of these beings, and in no way do I consider humans to be superior."

Paul stood up and paced the seawall. He and Bob slowly walked around English Bay, through the park. Paul carried the whalebone under his arm. He was huffing, and Bob could tell that he still had something to say.

Finally Paul stopped and glared at Bob. "No compromise! That's it! It's no more right to kill just a few whales or keep just a few in captivity than it is okay to have a tiny Auschwitz or just a few slaves. Time will bear this out, Bob. Someday it will be morally unthinkable to treat other creatures like that."

"So do you think that's Skana's bone?" Bob asked.

Paul paused, and then said quietly, "It's Skana."

"You're sure?"

"Yep."

Paul and Bob finally did drink a beer, including a solemn toast to Skana, at the stately Sylvia Hotel pub overlooking English Bay, where the grain and oil tankers waited anchor in the red sunlight of dusk.

"You're dealing with people's belief systems and their livelihoods, Paul," Bob said as they gazed out the window at the bay. "And in the case of the aquariums and the universities, you are dealing with people's self-image, status in the society, and desires for acceptance and success. Those are tough nuts to crack, Paul, and it isn't going to happen overnight."

"I don't believe that," said Paul. "Change can happen at the speed of thought. We *are* sentient. All we have to do is open our eyes and *see.* However, I must admit even Greenpeace seems to be going middle-of-the-road."

"It was bound to happen. Radical ideas don't take over the society, they seep in at best. Half the world is starving to death, Paul; do you think they're going to care about whales? Peasant revolts, colonial upheavals, blacks, women, every struggle faces this same reality. If Christ or Buddha could look down now and see what's happened with their ideas, how do you think they would feel?"

"Pissed!" said Paul.

"That's for sure." Bob grinned and clinked Paul's glass with his own. "Too bad the whales don't write history books, or you might be a hero. Better not to think about the results, but rather just say what you believe, do the work that inspires you. Perseverance furthers," Bob concluded, quoting the *I Ching*.

Paul placed Skana's vertebra on a shelf in a window of the house on Hanson Island where the afternoon sun glistened on its white fins and dorsal ridge. In the right light it looked something like an orca itself. The Vancouver Aquarium had already replaced Skana with two orcas captured in Iceland. With Canadian and U.S. waters closed to orca captures, the industry had moved its operations to Iceland, where between 1976 and 1982 over forty orcas had been plucked from the local population and sold to the highest bidder: Sea World, Marineland in Ontario, the Vancouver Aquarium, and England, Hong Kong, the Netherlands, France, and Japan. In 1965, when the first orcas were caught for display, the price was eight thousand dollars. By the summer of 1982 it was over two hundred thousand dollars. Sea World itself grossed a hundred and twenty million dollars annually from three oceanariums that held eight orcas. Orca displays were more than just a few people's "livelihood," they were full-fledged corporate gold mines.

The vertebra sat there in the window as Paul and Helena and their constant stream of visitors pursued their daily lives. The most pressing issue at the time was the battle with the logging company over their plans for Hanson Island. The Nimpkish Indians and archeologists confirmed that Hanson Island was rich in middens and historical artifacts. Preferring to keep an open dialogue with the logging company, Paul planned no media-oriented protests. In his conversation with the company public-relations officer, he elicited a promise to inform him of any plans to begin logging.

Nevertheless one day, while out in his boat showing a journalist the island, Paul heard the grinding roar of chain saws in the forest near Dong Chong Bay. He pulled into the shore and confronted the fallers who were cutting trees along a roadline. "Hey," Paul said, standing in front of a tree about to be felled, "what's going on here? I had an agreement that they'd let me know before they did any logging."

Paul pressed his point, and the loggers left. When the story appeared in the newspaper, however, Paul's communication with the company suffered a setback. He was reminded by a company official that a condition of his special-use permit was that he not disrupt any logging activity. Paul's diplomatic skills were put to the test.

After several phone calls and letters, and a visit to the corporate headquarters in Vancouver, Paul convinced the forestry executives, the corporate magnates who could ultimately decide the destiny of Hanson Island, to visit him, to see his operation, and to discuss, as Paul put it, "alternatives." Linda and Yashi offered to help. The giant trees had been, from Yashi's earliest memories, his "big friends." The grove of spruce trees and the colossal red cedar were cherished by Linda: They had represented, during the early years on Hanson Island, a sort of mystical guardianship, and she had often sat under their boughs.

In Vancouver, Linda had taken to clay sculpture, first as a hobby, then as a serious art form. She had produced a series of gnomes standing about two feet tall, usually sculpted with the faces of her friends but with the bodies, attire, and expressions of the forest's "little people." On a visit to Hanson Island with Yashi and Bill, Linda brought one of the clay gnomes and a long blue ribbon of the color that had been used to mark the boundary of OrcaLab's special-use permit. With Helena and Paul they plotted a strategy.

A week later, on August 25, when the forestry executives arrived, Helena and Paul took them to the lab and talked about Paul's work, the uniqueness of Hanson Island, the ancient middens, and other rational reasons for saving the forest, not the least of which was the public-relations value to the company. Then they led the party on a trek through the woods, along the paths cut by twelve years of meandering. When at last they came upon the towering cedar, the party stopped. Encircling the forty-foot circumference of the tree was the blue satin ribbon, tied in a bow that was held by the smiling gnome, pipe in hand, eyes right on the human visitors. Beside the gnome was a wooden tablet with a message that Bill had carved in Gothic script: BLESSED BE HE WHO LEAVES THESE TREES.

Perhaps more charmed than convinced, the executives passed a friendly afternoon with their hosts, lauding them for the wonderful work they were doing and promising to "seriously consider" their requests. After they left, Yashi noticed that Frank Luci, director of operations for the company, had written in the guest book, "And blessed are those that watch the Orcas." Ed Burton, the man who would make the final decision, had written "Save the Tree!" The polite protest seemed to have worked its charm on the men who could, with a wave of their hand, save or defoliate the forest of Hanson Island.

Paul phoned the next day and was told that the company would make some concessions. A letter followed that promised to move the cutting line back enough to "save the big tree." When company engineer Steve Lackey returned with a government forester to re-mark the cutting line, Paul went with them into the woods and further convinced them to move the line to the far side of a creek that supplied them with water. In the end, the boundary was moved twenty meters beyond the cedar tree, but Paul considered it a very partial victory. The clear-cut, if and when it came, would denude the forest down to the creek behind OrcaLab, and so near the cathedral grove that the delicate forest realm would never be the same. Paul was convinced that exposing the delicate creek bed to the sun would dry it up completely in the summertime, and they would be without water. He vowed to continue his efforts, a vow that would eventually lead him to the New Zealand offices of Fletcher-Challenge.

In the summer of 1982, a young Japanese woman named Haruko Sato came to visit Hanson Island. In the spring of that year, Paul had received a letter from the seventeen-year-old student who, like so many others, wanted to come to Hanson Island and visit the whales. This particular request, however, was unique in one startling respect. Haruko, as she recounted in her letter, had been nine years old in 1974, when Paul had first visited her school to present the Whale Show. She had been so moved by the arresting images and stories of the whales that her life course had been set on that day. She had thought, studied, and pursued little else in the ensuing eight years. Haruko's ambition was to become a marine mammal trainer. For four years she had worked and saved money for the trip to Hanson Island.

When Haruko arrived, shy and humble but bursting with excitement, she quickly established herself in the scheme of things around Hanson Island. She was invaluable in the lab, graciously helpful around the house, and unobtrusively dedicated to her studies.

Haruko was eager to see whales, but Paul's methodology was to study the whales without harassing them in boats, so he showed Haruko his recording lab and took her to the bluff where she could watch for whales along the entire sweep of Blackney Passage and into Blackfish Sound. For two weeks, Paul went about his work, leaving Haruko on her own. She slept in the little room above the lab and would sometimes stay up all night waiting for the orcas and recording them whenever she heard vocalizations over the speakers. Although orcas passed at night, for almost two weeks at the beginning of Haruko's visit, they did not pass OrcaLab during the day. Paul began to wonder if he should take Haruko out in the boat.

"I'm sorry," Paul said to her one day, "that you haven't seen the whales yet."

"Oh, Dr. Spong, don't worry," said Haruko. "I've been seeing whales every day."

"Oh?" Paul tilted his head quizzically, wondering if he had missed something.

"Oh yes, every day. Please, look." Haruko opened her notebook on the table to show the drawings that she had made each day on the bluff. With the patience and skill of a seasoned observer, Haruko had drawn, each morning, an outline sketch of the entire vista from the bluff, showing the full length of Blackney Passage. Marked each day on this series of sketches were the comings and goings of every marine mammal that ventured through these waters, and in her notebook were descriptions of their activities. She had traced the movement of Dall's porpoises, seals, sea lions, and minke whales. Although she had not yet seen an orca, Haruko's sketches were testa-

ments to the abundance of marine mammal life in Blackfish
Sound.

Paul was refreshed by Haruko's attitude. Over the years he
had accommodated hundreds of visitors who were impatient to
see the whales up close and from boats. Paul had often felt
uneasy about this. Now Paul saw in this competent young
woman the possibility of a whole new generation of benign
researchers, unfettered by old notions of science. He hoped
that her attitude betokened a coming new wave of sensitive,
nonmanipulative research, and it pleased him to see such benign intelligence at work.

As long as people were capturing and killing whales, Paul
realized his work would be political as well as scientific. He
did not know whether his ambition to follow an orca throughout its lifetime would ever be realized, but now he could see
that there would be others who would share his philosophy
and participate in his goals.

Before she left, Haruko did see orcas and included those
sightings in her daily sketches. She came to know Nicola and
her family and some of the other pods as they passed by the
cliff. Over the years, the family structure of Nicola's group had
slowly revealed itself, and Paul and Helena pointed out individuals to Haruko. Haruko was delighted with her close-up
view of this whale family. When she did depart to rejoin her
family and resume her formal studies in Japan, she promised to
return, and Paul assured her that there would always be a
place for her at OrcaLab.

From Japan, Haruko sent a letter to Paul and Helena telling
them that she had decided to abandon her plan to become a
marine mammal trainer in favor of studying whales in the wild.

On one of the last days of summer in 1982, Dong Chong Bay
was blown up, in a scene reminiscent of Dante's Inferno, pro-
ducing a huge mushrooming cloud of smoke and debris. The
blast followed more than a month's preparation by engineers,
who first cleared the land and drilled the rock, filling the holes
with precisely calculated quantities of explosives. The rock

went up, and came down again as rubble to be used for road construction.

Amid all the frenetic activity over the forest, Helena had become concerned that Paul, in the previous two years, had spent little personal time with the whales. He'd been too busy to go out with them, and his philosophical thinking was becoming increasingly set against people interfering with whales, however benign their intentions might be. Helena reminded Paul that it had been quite a while since he had kayaked with the whales. Maybe he was becoming too remote, losing touch. "You haven't been out with the whales in a long time, Paul," she said. "I think it would lift your spirits if you went out with them."

"Well . . ." Paul trailed off. After a silence, he began again. "I guess I feel that I don't want to be poking into their lives, intruding, plaguing them all the time. Look how many boats are always out there."

Paul conceded that he would go out, but only when the time was right. Several days passed, and one morning Paul, Helena, and Anna sat at the table eating breakfast. The sky was a brilliant azure blue, and white puffy clouds drifted over Blackfish Sound. Inside, they could hear Joel and Louise chopping wood on the other side of the bay. A horde of gulls scoured the slimy rocks exposed by the receding tide, gobbling their own breakfast of bugs and crustaceans.

The chopping stopped, and Paul saw Joel running out to the rock ledge in front of the cabin. "Orcas!" shouted Joel. Paul and Helena, with Anna running ahead, walked quickly out to the lab. Paul started a recording and then joined Helena and Anna on the front lab deck. Helena was looking through binoculars.

"It's a perfect day," said Helena. "Why don't you go out?"

"Oh, I don't know," said Paul. "Who is it?"

"It's the B's; there's B1, and B2, and B5; it looks like all B-pod is there," said Helena.

"Oh, the B's," said Paul impassively. "Those guys are so serious. If it was Nicola's gang I'd go out."

"Give me a break!" said Helena.

"No, really, if it was A-pod I'd go out."

An instant later Helena started laughing and Paul stood speechless, watching as Nicola and all the other individuals of the subgroup of the A-pod known as the A1s—the females A30, A36, and A12, with their juveniles and calves, and the newly adult male, A6—all surfaced at once in a line, and stopped, directly in front of and below the lab.

Helena laughed. "Well, I guess this is the morning you go out."

Paul, without a word, turned and ran to the beach, carrying his kayak down to the lapping low tide. By the time he was out in the middle of Blackfish Sound, the orcas were well ahead of him, and he soon tired, having gone so long without kayaking. Paul stopped paddling, knowing that he could not keep up with the whales, deciding just to let them go. Then, as he drifted with the tide, watching the whales recede, all the whales turned together and came back toward him. Nicola was the first to approach, and she came within twenty feet of his kayak before diving and coming up in front of him. "Nicolaaaaa!" Paul called, and the matriarch, the grandmother, spyhopped just in front of Paul's kayak, fixing her eye on him and slipping back silently into the water. The eight B's cruised in a tight group twenty meters to the outside, their massive breaths enveloping him. Paul followed Nicola as she re-joined the A30 group, her immediate family. A30 was presumed to be the daughter of Nicola, and the young male, A6, was A30's son, Nicola's grandson. Swimming closely with them were A30's other children, A37 and A39, juveniles still too young to be identified by gender. It was becoming more and more obvious that the orcas grouped themselves around their mothers. Sons tended to stay with their mothers throughout their lives, and mature females traveled as subgroups with their young.

The orcas enveloped Paul in their band and continued back through Blackney Passage, in the direction from which they had come. Paul paddled effortlessly, and the whales traveled no faster than he did. As he paddled back past OrcaLab, he was surrounded by the whales, the A30 group on the inshore side and the B's on the outer, with the rest of the A1s, the A36s and the A12s, following close behind. As they moved toward

Johnstone Strait, Paul could feel the whales holding the pace for him as he watched their sleek, radiant bodies glide through the blue water. One calf swam close to the kayak, surfacing as Paul lifted the paddle on that side, and although its mother swam nearby, there was not the slightest sign of panic or urgency. Paul felt completely accepted and welcome, awash in the general state of grace that pervaded orca society.

Again Paul noticed the breathing groups, several whales all diving, rising, and breathing together in absolute cadence, like well-rehearsed, impeccably trained ballet dancers moving to some silent fugue. When a whale surfaced close by, Paul could see its eye peering up at him through the water. He did not worry in the slightest that he might hit a whale with his paddle, as the orcas were so obviously in such competent control of their bodies and so keenly aware of the space around them.

Paul, however, eventually grew tired. As the whales headed toward Robson Bight, Paul—knowing that he faced a long, up-tide paddle home—turned back. It was late afternoon, and nearly high tide when he beached the kayak in front of the house and walked back inside, where the fires were going and supper was being prepared. Paul resolved that he would make at least one trip each year in his kayak with the whales.

In the spring of 1983, the logging roads were put in at Hanson Island. The forestry company had "compromised" with Paul, allowing the cathedral grove of giant spruces and the ancient Big Cedar to stand. They also agreed with the Nimpkish Band in Alert Bay to preserve a few middens at Dong Chong Bay, but much of Hanson Island was still slated for clear-cut logging, including most of the forest surrounding OrcaLab. Paul and Helena left Hanson Island during the road construction, not wanting to be subjected to rock blasting and the maddening roar of bulldozers and chain saws and the thundering crack of trees being cleared for the roads. During this time they traveled to Boston and Washington, D.C. When they returned in July, it was to hear stories of rocks flying into the bay, narrowly missing buildings, boats, and people and of a confused bear walking up to the house along the beach, and to experience for

themselves the last days of the terrorizing "construction"
phase.

"And that was the best part," said Paul grimly to Helena a
few nights after the silence returned. The forest itself now
seemed ominously silent; the owls and ravens had gone, and it
was a long time before Paul felt peace returning to his home
and being. He could scarcely bring himself to walk in the
woods, as he could not bear the sight of the logging roads cutting their ominous swath through once-pristine forest glens.
Moreover, he found himself getting confused and lost, as old
landmarks were now gone. "It's all a reflection of one of the big
differences between us and the whales," Paul told a friend one
day. "The land is owned; but the ocean is not owned, it is
shared. The virgin forest of British Columbia is one of the last
great forests in the world. The logging companies plan, and it's
now government policy, to fell every old-growth tree in B.C. by
1990. That's just as crazy as killing all the whales. And just like
the whalers, when cutting down trees is no longer profitable,
the companies will move their capital into something else.
These people must know what they are trampling on. Where
will salmon spawn? Where will the eagles go? Where can the
eye fall on something unmanipulated by human minds and human hands? I see more intelligence at work in the wildness of
the forest than I see in most human enterprises."

Fortunately for Paul, he received much-needed solace and
support during this time from his family and from his orca
friends. Milora had turned three at the end of 1982, and Anna
celebrated her third birthday in the summer of 1983. The two
girls had become close friends, and their development was a
great joy to Paul. Yashi was growing into a secure, solid young
man.

On Wednesday afternoon, June 8, 1983, Paul, accompanied
by Helena, Anna, and Yashi, joined a gathering of colleagues
from around the world at Boston, Massachusetts. The conference, co-sponsored by the International Whaling Commission
and hosted by the Boston Aquarium, was called "Whales
Alive." It marked a new and historical departure for the IWC,

an organization that hitherto had been concerned solely with the question of how many whales could be killed. The subtitle of the conference, "The Non-consumptive Utilization of Cetacean Resources," set the theme of the meeting. It was co-chaired by Sidney Holt, Dr. Robbins Barstow from the Connecticut Cetacean Society, Dr. Patricia Bernie from the department of international law at the University of Edinburgh, and Dr. Francisco Palacio from the Tinker Center for Coastal Studies in Latin America.

Dr. Holt said in his introductory address, "Many people are coming to think that cetaceans have something to teach us, so, therefore, they have value, and that they stand at the pinnacle of one track of evolution." His comment set the stage for the introductory paper, "Whales Are Not Cetacean Resources," by philosophers Dale Jamieson and Tom Regan. And that paper established the mood of the meeting.

Jean-Paul Fortom-Gouin introduced Dr. Roger Payne, whose paper was on "Recently Developed Benign Research Techniques for Assessing and Modelling Whale Populations." Dr. Georgio Pilleri's paper on "Cetaceans in Captivity" stressed that the scientific rewards of working with captured whales are negligible and are far outweighed by the disruption to cetacean families and to individuals. Phoebe Wray discussed "The Pleasures of Tradition," speaking to the educational and cultural values of whales. Dr. Peter Beamish spoke on "Live Whales as Optimum Producers of Human Recreation."

Dr. Masaharu Nishiwaki from Japan presented a paper on "Recent Aquarium Activities on Smaller Cetaceans in Japan," a welcome sign that the Japanese were at last willing to discuss the value of whales as other than a harvestable resource. Sidney Holt outlined the development of the Indian Ocean Sanctuary, established by the IWC. Research in the sanctuary was restricted to "benign techniques." James Hudnall from the Maui Research Institute presented the accumulated knowledge on "Interpersonal Contacts with Free Cetaceans: Where We Are Now, and the Emerging Possibilities." Maxine McCloskey delivered a paper on the benefits of "Recreational Whale

Watching" in the wild, for human enjoyment, education, and research.

Paul's paper was entitled "Non-consumptive Abuses of Cetaceans," the irony of which was fully intended. The conference had been called to discuss what could be done with whales other than to kill them. Paul's point was that it is possible to abuse whales in many other ways than by killing them. If whales were viewed as free individuals and members of communities with rights of their own, then any denial of these rights constituted "abuse." Paul well knew that he himself could be accused, as much as anyone there, of having abused cetaceans in this sense, and he was speaking directly to the methods used by himself and his colleagues.

To illustrate his point, Paul played a tape of the sound made by his own boat engine underwater, and the loud, decidedly unpleasant sound filled the crowded auditorium. Paul was prepared to go on for two minutes, but stopped after thirty seconds, because the audience had clearly had enough. "For the whales," Paul said, "this is what they hear *all* day, and *every* day; the only peace comes at night, when the scientists and whale-watchers have gone away." He felt a stir in the audience, and knew his message had hit home.

"Now we know them," Paul concluded. "Let's leave them alone."

The "abuses" to which Paul spoke included interruption or invasion of the privacy of their breeding and birthing grounds, noise pollution from engines, safety hazards such as propellers, keels, and nets and other human equipment, capturing for research purposes, and in any way denying whales the right to complete freedom. "When we talk about whale sanctuaries," Paul admonished, "let's make sure we are not talking about a cool place for 'whale-watchers' to hang out and annoy whales, run their boats up their backs. Sanctuaries should be *sanctuaries:* quiet, peaceful, a place where whales can get away from humans and be completely undisturbed."

Paul pointed out that Sea World, by comparison, was seeking a permit to capture one hundred orcas in Alaskan waters. Sea World's plan involved hoisting the captured whales onto the deck of a research boat, pumping stomachs, extracting teeth, analyzing stomach gases, recording heartbeats, and taking blood samples, after which the whales would be kept in pens for further study. Ten orcas were then to be kept permanently for a "breeding program," designed to provide the aquarium market with orcas. Such "research," Paul told the delegates, was "disrespectful, insensitive, arrogant, ignorant, and outrageous." He went on, "Sea World's research and breeding program is a scientific ploy in a big-money game. Below the scientific surface one easily sees that the primary, perhaps the sole, reason for the exercise is the rigorous examination and screening of a large sample of orcas in order to select the best of them for permanent placement in captivity." With this presentation, Paul launched a campaign to save the orcas of Alaska from the massive planned capture by Sea World. Furthermore, Paul convinced the meeting to list among its recommendations "an end in due course [to] the keeping of cetaceans in captivity."

The issue of keeping cetaceans in captivity sparked the most controversy among the assembled participants. Though taking cetaceans from the ocean and displaying them in tanks is not "nonconsumptive," it is arguably "low-consumptive," and clearly preferable to the wholesale slaughter still going on in various parts of the world. Some speakers passionately addressed the educational value of keeping cetaceans in captivity. Paul, while acknowledging the debt owed to dolphins in tanks and their exhibitors, admonished the meeting, "Just because we once made fire by rubbing sticks together is not a sufficient reason for us to continue the practice in the present day."

In the end, Paul's opinion held sway. For the first time, a prestigious international gathering expressed the opinion that captivity would in the future be socially unacceptable. The threat of this was obvious to the representatives of the captive industry who attended the meeting, and immediately afterward they began to organize, holding their own meeting of experts, which of course concluded that holding cetaceans in captivity is humane, necessary, and beneficial. The scientific community became quickly polarized, leading Paul inevitably to further conflict.

After leaving the Whales Alive Conference in Boston, Paul carried his campaign against orca captivity to Washington, D.C., where he lobbied senators and congressmen and government officials, urging a public inquiry into the Sea World plan to capture Alaskan orcas. As a result, a public hearing was scheduled for Seattle in August, and Congressman Rod Chandler of Washington State introduced an amendment to the Marine Mammal Protection Act that would prohibit the capture or import of orcas for public display.

In August, Paul traveled from Hanson Island to Seattle, Washington, for the public hearing on the Sea World proposal that had been convened by the U.S. National Marine Fisheries Service. The state of Washington formally opposed Sea World. Messages were read from the governor and from Senator Slade Gorton, the man who'd brought the 1976 court action against Sea World as attorney general for the state. Ralph Munroe, the leader of the 1976 opposition, was now Washington's secretary of state, and eloquently appealed for a decision against Sea World. Paul presented a report from a workshop he had convened at OrcaLab, arguing that the Sea World plan was, in truth, an effort to screen orcas for captivity, not to study them, and that not enough was known about orca breeding to successfully select and breed them in captivity. The vast majority of speakers at the hearing was opposed to the Sea World plan. Nevertheless, in November of 1983 Sea World was issued a permit to capture one hundred orcas in Alaskan waters.

That summer, whale magic remained alive and well at Hanson Island. A film crew from Germany came to British Columbia to shoot a segment for a film about Greenpeace. Since they wanted to get some "live whale footage," Patrick Moore, who was now the president of Greenpeace Canada, brought the film crew to Hanson Island with Bob Hunter, chartering the original Greenpeace boat, the *Phyllis Cormack,* now an Alert Bay seiner, for a day. Pat, following the advice of Mel Gregory, told the Germans—hardly a mystical bunch, but eager to photograph whales on a tight schedule—that the way to get the orcas to come around their boat was to blow on kelp horns.

Pat showed the Germans how to make the kelp horns. Back out on the *Phyllis Cormack,* anchored just offshore at OrcaLab, Pat and the German film crew began to blow the horns, in an assorted variety of sizes and tones, and a low, reverberant hum echoed off the cliffs. If told by some, the story very likely would not have been believed, but the eminently rational Dr. Moore later confirmed that the orcas showed up within five minutes of their beginning to blow the horns. *"Five minutes* at the most! They were leaping and jumping all around the boat as if they were circus performers. The Germans went crazy, cameras buzzing and tape recorders rolling; the orcas played on the bow of the boat; they splashed us; it was incredible!" Later, all Mel would say was, "What do you expect?"

In the spring of 1984, Paul made three trips to Juneau, Alaska, to continue his opposition to the Sea World scheme. In Alaska, Paul found a friendly legislature and a supportive populace, appreciative of the natural environment. A citizens' group formed, calling itself Organized Resistance to Captures in Alaska (ORCA). ORCA promised to disrupt any attempt that Sea World made to capture Alaskan orcas. Furthermore, Alaskan State Fish and Game officials were sympathetic, not wanting to defend Sea World, "a California bunch," against the boats or potentially even guns of the Alaskan people. Eventually Governor Bill Sheffield stated emphatically, on behalf of the Alaskan people, his opposition to the Sea World plan. The state of Alaska took Sea World to court, charging that they had not done an environmental-impact study relevant to the proposed capture. Soon a judicial decision revoked Sea World's capture permit, and although the decision was appealed, Sea World quickly abandoned the hunt, even terminating a "benign" research program associated with it.

The day after Paul's return from his last trip to Juneau, hopeful but uncertain what the results of his work would be, Bill Wheeler brought him a gift that had washed up on the beach in his absence. Bill was a friend who had been caretaking the island for several years, building himself a cabin across the bay from the lab and house. The gift was an old wooden-handled harpoon lashed with frayed rope, with a metal head and hinged brass barb. Obviously it was a weapon used to kill marine mammals, quite possibly whales.

Paul pondered the discovery. "Well," he said, "how many thousands of miles of coastline do you suppose there are in British Columbia? Sixteen thousand miles of coastline, not counting the islands. How many islands?" Paul went on. "Thousands. How many beaches? And this harpoon washed up on *this* beach. So what am I supposed to think? What's the message?"

Bill shrugged his shoulders and said nothing, cocking his head and smiling.

"Well," Paul continued, answering his own question, "maybe it's a signal of the final surrender by the whalers—you know, 'We give up, we'll stop killing whales.' But maybe it's 'We're still out here killing whales, and we aren't going to stop.' And if that's it, then the final message is *we* can't stop either!"

In October of 1984, Paul left Hanson Island and flew to Melbourne, Australia, where plans for a huge new oceanarium were being discussed. The developer had built similar tourist facilities in Hong Kong and Indonesia and had a poor history of keeping captive cetaceans alive. Paul was invited by Alison Kelty on behalf of Greenpeace Australia and Project Jonah, the main groups that opposed the development. Kelty organized Whale Shows for Paul in Melbourne, Adelaide, and Sydney and arranged a hectic schedule for him. As the debate heated up, the promoter flew in Dr. Ken Norris from California to defend cetacean captivity. Dr. Norris and Paul followed each other around on the same circuit for two weeks, lobbying with politicians and officials and talking to the media. Their only face-to-face meeting came during a television debate in which they sat in studios in Canberra and Melbourne. During the debate, Paul charged that the oceanarium was not a scientific project but a glorified circus. "What do you learn from whales in captivity?" Paul asked. "You certainly learn nothing of their real nature."

The Greenpeace and Project Jonah people were happy, feeling that Paul had won the debate, and in November the Australian federal Minister of Environment, Barry Cohen, denied the promoter a permit to capture dolphins and orcas in Australian waters. The battle continued, as states could allow captures in their local waters, but the Australian policy was becoming encouragingly pro-whale. A year later, a Senate Select Committee would side with Paul and recommend that no new captive facilities should be built in Australia, and that the existing facilities should be phased out.

Seeing the possibility that Australia might be persuaded to lead the way for the world and begin to rehabilitate and release captive cetaceans, Paul traveled to Warragamba, a former industrial boomtown gone bust in the dry foothills of the Blue Mountains two hours west of Sydney. Two roadside animal exhibits there had been a boon to the local economy when they were built in 1973. Paying the five-dollar admission, Paul was depressed and angered by the sight of more than a dozen thirsty lions lounging around in the dust, other lions being herded by a zebra-striped "safari" vehicle, and a glazed-eyed brown bear pacing in a frantic circle on a hot paved surface behind a chain-link fence.

In 1975, the owner built a thirty-foot-diameter pool and captured an eleven-year-old female dolphin and her newborn calf to add to his exhibit. Sally, as she was known, had lived for nine years in this pool by the time Paul first saw her. Her infant, Squeak, captured with her, survived for five years and died suddenly. Two males were then introduced into the pool. Sally conceived, and another calf was born in 1981. Sally was eight feet long, so regardless of where she was in the pool, the wall was no more than eleven feet away from her body. She hardly moved. For amusement, apart from Sally's public stunts, there was a soccer ball and a propeller and an occasional splashing game with one of the staff. One of Sally's games was to take the soccer ball to the bottom of the pool and hold it there for a long time; eventually she would let it go, and it

would fly out of the water. This is what Sally did to her baby
when it was born, but the baby, of course, did not come up; it
drowned. Sally got pregnant again and drowned that infant as
well. When Sally gave birth for the third time in the Warragamba tank, the staff separated her from the baby immediately, but the young dolphin, poignantly named Bumper,
crashed into the walls so many times, his head became lacer-
ated and infected; he died after six weeks. In four years, four of
Sally's babies had died, two by her design.

Paul wanted Sally rehabilitated into her natural ocean environment before another calf suffered the fate of the previous
four. He outlined a program to the New South Wales government for reintroducing Sally and her two male companions
back to the ocean environment by way of a "halfway house" in
a sheltered bay, in which she would be trained to catch live
fish and observed for a period before her release. The question
of why Sally had drowned two of her offspring seemed self-
evident. "It appears," Paul said, "that cetaceans in captivity
become lethargic, despondent, neurotic, even, by our definition,
insane. I hold Sally no more responsible for those deaths than I
would a human mother driven to madness by the torture of
imprisonment and isolation. Besides, we have to consider the
possibility that in her ethical judgment, she could not commit
her child to suffer a short, miserable life in the confinement of
the Warragamba pen."

"In an age," Paul told the Sydney magazine *Simply Living*,
"where memories of the Cambodian horror and images of
starving Ethiopian millions stir our conscience and fill our television screens, this attempt to arouse people and governments
to action over the question of confining a few dolphins and
other whales, even of condemning them to an early death,
might be seen as trivial. So, taking such a risk, let me say that
to me this is a completely serious and desperate matter. Sally
is a loving, thinking, caring, sharing, exquisitely aware, conscious creature who has been snatched away from her family,
her security, her free life in the ocean. She is trapped in a space
less than four times the size of her body, shut off from every
friend she ever had, and from every natural sound she has ever

known. She has been driven to this state of desperation or insanity or whatever it is by the conditions that human beings have forced upon her. Sally should be set free so that she and her future children can live in peace and freedom among their kind.

"And what is the worst case?" Paul posed the obvious question himself. "The worst case is that through confusion, illness, physical damage, or other mishap, Sally would be unable to survive. We often hear this argument. Well, if Sally did perish, I would suspect that even a short stay in the ocean, surrounded by natural sound, with fish to chase and rocks and sand to rub against, would be better than all the empty days ahead at Warragamba, and the final, lonely end, death in that desolate pool."

Before returning to Canada, Paul flew to New Zealand, where he campaigned briefly and futilely against the issuance of a permit by the government for the capture of four new dolphins for the only dophinarium in that country. He also had one final item on his agenda, a visit with Ron Trotter, chairman of the board of Fletcher-Challenge, the multibillion-dollar resource company that owned the timber rights on Hanson Island. An old school friend, working for the newly elected government, phoned ahead for Paul and set up an appointment through Mr. Trotter's secretary. However, when Paul phoned on the day before the promised appointment, the secretary told him that Mr. Trotter would be away the following day and unable to see him. Paul's airplane reservations were set, and he could not delay his departure, so he launched into a last, desperate attempt to see the man who could decide the fate of his home.

In late afternoon, at the Wellington airport, Paul hurriedly changed clothes in a public washroom. He stored his luggage in a locker and took a cab into downtown Wellington, asking the driver please to hurry. As the cab sped toward his destination, Paul typed out a letter on a portable typewriter balanced on his lap, a letter introducing himself to Trotter. Hurrying into the upper-floor office suite of the chairman of Fletcher-Challenge,

Paul signed the letter and handed it to the chairman's secretary, who disappeared briefly and then returned. "Dr. Spong," she said, "Mr. Trotter will see you in a moment."

The chairman was a big man, tall and healthy, with a steady gaze. He walked from behind his desk in the spacious office with its wall of glass overlooking Wellington Harbor and shook Paul's hand. The two men sat down in a corner nook in large, comfortable chairs. Paul showed him photographs of Hanson Island, of the whales, and showed him the clear-cut aftermath on Cracroft Island. Trotter listened with genuine interest, and they talked for nearly forty minutes, Paul appealing to the businessman that any gesture on his part to preserve the forest on Hanson Island could only help the company's public image in British Columbia and the world. By the time Paul was back on the airplane, heading for home, he felt very hopeful that Hanson Island might have a friend in Mr. Trotter.

Back on Hanson Island, Paul and Helena hosted a visit by Ken Takahashi, who brought with him an interpreter and a representative of a major Japanese corporation that was interested in sponsoring the proposed orca feature-film project. The visit was a success, and the company agreed to invest in the film, provided other partners could be found. Soon a script would be written. The tentative title of the film was *Message from the Whales*. The "message" was to be brief: Give us space. Paul liked the idea, as it fitted well with his evolving thoughts about whales and people's relations with them.

Paul also saw in the film an opportunity to launch a new strategy to free Orky and Corky, the A-pod orcas that were confined at Marineland of the Pacific in Los Angeles. Corky was pregnant with her fifth calf since being captured with A5 in 1969. All four of Corky's previous calves had died at birth or within a few weeks. Paul's proposal was that the two adults and the infant would be moved immediately after the birth and reintroduced to the ocean in Blackfish Sound. The first step would be to place them in a "halfway house," where they would be trained to catch live fish, and for release and recall. Eventually they would be released back to their pod. Paul saw the possibility that they could carry cameras and sound equipment that would document their new life among their old family and provide incredible, exciting imagery for the Takahashi film. Paul was certain that if it could be done, the film would be a sure commercial success. The only problem was how to persuade Marineland to let go of its star attraction. Again, Paul was hopeful, as Marineland was owned by a single person, a Hong Kong businessman named Dicky Chieu. Paul set out to track Chieu down, hoping to persuade him to participate. Immediately, Paul ran into a blank. Dicky Chieu could not be located. There seemed to be no record of him in Hong Kong, and Paul wondered if he would have to travel there himself to take up the search.

Meanwhile, he knew that time was running out. Corky had been held captive for nearly sixteen years, and statistically was already living on borrowed time, though by ocean standards she was still young. Within a few years, all the West Coast captives would be dead, and because it was unlikely that any more would ever be taken, Paul knew that the chance of conducting the unique experiment would soon be lost forever.

Paul sat on his sofa, looking out at the fir trees around the bay as he contemplated the fate of Orky and Corky. His thoughts drifted with the images outside and the sounds in the house. The sky was slightly overcast, shedding a soft, brilliant glow over the water and the forest. A few drops of rain fell in the breeze. On the shelf, in front of the window, Skana's white vertebra with sweeping fins was irradiated with soft light. Next to the whalebone sat the guest book that had been at Hanson Island for twelve years, with names and messages from hundreds of visitors. Paul could hear Anna playing outside. Helena was chopping vegetables in the kitchen.

Staring at Skana's bone, Paul felt the rumblings of his past anger over her lonely death, the confinement of Corky and Orky, and the slaughter at sea that he had witnessed. That anger rising in his stomach was familiar to Paul. He recalled how Skana had taken his hand in her mouth to calm him down the day they told him his ideas were "wacky." Skana. She had certainly been as much a teacher and friend as anyone he could remember.

Paul went outside and brought in wood for the kitchen stove. Anna trundled in behind him, carrying a small piece of wood in each hand. In the kitchen, Paul lit a fire and put on the kettle for coffee. While Anna and Helena sat down to play with a puzzle at the dining-room table, Paul stirred the frying noodles and vegetables and made a salad picked fresh from the garden. He smiled to himself, watching Anna's angelic face as she worked with pleasure and enthusiasm at the puzzle before her on the table.

When the food was ready, Anna helped Helena set the table. Paul sat down and began to serve, holding Anna's plate and dipping into the dish.

"Orcas!" Helena called, pointing outside through the window.

"Orcas, orcas!" Anna was jumping up from her seat, running to get her shoes. Leaving their dinner on the table, Paul, Helena, and Anna grabbed their coats and boots and hurried outside. The rain had begun to fall more heavily, and the three of them huddled under the eaves of the lab.

Helena looked out through the spotting scope. "There's A30 and the new calf. There's A20." She called them out as the whales came by, three generations of orcas, rising, breathing, and diving together, in their own world, subject to their own mysterious laws and order.

"There's Nicola," said Helena as the elderly matriarch swam by.

"Nicola!" squealed Anna.

The rain made a steady patter on the cedar shakes of the lab roof and dripped down in front of them as they sat on the bench and watched the silent whales slip through the gray water with their steady, eternal pace. Helena and Paul held close together as Anna straddled both their knees. A heron stood motionless in the shallows, unperturbed by the drizzle, poised, waiting for its meal to swim by.

"WaaaaaAAAaaaup!" The single call came over the speakers.

"Whoooooooop!" howled Anna.

They stayed there, nestled inside their coats as the rain washed down over the water and the hills beyond. The heron caught a fish, raised its head, and swallowed it. "Let's eat," said Helena, and the three of them walked back into the house, where they finished their supper. They played a memory game on the floor by the fire as the evening sky cleared and the rain stopped. When Anna fell asleep, Paul put her to bed. Paul and Helena sat up by the fire for a while until Helena began to yawn and stretch. "I think I'll go to bed," she said.

"I'm going to stay up awhile," said Paul as he smiled and said good night.

The waxing moon was three-quarters full in the sky, and the light fell through scattered clouds. Paul did not feel alone. He felt the presence of Helena and Anna as they slept. He felt the presence of the forest birds and orcas. All around the world he had a great network of friends who believed, as he did, that the long human loneliness was only a myth of separateness. We share our intelligence with the wild intelligence of the forest and with the sublime intelligence of the whales. As Paul sat back on the comfortable, billowing pillows, a shaft of moonlight fell on Skana's bone. Paul no longer felt angry, or even sad, as he gazed at the last remnant of his friend, but rather thankful that she had opened such vast worlds to him. Human experience is limited by the way we exercise our power to imagine worlds we have not seen, to penetrate the mystery with our wonder. "Yes, Skana," he thought, "I *am* grateful."

Paul closed his eyes and leaned his head back onto a cushion. After a few minutes of rest, he got up to go to bed. Passing the enigmatic bone, he reached out to touch it, thinking, "We still have work to do."